THE BEST OF BIRDS & BLOOMS 2009

Marie Read

The Best of Birds & Blooms 2009

Editor: Kirsten Sweet
Art Director: Joseph Handy
Managing Editor: Stacy Tornio
Editor, *Birds & Blooms*: Heather Lamb
Art Director, *Birds & Blooms*: Sue Myers
Copy Editor: Susan Uphill
Contributing Editors: Melinda Myers, George Harrison, Tom Allen
Art Associates: Tonya Limberg, Dena Ahlers
Photo Coordinator: Trudi Bellin
Assistant Photo Coordinator: Mary Ann Koebernik
Creative Director: Sharon Nelson
Vice President, Executive Editor/Books: Heidi Reuter Lloyd
President, Home & Garden and Health & Wellness: Alyce C. Alston
President, North American Consumer Marketing: Dawn M. Zier
THE READER'S DIGEST ASSOCIATION, INC.
President and Chief Executive Officer: Mary G. Berner

5400 S. 60th St. Greendale WI 53129
International Standard Book Number (10): 0-89821-722-9
International Standard Book Number (13): 978-0-89821-722-3
Serial Number: 1553-8400 Printed in U.S.A.

To order additional copies of this book,visit *www.countrystorecatalog.com* or call 1-800-344-6913.
Learn more about *Birds & Blooms* at *www.birdsandblooms.com.*

Magazine covers this page, clockwise from top left: Richard Day/Daybreak Imagery, Francis and Janice Bergquist, Carol L. Edwards, Maslowski Wildlife, Maslowski Wildlife, Skip Moody/Dembinsky Photo Assoc.
Magazine covers opposite page, clockwise from top left: Rolf Nussbaumer, Greg Lasley/KAC Productions, Rolf Nussbaumer, Rolf Nussbaumer, Rolf Nussbaumer, Maslowski Wildlife

Front cover photos, from top left: Sam Alfano, Richard Shiell, Carol L. Edwards; bottom photo, Donna and Tom Krischan
Back cover photos, from left: Frank Moegling/The Image Finders, Alan and Linda Detrick, Maslowski Wildlife

*W*ELCOME

You hold in your hands the very best stories from the past year of *Birds & Blooms* and *Birds & Blooms EXTRA*. We've packed this book with the best stories, the best advice and the best photos. They're all conveniently in one place for you to keep as a reference that's both useful and enjoyable.

Among these pages, you'll find great ideas for attracting more birds to your backyard, advice from green thumbs about growing a better garden, and solutions from our experts to backyard problems. And don't forget to watch for our popular "Editor's Picks" throughout the book. These honor some of our favorite features.

Be sure to check out our Bonus chapter, starting on page 220. We've added 12 fresh features, including a bird feeder plan, easy container recipes, and the best annuals and perennials for attracting birds.

You've shared your best stories, advice and photos. Now it's time to sit back and enjoy the results!

Heather Lamb

Heather Lamb
Editor, *Birds & Blooms*

Contents

Norway map
Adam Gib
KAC Productio

Monar
Ellen Kemb

Bald eagle
Bill Houghton

Photos of the Year

We've gathered a collection of the most striking images of the year.

Black-capped chickadee
Marie Read

Black-eyed Susan
Judy Kennamer

Blue jay
Carol Edwards

Common loon
Marie Read

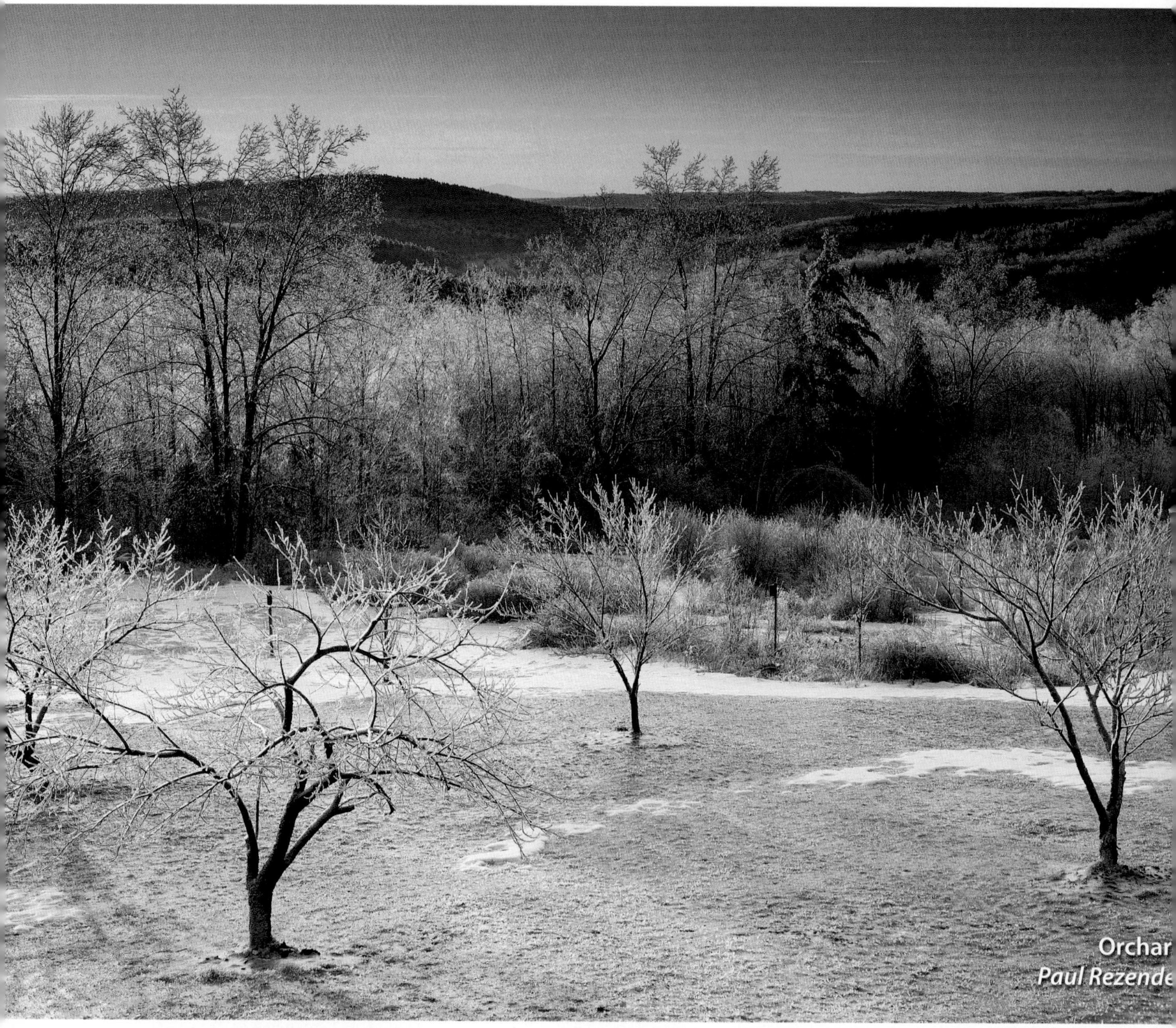

Orchar
Paul Rezende

Iris
Charles Martin

Photos of the Year

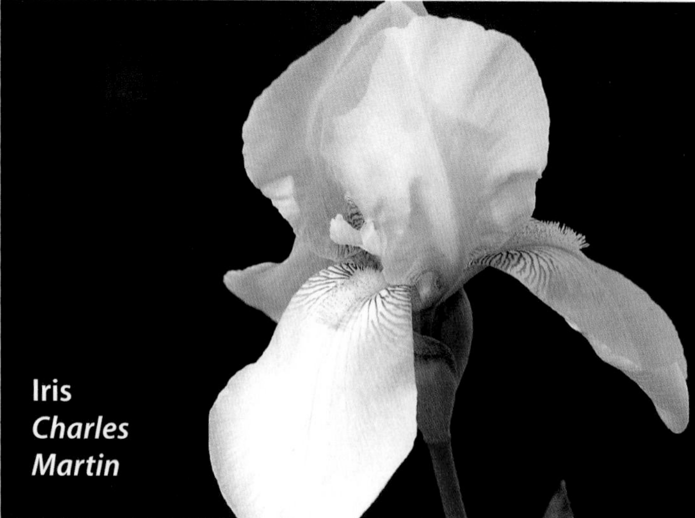

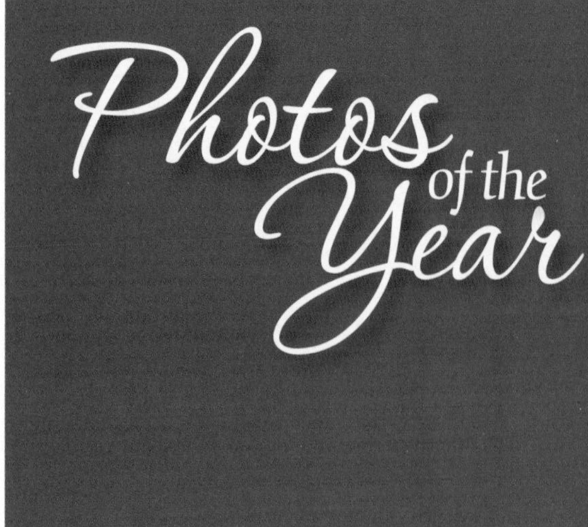

Western meadowlark
Richard Cronberg

American robin
Jan Master

Luna moth on dahlia
Nancy Rotenberg

Green-winged teal
Greg W. Lesley
KAC Productions

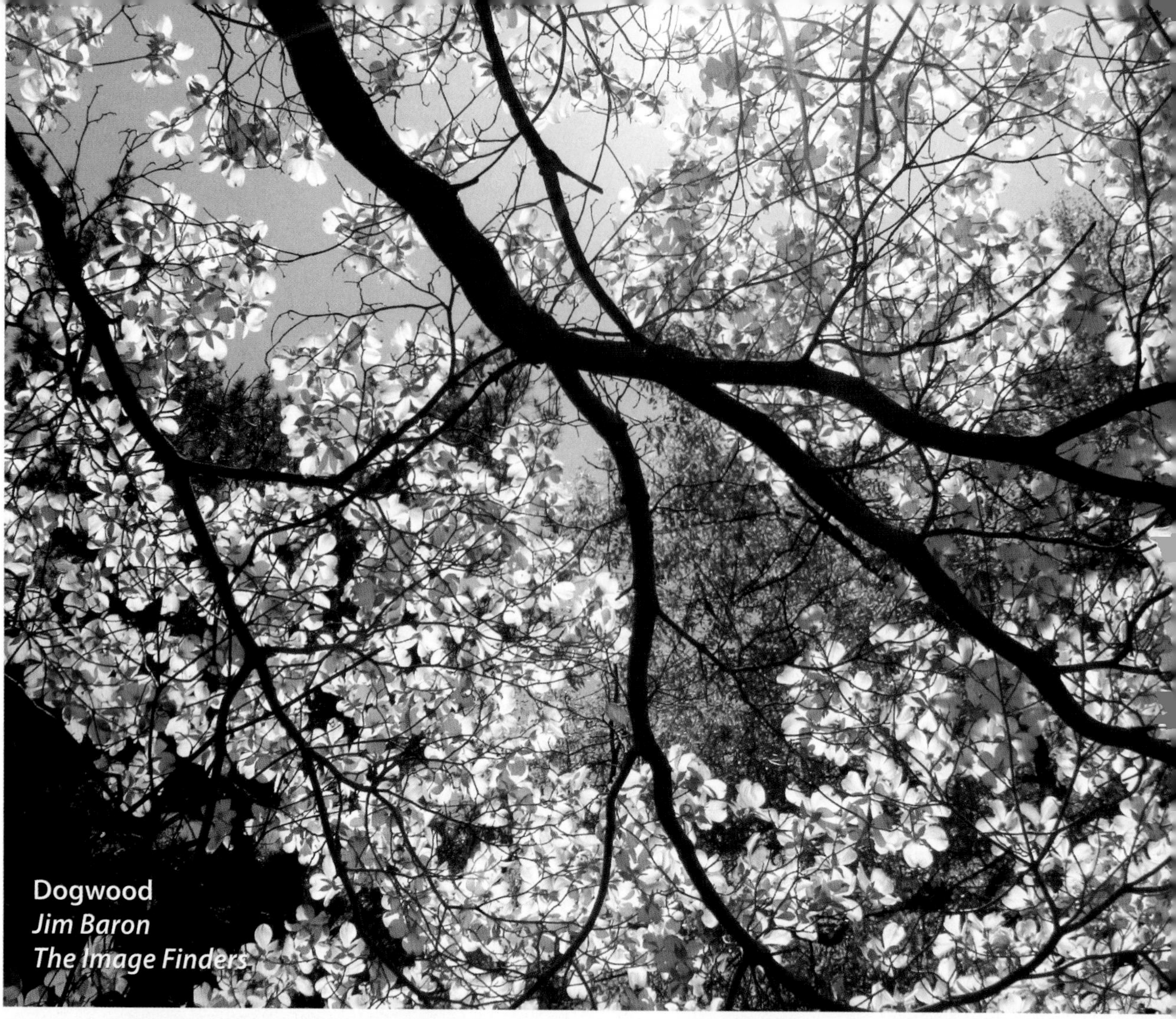

Dogwood
Jim Baron
The Image Finders

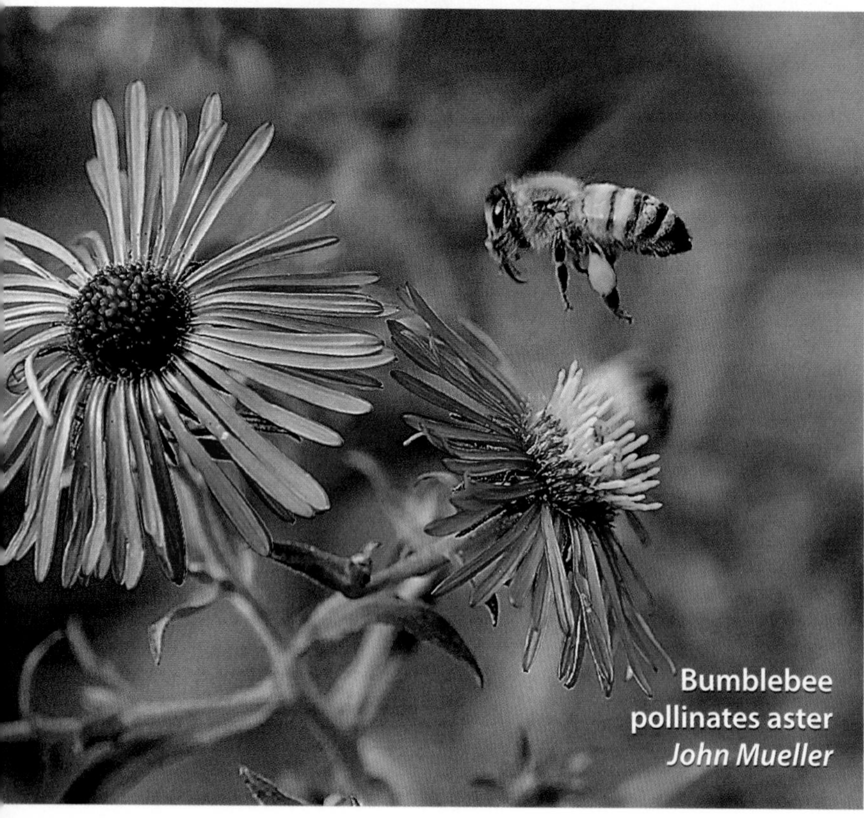

Bumblebee pollinates aster
John Mueller

Bleeding hearts
Norma Van Alstine

Photos of the Year

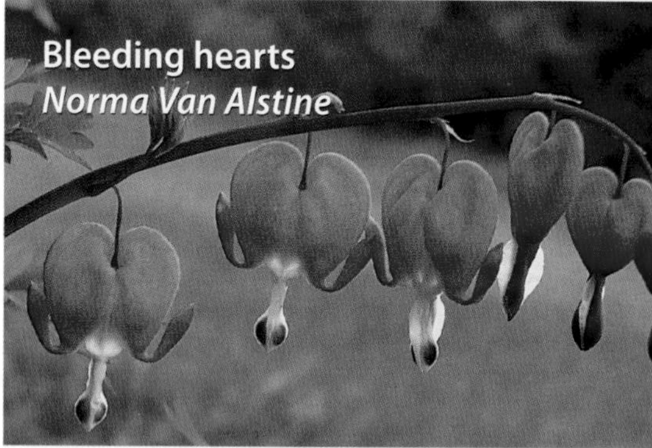

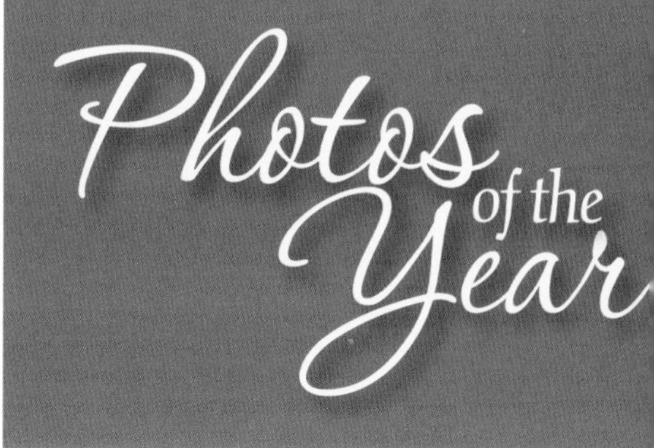

Geranium
Cathy Zoulek

Least bittern nestlings
Maslowski Productions

Hollyhocks
judywhiteGardenPhotos.com

Turkey among tulips
Joyce Sims

Tulip
Catherine Sprotberr

Zinnias
Mark E. Gibson
The Image Finders

Baltimore oriole
Wilber Suiter

Tuli
Ken Thomme

Aphid on
Mexican sunflower
Ray Minnick

American goldfinch
on daylily
Carol Edwards

Sunflowers
Darryl R. Beers

34

26

31

20

40

Chapter 1
Top Billing

Photos: American kestrel, George Harrison; kingbirds, Bill Leaman/The Image Finders; house finch, Bill Leaman/The Image Finders; Canada goose, Marie Read; ruby-crowned kinglet, Anthony Mercieca; red-bellied woodpecker, Skip Moody/Dembinsky; red-tailed hawk, Francis and Janice Bergquist; northern Bobwhite, Larry Ditto/KAC Productions.

American Kestrel

Colorful falcon has charmed its way into backyards across the country.

By George Harrison
Contributing Editor

Anthony Mercieca

At a Glance

Size: 9 inches long with a wingspan of 22 inches.

ID Tips: Long, swept-back wings and tail. Both sexes have a russet back and tail, and double black stripes on a white face. Male has blue-gray wing coverts and cap.

Voice: Call is "killy, killy, killy."

Nest: Kestrels use little or no nesting material in their cavities. Females incubate the 4 to 5 cinnamon-colored eggs for 29 to 31 days. Young remain in nest another 28 to 31 days. Both parents feed young.

Diet: Mostly large insects such as grasshoppers; also small mammals, birds (their name used to be sparrow hawk) and even reptiles.

Fun Facts: After their parents leave them, juveniles gather in groups with young kestrels from other nests.

Backyard Favorites: Large birdhouses on poles or trees in open areas.

If you see a little falcon perched on a utility wire along the highway, chances are it's an American kestrel. The kestrel is the best-known and smallest bird of prey in North America, measuring just 9 inches long.

Don't think the bird is overlooked, though. The kestrel's blue-gray wings and bold-patterned head make it unforgettable.

Donald Bauer remembers watching the antics of American kestrels on the power lines near his neighbor's home in Walla Walla, Washington.

"One day, I saw a kestrel suddenly drop to an overgrown grassy area," he says. "It hovered for a few seconds, snatched a grasshopper and returned to its perch on the wire."

Donald watched the kestrel devour its meal. As soon as it finished, the bird went back for more until it finally had its fill 15 minutes later.

It's not uncommon for American kestrels to live near humans. In fact, they're so friendly they will sometimes go to bird feeders for food.

While she was living in Las Vegas, Nevada, Wanda Daura of Payson, Arizona learned how friendly American kestrels are.

"We always fed mealworms to mockingbirds," Wanda says. "Then, suddenly, the worms were disappearing twice as fast as usual."

Laura quickly discovered the culprit.

"One morning, I looked outside the kitchen window, and I could hardly believe my eyes," she says. "A female American kestrel was eating the mealworms. She ate every last one of them."

American kestrels are unique when it comes to nesting, too. Unlike most hawks, kestrels will nest in natural tree cavities like old woodpecker holes and will also use nest boxes.

I remember finding a pair of nesting kestrels myself a few years ago. I was producing a PBS special on backyard birds, and I discovered a family nesting in a birdhouse on a utility pole.

I watched the birdhouse until the young fledged, and then nearly injured myself trying to find one of them for a picture. Finally, I spotted two cute little imps perched quietly on a stump. They froze there long enough for me to get some photos (above right), despite the scolding from their parents overhead.

As common as they appear, American kestrel populations have declined slightly in recent years, according to the North American Breeding Bird Survey.

You'll still find these beauties perched along highways, though perhaps not as frequently as you used to. Nevertheless, I hope you get the chance to enjoy their antics, too.

NESTING NOTES

American kestrels seem to like nesting near people. They will readily move into a large birdhouse on a pole or in a tree, 10 to 30 feet above the ground. Much like birdhouses for screech-owls and wood ducks, nest boxes for American kestrels are 10 inches long, 10 inches wide and 24 inches high. The boxes have a 4- by 3-inch elliptical entrance hole.

LOOK AT THIS FACE. Even as youngsters, you can see that these American kestrels are beginning to develop the distinctive markings for which the adults are known.

George Harrison

Summer
Year-round
Migration

Roadside fields and grassy areas are perfect hunting grounds for this insect-eating hawk.

Anthony Mercieca

Photos by Maslowski Productions

Hairy Woodpecker

It's easy to attract one of the most widespread birds in North America to your yard.

By David Shaw
Fairbanks, Alaska

The air was cool and wet in the high-elevation Costa Rican forest. Beneath the overcast sky and low canopy of dense surrounding woods, it was nearly dark. From somewhere in those depths, I could hear a bird calling, strangely familiar in that otherworldly tropical jungle.

For some time, I clambered around, binoculars in hand, trying to get a glimpse of the bird. Eventually, through a narrow passage between the dripping, twisted branches, I saw it and immediately understood why the call seemed so familiar. It was a hairy woodpecker, smaller than I'm used to and oddly sooty colored, but unmistakable. I was shocked—this was the same species that regularly visits my suet feeder back home in Alaska.

I pulled out my tattered guide to the birds of Costa Rica. Sure enough, the information indicated this nonmigratory species had an enormous range, reaching from the farthest extents of the boreal forest in Alaska and Canada to the mountains of western Panama.

Previously, I had encountered this species in the high pine forests of the Cordillera Central in Mexico. I had also seen them in old-growth spruce forests of the Pacific Northwest, and found them foraging in the hardwoods of the eastern United States. I hadn't realized just how far their range extended.

Easily Mistaken

Due in large part to the hairy woodpecker's extensive range, the species is highly variable. In the far southern parts of its distribution, in southern Central America, it is small and gray colored. In Alaska, hairies have an immaculate white breast and are huge, weighing a third or more than populations in the lower 48 states and twice as much as those in Central America.

This extreme variability from one region to the next, from one population to another, can make identifying hairy woodpeckers a challenge. Downy woodpeckers, the hairy's smaller cousin, are very similar in appearance and occur in many of the same habitats.

Subtle Differences

Luckily, there are a few characteristics that make distinguishing these two species a bit easier. First is their size: Hairies are substantially larger. However, assessing size is not always straightforward, and it is often necessary to look at other characteristics.

So, take a look at the bill. Hairy woodpeckers have a bill that is as long or longer than the length of their head, while a downy woodpecker's bill is considerably smaller. It's rarely greater than the distance from the front of the head to the back of the eye. (In the photo at right, the hairy is at the bottom.)

Though the plumages of the two species are nearly identical (both have black backs speckled with white, and the males bear red on the backs of their heads), there is one other difference worth noting. Downy woodpeckers always have black bars in the white outer tail feathers, while this is generally lacking in hairy woodpeckers.

As I mentioned earlier, hairies are diverse, and this is true of behavior as well as appearance. A species as widely distributed as this one needs to adapt to many different habitats and climates. Like other woodpeckers, they feed primarily by climbing up and down trunks of trees searching for insects.

Hairies regularly use a method called "percussion" in which they tap lightly on the side of the tree as they climb up and around. They are not collecting food, but searching, listening for the telltale hollow sound of a grub or insect embedded inside. After encountering a likely spot, they will spend all the time necessary pecking, prying and excavating the wood to extract the morsel.

BIRD-WATCHER'S SECRET

Hairy woodpeckers love insects, but they can hardly resist backyard feeding stations, especially when they're stocked with suet, sunflower seeds, meat scraps and peanut butter. But don't confuse this visitor with its smaller cousin, the downy woodpecker. They are very similar in appearance, with only a few subtle differences.

CAN I GET SOME OF THAT? Suet will attract both hairy and downy woodpeckers (below) to your backyard. To tell the difference between the two, look at the overall size of the bird and its bill. Hairies (bottom of photo) are larger and have a longer bill.

Crafty Techniques

Though this foraging strategy is typical, it is not the only one used. Hairies have been observed catching insects in flight, eating ants off the ground, picking bugs out from beneath scales of bark, delicately prying open sunflower seeds on bird feeders, and thieving sap from the tree carvings of yellow-bellied and red-breasted sapsuckers.

In spring, I find hairy woodpeckers most often when I hear their rattling call and loud drumming. Drumming displays are used to establish territories, much like a singing songbird, and are an indicator that a nest cavity, excavated from a dead tree, is somewhere in the vicinity.

Hairies establish monogamous pairs and may remain bonded to the same individual throughout their lives. Once a pair establishes a territory, they won't wander very far and can often be found, season after season, year after year, inhabiting the same patch of woods.

Recoveries of banded birds suggest that hairy woodpeckers rarely wander more than 30 miles from their home territory. In fact, a pair of hairies lives in the forest surrounding my home near Fairbanks. I can find them just about any day, whether it's a cold January day or a hot one in July.

From Sea to Shining Sea

As I sit here now on the opposite side of the globe in Alaska, looking out at the snow, I think back on that day I discovered the hairy woodpecker in Costa Rica. I can picture the tropical forest strewn with bromeliads and moss, the trees crooked from the wind. When I saw the hairy that day, the place no longer seemed so foreign. I knew then, that in that strange jungle lived a bird that also resided around my home 5,000 miles to the north.

This knowledge made me feel far more connected than I had before to the greater world. Even years later, I can still feel that strong connection between two faraway places. Now, each time I hear the call of a hairy woodpecker as I stroll through a snowy Alaskan forest, I think of another one in Central America, drumming back.

At a Glance

Size: Bird is 9-1/4 inches long and has a 15-inch wingspan.
ID Tips: The hairy has a black and white checked back. It's almost identical to the downy, but is noticeable larger. The hairy has a longer, heavier bill and an inconspicuous tuft. The females look similar to males, but they lack the red mark on the back of the head.
Voice: A strong "peek" or "peech," sharper than the downy.
Nesting: Pairs work together to excavate the cavity. The females usually lay four white eggs. Young leave the nest after roughly a month.
Diet: Insects, larvae of wood borers, fruit and nuts.
Fun Facts: This bird can look quite different in its varied regions. Across its huge range, there are over 17 subspecies.
Backyard Favorites: Visits feeding stations for suet, sunflower seeds, meat scraps and peanut butter.

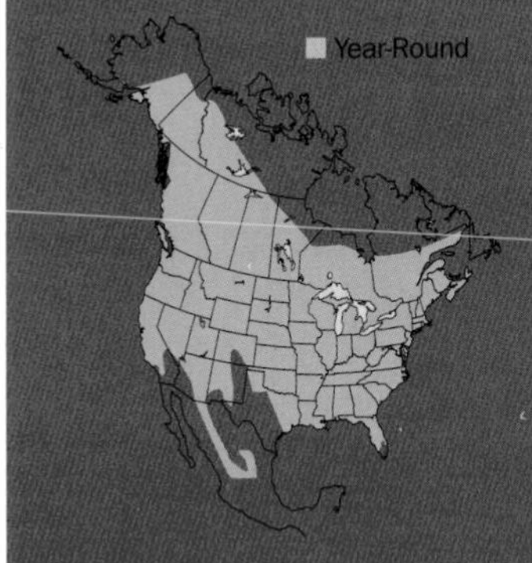

Kingbird

Eastern and western species take the crown when dinnertime rolls around.

By George Harrison, Contributing Editor

Bill Leaman/The Image Finders

Fishing is never boring when kingbirds are around. Every summer, I go boat fishing on the little lake near my house, and the eastern kingbirds keep me entertained.

The striking black and white birds with white outer tail feathers will perch on a cattail spike until they spy an insect flying over the water. Then in a flash, they dart out, grab the prey in their bills (I can hear the snap from 50 yards away) and flit back to their perch. This happens dozens of times between each bluegill I catch from the lake.

Take-Charge Attitude

Both the eastern and western kingbirds hunt insects in this flycatcher-like fashion. They are very aggressive birds as well—thus, their "kingbird" moniker.

One day last spring, I heard a ruckus above me and looked up into the sky to see an eastern kingbird attacking a red-tailed hawk. The bird was going after that hawk with such venom that it looked like it was going to kill that poor raptor. The kingbird was totally fearless, even though it was a fraction of the hawk's size.

Randy Dettmers is an ornithologist in Shutesbury, Massachusetts, and he has seen similar attacks by kingbirds many times. Most recently, he heard several birds calling out noisily in a nearby pine stand. A few minutes later, a crow flew out of the trees with a pair of eastern kingbirds following it in hot pursuit.

"There was no doubt about it, those kingbirds were mobbing that crow," Randy says. "It was quintessential kingbird behavior."

Divided by Appearance

Eastern and western kingbirds are very much alike except in appearance. The eastern is a black and gray bird with a white breast, belly and tips on its tail. The western is a gray and olive bird with a white breast, yellow belly and white outer-edge tail feathers. Both have a hidden spot of red feathers on the tops of their heads, too.

Dave Hansen of Irene, South Dakota was lucky enough to see this red crown patch on a western kingbird.

"Now each spring, I await the return of this common, plain bird with hopes that I might be able to catch another glimpse of its hidden red crown."

Chris Patenaude of Perley, Minnesota has another reason

"Kingbirds are definitely in a class by themselves."

NESTING NOTES

Even though kingbirds are aggressive by nature, they are actually social nesters. You'll often find their bulky, poorly constructed nests in trees or shrubs shared with other birds.

Ted Rose/Unicorn Stock Photos

At a Glance

Size: Roughly 8-1/2 inches long with a wingspan of 15 inches.

ID Tips: Eastern and western birds do not look alike.

The eastern is black to gray on the head and back, with a white breast and belly; the western is gray to olive on the head and back, with a white breast and yellow belly.

Voice: Eastern is a series of "kit, kit, kit," or "dzee-dzee-dzeet." Their call note is a "tzeeb."

Western sings a lower-pitched, squeaky "pidik, pik, pidik, PEEKado."

Nest: A bulky, poorly constructed nest with a shallow cup of course twigs, saddled in the crotch of tree or shrub 5 to 17 feet above the ground or sometimes over water.

Females lay two to three seashell-pink, spotted eggs. Females incubate eggs for 12 to 14 days, and then the male helps feed for 16 to 18 days until the birds make the first flight. Parents may attend fledglings for more than a month after they leave the nest.

Diet: Mostly insects caught on the wing in typical flycatcher fashion.

Fun Facts: The name kingbird is derived from their "take-charge" behavior.

Backyard Favorites: Dead snags on tree and shrubs from which they can launch their attacks on flying insects.

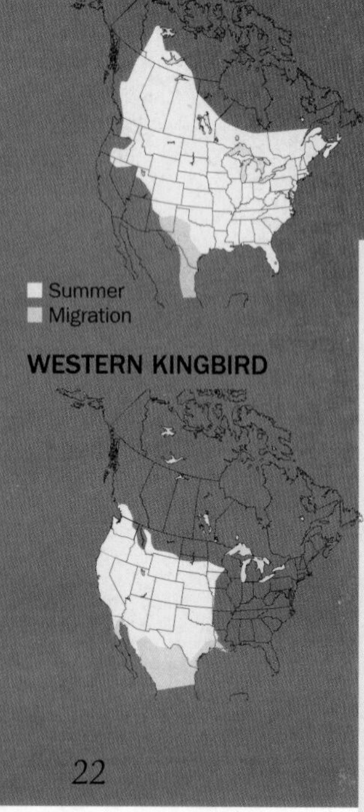

Bill Leaman/The Image Finders

MULTIPLE KINGS. You can find the western kingbird (above) across most of the western half of the United States. The Cassin's (right) is a Southwest species, and the gray kingbird (below) is mostly in Florida.

to keep a close watch on kingbirds in her area. One year, she watched as a western kingbird robbed a golden digger wasp of its prey.

"The wasp would leave its prey in the opening of its nest burrow while it checked the tunnel," Chris says. "In that brief, 5-second window, a kingbird would fly by with the speed of a falcon and nab the insect."

Despite their aggressiveness, kingbirds are social nesters. It may be surprising, but not unusual, to find kingbirds nesting in a tree or shrub with other birds.

My dad, Hal Harrison, found an eastern kingbird nesting in an apple tree very close to the nests of a Baltimore oriole and yellow warbler. And in Tucson, Arizona, he found a western kingbird nesting in the same Mexican oak tree with a dusky-capped flycatcher, acorn woodpecker and hooded oriole. Eastern and western kingbirds migrate a long distance to South America in fall.

Larry Dech

Kings in Other Regions

Of the seven kingbirds found in North America, the eastern and western kingbirds are by far the most common.

Tropical and thick-billed kingbirds are found on the Arizona/Mexico border, and the Couch's kingbird on the Texas/Mexico border. And then there's the Cassin's kingbird that is well established in the Southwest, and the gray kingbird found in Florida.

No matter which kingbird you have in your area, these birds are definitely in a class by themselves. Many people refer to them as tyrant flycatchers. It seems fitting. After all, they are kings.

Roland Jordahl

House Finch

©Tom Vezo.com

Red-faced birds are taking over North America.

By George Harrison
Contributing Editor

Once upon a time, there was a healthy population of house finches living around ranches in canyons and bottomlands throughout the American West. Then one day in 1939, a bird fancier in southern California trapped some of them and put them in cages.

The caged house finches adapted well to captivity, thriving on a diet of canary seed. They did so well, in fact, that the bird fancier trapped more house finches and began selling them as "Hollywood Finches" to pet stores in the East.

The only problem was that the Migratory Bird Treaty Act protects house finches and other native songbirds from being kept in captivity.

Maslowski Productions

John and Gloria Tveten/KAC Productions

John and Gloria Tveten/KAC Productions

FLOCK TOGETHER. In winter, house finches may travel in groups, like those on a barbed-wire fence at top. Male house finches (middle) have reddish faces and rumps. Females (bottom) are striped.

Free the Birds

So one day in 1940, a U.S. Fish and Wildlife Service law enforcement agent raided a pet store on Long Island, New York that was selling house finches. But as the agent entered the front door, the store owner released the house finches out the back to keep from being arrested.

The liberated house finches adapted well to the new area, and people soon found the birds nesting in Babylon on Long Island. During the 1940s and 1950s, the house finches did so well in their new eastern habitat that they began to radiate out along the Atlantic coast, up major river valleys and down highways leading to communities where people maintained bird feeders.

On first sighting, most people thought they were purple finches, a common feeder bird in the East with a similar red face among males and brown stripes among females. The subtle differences in bill shape, body shape and brighter red-orange coloring of the house finch was not yet obvious.

By 1961, the population of eastern house finches had moved into Pennsylvania, and they didn't stop there. In 1964, they reached Ohio. It was 1972 when they moved into Chicago. In 1981, the birds were in Missouri; 1985, Wisconsin. By 1988, they had spread all the way to the Mississippi River.

Meanwhile, back at the ranches, western house finches had spread eastward, as if reaching out to their wayward kinfolk. By the early 1980s, the western population of house finches had crossed the Rockies and were heading east to the Missouri River.

In the spring of 1988, after 48 years of separation, the two populations of house finches met on the banks of the Missouri River at Council Bluffs, Iowa. They were finally a family of one.

This tale of the house finch is not only true, but it's also unique in the annals of North American ornithology. This is the only time that a species has split into two continental populations and then reunited. And it all happened in less than 50 years.

Today, house finches are common in every state in the continental U.S., parts of southern Canada and northern Mexico. They gorge on various types of birdseed at virtually any backyard feeder.

Learning to Adjust

D.A. Lombillotte of Sandusky, Ohio even found the birds eating from her goldfinch feeder. She usually has two tube feeders out for the birds—one standard design and another upside-down style for goldfinches.

BIRD-WATCHER'S SECRET

Since house finches don't migrate, they can easily be found year-round in most of North America. If you don't already have these common backyard visitors in your yard, attract them with tube feeders filled with seed, and a birdbath for them to bathe and drink. If you're lucky, a nesting pair might settle in your backyard.

Maslowski Productions

GAINING GROUND. House finches are quickly becoming one of the most popular feeder birds in North America. They aren't picky when it comes to seed and will happily munch on cracked sunflower or nyjer. They have several broods each season, a factor contributing to their rapid expansion.

Richard Day/Daybreak Imagery

When her regular tube feeder developed a crack, she had to take it down for repairs.

"This left only the upside-down one for the birds," she says. "The house finches were genuinely confused when they first landed on that feeder. But after a few days, some of them began copying the goldfinches and started hanging upside down from the perches. Soon, several were successfully feeding alongside their cousins."

One reason house finches spread across the country so quickly is that they are very prolific. One house finch pair can produce up to three or more broods per year, of four to five young each. They will nest anywhere from hanging flowerpots to door wreaths and more. One day, my neighbor Betty Kindem asked me if she could still water her potted flowers while the birds were nesting inside.

I was happy to tell her that she could keep the birds and flowers, as long as she watered the outside edge of the flowers without soaking the nest.

Sticking Close to Home

Jacqueline Sue Paine lives in Colorado Springs, Colorado, and a few years ago, she had a pair of finches nest in a small suction-cup feeder hanging on her kitchen window.

"All was going well until we heard an unusual amount of chattering one day," Jacqueline says. "We looked out and saw the feeder hanging by only one suction cup!"

Reaching out the window, she was able to reattach the loose suction cup securely back on the window.

"Within 30 minutes, the adult finches returned to care for their young, and once again sang their loud chorus," she says. "It was music to my ears."

House finches don't really migrate. In the West, they move to lower elevations in winter. In the East, they move around a great deal, like American goldfinches, but there doesn't seem to be an organized pattern of north or south movement.

From my own experience, I know that I see fewer house finches at my Wisconsin feeders during winter. I do see some, though, and at times, small flocks even gather to feed heavily during cold days.

You don't really need to send out invitations to bring house finches to your yard. They will invite themselves if you're already feeding other birds.

With their history, if they are not already the most common feeder bird in North America, they will be very soon.

At a Glance

Common Name: House finch.
Scientific Name: *Carpodacus mexicanus.*
Length: 6 inches.
Wingspan: 9-1/2 inches.
Description: The gray-brown striped male has an red-orange forehead, face, breast and rump; female is grayish brown and striped overall.
Voice: A very melodious, sweet, canary-like song; a sharp "queet" is the call note.
Nesting: They nest in a variety of sites, including hanging flowerpots, holes in buildings, and in trees and shrubs. Females build most of the nests and incubate the eggs for 12 to 14 days while the male feeds her. Like goldfinches, house finches feed their young partially digested seeds, sometimes called canary milk. Young leave the nest in 2 to 3 weeks.
Diet: Mostly seeds, including thistle, dandelion and noxious seeds from old fields.
Backyard Favorite: Tube feeders, filled with medium cracked sunflower seed or nyjer (thistle). A birdbath draws them to bathe and drink.

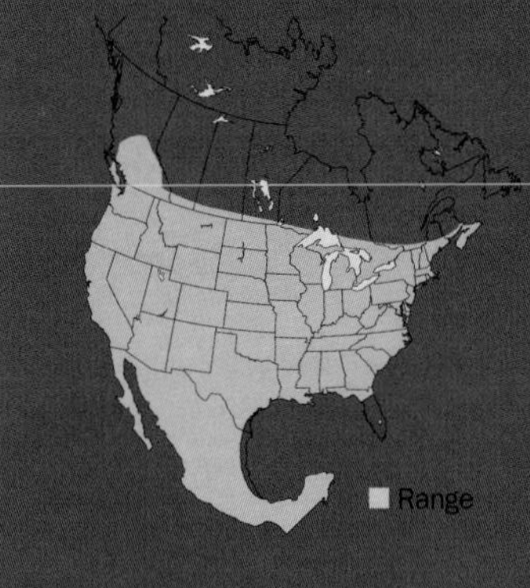

Canada Goose

Meet one of the most controversial birds in North America.

By George Harrison, Contributing Editor

Marie Read

The honking of Canada geese used to be one of the most romantic sounds in all of nature. Don and Elaine Jay of Parsons, Kansas would agree.

While out for a drive a couple of years ago, they saw a huge flock of Canada geese silhouetted against the evening sunset. They drove toward them, eager to watch the birds heading for a nearby pond.

"By the time we arrived at the north end of the pond, the 500-plus geese were already making their final approach," Don remembers. "They created such a din of honking that we stopped trying to talk over them. Instead, we rolled down our windows to experience the full effect.

"As they splashed down, it looked like rain drops from a summer storm. My wife and I sat quietly and savored the wonderful display of wild nature."

Not everyone shares Don and Elaine's affection for the Canada goose. The birds and their honking aren't as loved as they once were. Some people even call them flying rats.

So, what happened? Why was there such a dramatic change in attitude toward Canada geese? Simply put, the population of one of the breed's subspecies, the giant Canada goose, exploded.

The giant Canada goose is one of 11 subspecies found throughout North America. The giant is a nonmigratory resident goose that lives year-round in the lower 48 states. Because of its large size (up to 24 pounds), it has an enormous appetite, requiring at least a half pound of food a day.

Taking Over

During the last 2 decades, the giant Canada goose has reproduced faster than any other goose. Now, they are throughout much of the U.S., and they raid golf courses, corporate lawns, lake properties, corn and wheat fields and backyards for food. And as anyone who has these birds around can attest, wherever they eat, they also leave their droppings.

The tragedy of this goose dilemma is that only the resident giant Canada geese are thriving to the point of multiplying out of

"One swallow does not make a summer, but one skein of geese, cleaving the murk of a March thaw, is the spring."

—Aldo Leopold

Bill Carter

Larry Ditto/KAC Productions

Adam Jackson

FORAGING FOR FOOD. Once the grass or field crops start to appear, it's not unusual to spot Canada geese, like the pair at top right, searching for food in any open area. Above, a young gosling will stay with its parents for a year before leaving to find a mate of its own.

control. The traditional migratory subspecies—those that nest in Canada and winter in the U.S.—are experiencing depleted populations due to a lack of food on their northern breeding grounds. They also suffer because of overhunting during fall migration.

Wild Goose Chase

Waterfowl managers have been unable to design a hunt that will help control the population of pesky resident geese while preserving the migratory birds. Not only is it nearly impossible to tell the difference between the two birds, but the nonmigratory geese also tend to stick to urban and suburban areas during the day where they can't be hunted.

It's too bad the giant Canada goose has given all Canada geese such a bad name. The migratory species really is an interesting breed.

These birds have strong family bonds, and the young stay with their parents for a year before venturing out on their own. They often return to their original nesting sites, where the yearlings form new flocks.

Females build their nests on the ground and near water. They lay five to six creamy-white eggs. The female incubates the eggs for 28 days while the male stands guard nearby. After hatching, the parents lead the fuzzy youngsters to water, and then they can fly 42 days later.

Whether you love or hate Canada geese, there's no denying their reliability. Every year, they're always back with their honking.

Fond Memories

Debbie Curtis of Walterville, Oregon says she's been watching geese with her dad for as long as she can remember.

"Going with my dad to watch the geese is one of my most treasured memories," Debbie says. "He called whole flocks his pets, and whenever we'd see geese flying, he'd say, 'There go my geese.'"

Now, Debbie loves to watch her dad show "his geese" to her daughters. And even though they can't distinguish the migratory geese from the pesky giant ones, they enjoy them just the same.

At at Glance

Size: Length of 25 to 45 inches; wingspan of 43 to 60 inches.

ID Tips: Brown-gray back and lighter below; black bill, neck, legs and feet; distinct white chinstrap; longer necks and bills than most migratory species.

Voice: Their famous call, a clarion, musical, honking "ka-ronk," is one of the most haunting sounds in nature. When defending its nest, it hisses at intruders.

Nest: Builds near water on low stumps, mounds and muskrat houses using sticks, reeds and grasses. Females incubate the five or six creamy- to dirty-white eggs for 28 days while the male stands guard nearby. The young leave the nest hours after hatching and are able to fly 42 days later.

Diet: These grazers relish the fresh green sprouts of winter wheat as well as waste grain, and a variety of aquatic vegetation, wetland grasses and clovers. They graze on green grasses in urban areas.

Fun Facts: Canada geese often run on water for a step or two before leaping into the air.

Backyard Favorites: Green grass, cracked corn.

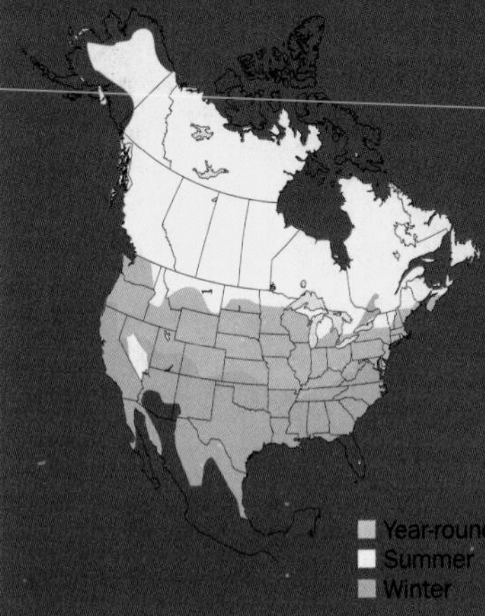

Ruby-Crowned Kinglet

Don't let its size fool you—this little bird has a huge voice.

By David Shaw
Fairbanks, Alaska

At a Glance

Size: Length of 4-1/4 inches and a wingspan of 7-1/2 inches.
ID Tips: Olive bird overall; males have a red crest, but it doesn't always show.
Voice: Whistled chant of "sii si sisisi berr berr berr pudi pudi pudi."
Nest: Ruby-crowned kinglets nest high in the tops of evergreens. They build small cup nests where the female will lay 5 to 12 eggs, the most of any North American

Anthony Mercieca

In my work as a wildlife biologist, I spend a lot of time outside, standing still in the early light, listening. For a fixed period, I note what birds I hear, then move on to another spot and listen some more.

These "point counts," as they are called, are a method biologists use to detect birds, assess populations and look for changes over time. For me, it is a springtime treat to stand in a quiet forest and listen to the chorus of birdsongs.

In interior Alaska, where I work, there is one species that I can almost always hear. Incredibly loud and boisterous for its diminutive size, you can hear the ruby-crowned kinglet's song from hundreds of yards away.

If I'm close to the singer, a male, usually perched out of sight in the top of a spruce tree, the volume of his song can drown out the rest of the birds in the nearby forest. The noise can even affect my data, but I don't resent his enthusiasm. Any 7-gram bird that can belt out a song like that has my respect.

Early to Rise

Here in Alaska, the ruby-crowned kinglet is one of the first migrants to arrive each spring. I've always found this early arrival, sometimes when there is still snow on the ground, rather remarkable.

As I mentioned, ruby-crowned kinglets are small—very, very small. They are equipped with thin bills for eating insects and yet arrive on the breeding grounds before most of their prey has emerged for the season.

This past spring, I watched a newly arrived ruby-crowned kinglet high in a white spruce near my home. He intermittently foraging and letting cry his raucous song. While foraging, he patrolled the branches of the tree, peering underneath scaly pieces of bark and probing into the spruce needles with his fine, thin bill.

Hidden Red Crest

Occasionally, through my binoculars, I could see him raise his bill and swallow a tiny insect. The forest was alive with birdsongs, and I could hear other kinglets singing nearby. Each time another kinglet sang, the bird I was watching raised his red crest, lifted its bill to the air and responded with some notes of his own.

"Any 7-gram bird that can belt out a song like that has my respect."
—David Shaw

songbird.
Diet: Insects.
Fun Facts: Ruby-crowned kinglets are one of the smallest songbirds in North America. Some hummingbirds even weigh more!
Backyard Favorites: Offer water for the best chance of spotting this beauty in your backyard. To increase your chances, keep a close watch during spring and fall migrations.

George E. Stewart/Dembinsky Photo Assoc.

Hidden Accessory

An otherwise drab, olive-colored bird, the ruby-crowned kinglet is named for the flash of brilliant crimson that graces the crest of the male's head. Don't look too hard, though. You will only see the bird's red crest during courtship or when it's agitated.

Time to Fly

As the summer breeding season turns to fall, ruby-crowned kinglets begin moving south in large droves. They are not choosy when it comes to winter habitat, which can be found everywhere from the forests of the Pacific Northwest to the dry woodlands of Texas. You can even find these birds in the warm swamps of the Southeast.

> **NESTING NOTES**
>
> **Ruby-crowned kinglets lay so many eggs (up to 12 in the Northwest) that their combined weight is often greater than the female herself!**
>
> **They build their nests very high in the trees, making them notoriously difficult to study. That's why biologists know very little about their breeding behavior, nests or survival of their chicks.**

During migration and the winter months, the species spends a lot of time foraging in mixed-species flocks where they mingle with golden-crowned kinglets, as well as chickadees, warblers and other small birds.

When I lived in western Washington, I regularly encountered this species during my many walks through the wet Pacific Coast forests. Quite a few ruby-crowned kinglets spend their winters in the Northwest. Though they do not sing during the winter months, I became accustomed to hearing the high-pitched, airy calls that round out the ruby-crowned's vocal repertoire.

This tiny, tough songbird livens up the forest unlike any other migrant bird. Though most people enjoy looking for this bird's hard-to-see crest, it is the song that I most associate with the ruby-crowned kinglet.

The sound is not so beautiful as the flutelike hermit thrush, nor as melodic as an American robin, but it rises loud, fast and boisterous, much like the spring season itself. That, perhaps, is the main reason I love the ruby-crowned kinglet. They remind me, with each thunderous note, to stop, watch and listen before the season fades away.

Year-round
Summer
Winter
Migration

Kathy Adams Clark/KAC Productions

Maslowski Productions

Don't let this assertive bird's name fool you.

By George Harrison
Contributing Editor

Red-Bellied Woodpecker

"Hey, George, look at that red-headed woodpecker up in our tree," my neighbor Sue Wendelberger called over the fence.

"That's not a red-headed woodpecker," I said. "It's a red-bellied."

"Really? But where is its red belly?" Sue questioned.

Without realizing it, Sue had hit upon the challenge of identifying this flashy bird.

If any bird was ever misnamed, it's the red-bellied woodpecker. Go ahead and take a close look. You can search with the best binoculars on the market, but chances are, you're not going to see this bird's red belly.

Though the adults do have a red wash on their

Skip Moody/Dembinsky Photo Assoc.

THERE IT IS! While its namesake coloring is often hidden from view, you can catch a glimpse of this bird's red belly from the right angle (above). Females (above, right) have red napes, while male red-bellies have red extending to the top of their heads.

lower bellies, you seldom see it. The bird has to be clinging to a tray feeder with its upper breast and belly angled just right.

I think this bird's name would be more accurate if they had called it the zebra or ladder-backed woodpecker. After all, the black and white bands that cover its back, wings and tail are its most distinguishing feature.

I see red-bellied woodpeckers every day in my Wisconsin backyard, but I only catch glimpses of their red bellies about twice a year. One of those times occurred a couple of years ago when a pair of these birds decided to nest in the basswood tree outside my window.

The male and female were working together excavating a nesting cavity. I enjoyed watching them, the female with her red nape and the male with his red extending from nape to bill.

Nesting Cut Short

I was anxious to watch the whole nesting pageant from start to finish. Females typically lay four to five white eggs in a cavity. The young don't leave the nest until 3-1/2 weeks after hatching, so all in all, it's a good month of entertainment.

Unfortunately, that didn't happen. Shortly after they completed their cavity, a pair of European starlings arrived on the scene. The battle between the four was fierce and went on for days. At first, it seemed that the red-bellies were winning because I could see the female sticking her head out of the cavity.

In the end, all the birds left. Sadly, the space remained empty until autumn when a gray squirrel filled it with leaves in preparation for winter.

Don't let this outcome fool you, though. Red-bellied woodpeckers aren't the type to give up a fight. In fact, Mary Jane Dennis of San Saba, Texas can vouch for that.

A few years ago, a red-bellied woodpecker showed up to her empty bluebird nest box. The entrance hole was much too small, so the bird took matters into its own bill, so to speak. Soon it had doubled the entrance hole.

"My husband and I enjoyed watching the woodpecker renovate this nest box and have left it up in hopes that it would return with a mate in spring," Mary says.

All About the Bill

With all the pounding and drilling the red-bellied does with its bill, it makes you wonder how they're physically able to do this. It's actually quite simple.

To begin with, woodpeckers literally have thick skulls. Add to the equation the strong muscles around their skulls and bills that absorb the shock of pounding, and you can see how they can withstand the hammering.

While impressive, this amazing bill sometimes gets woodpeckers in trouble. People can hear their racket up to a mile away. And even though they're only courting and declaring territory with this

Maslowski Productions

noise, it can also damage the surface they're drumming on, which is troubling especially if it's the siding on your house.

Expanding Their Range

Red-bellied woodpeckers are relatively new to the North. Like northern cardinals, northern mockingbirds and tufted titmice, these birds are native to the Southeast.

It's only been in the late part of last century that they pioneered northward. I recorded my first red-belly in southeastern Wisconsin in December 1975. Since then, we have seen these birds in our backyard every year.

Red-bellies are now common through the Upper Midwest and Northeast from the Great Plains east to New England.

Some ornithologists believe that the increased availability of feeder food has contributed to their expansion. I know from my own experience that these birds have adapted their eating habits quite a bit.

When they first arrived in our region, they only seemed interested in suet. It was a shock when I spotted one clinging to my tube feeder one day, removing a cracked sunflower seed.

Apparently, they've developed a sweet tooth, too. Red-bellied woodpeckers have been known to eat oranges intended for orioles and sugar water from hummingbird feeders.

Judy and Charlie Claggett even serve biscuits to their red-bellied friend in their Louisville, Kentucky backyard.

Feeding "Big Red"

For the past few winters, a male red-bellied woodpecker has visited the Claggetts' place every morning. They call him "Big Red." He announces his daily arrival by landing in a tree and "barking" a loud call to get their attention.

This tells the couple they need to put out more biscuits on their empty feeding tray.

"The bird does this several times a day and is often with a downy woodpecker companion, although it's always Big Red who does the ordering," Judy says.

Whether it's for suet, birdseed, biscuits, oranges or even sugar water, red-bellied woodpeckers are always welcome in my backyard. They provide hours of entertainment, and with or without their red bellies showing, they're always a gorgeous sight in winter, spring, summer or fall.

BIRD-WATCHER'S SECRET

Ever wonder where the red belly is on a red-bellied woodpecker? Truth is, the red belly is there, but the upper breast and belly have to be at a certain angle for it to be seen.

To attract this visitor to your yard, put out suet, cracked sunflower seeds, orange halves or sugar water. Yes, they share a favorite food with the hummingbirds.

Joanne Williams/The Image Finders

At a Glance

Common Name: Red-bellied woodpecker.
Scientific Name: *Melanerpes carolinus.*
Length: 9-1/4 inches.
Wingspan: 16 inches.
ID Tips: Males have a zebra back, red hood and nape with a reddish tinge on their bellies. Females are identical, but only their napes are red.
Voice: Like other woodpeckers, both males and females drum on trees and siding to "sing." They also have a call note that sounds like "chiv, chiv, chiv."
Habitat: Bottomland woods, swamps, coniferous and deciduous forests, and shade trees in backyards.
Nest: Both sexes drill a nesting cavity in a tree, utility pole or wooden building. The female lays one pure-white egg each day until the clutch of four or five is complete. Both parents incubate the eggs for about 2 weeks before hatching. The young remain in the cavity for another 3-1/2 weeks before fledging.
Diet: Larvae, insects, acorns and berries.
Backyard Favorites: Medium cracked sunflower seeds on a tray feeder, suet, orange halves and sugar water.

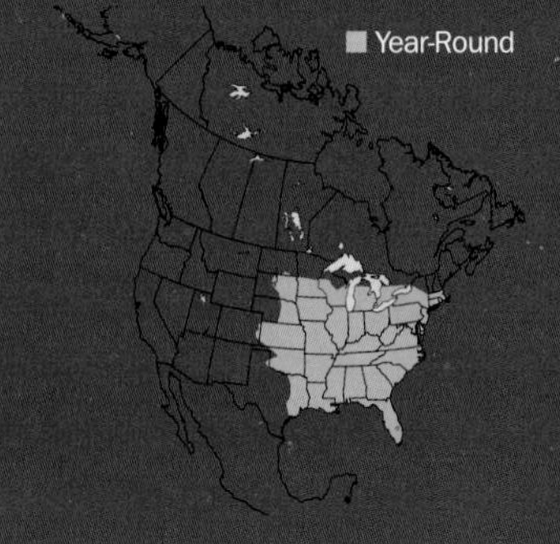

Northern Bobwhite

This understated member of the quail family is a southern favorite.

By George Harrison
Contributing Editor

It's 5:30 in the morning, and Roland Lancaster is quietly walking through the woods on his property near Ada, Oklahoma. Suddenly, he hears a clear, sweet whistle penetrate the chilly morning air: "bob-bob-white."

He smiles, instantly recognizing the northern bobwhite's call of its own name. Roland wets his lips and returns the whistle: "bob-bob-white."

He climbs the steps to his tree stand and settles in to wait. It's deer hunting season, and while many people think of bobwhites as game birds, this barely crosses Roland's mind. Today, the bobwhite is his morning companion as the sun rises.

Plainly Popular

Roland's admiration for the bobwhite is not unusual. I've never known a game bird more popular. It might not be much to look at, compared to the stately ring-necked pheasant or drake wood duck, but it doesn't matter. People love this round, stocky flier.

Hunters and nonhunters alike refer to the bird as simply "quail" most of the time. It is, in fact, one of six species of native quail and the only one found east of the Rockies.

Larry Ditto/KAC Productions

Rob Curtis/The Image Finders

POWER IN NUMBERS. Bobwhites live in coveys, which consist of several bird families and as many as 30 birds. Above, bobwhites gather in a tight circle. At right, you can tell the difference between males and females because males have white markings on their heads.

NESTING NOTES

Northern bobwhites are ground nesters. They find an impression in the ground and line it with grasses, then build a weaved arch over the cavity. Northern bobwhite chicks leave the nest almost immediately after hatching and never return. But they definitely don't wander off alone. Families join other families and live in coveys, or groups, of up to 30 birds.

You can easily recognize the bobwhite from its song. To attract mates and defend territories, males perch on fence posts and stretch their bodies to full length, raising their crests and sounding off with a clarion "bob-bob-white."

I'll never forget hearing that crystal-clear call while experiencing a really bad day in the 1950s. I was a U.S. Army officer cadet at summer training in Virginia. My colleagues and I were suffering through one of those scorchingly humid days common in the South.

Just when I thought I was about to die, the melodious whistle of "bob-bob-white" pierced the moist air. At that moment, I suddenly regained the spirit to forge ahead.

Covey Life

While most birds live in flocks, bobwhites live in coveys. This consists of several families, totaling up to 30 birds, that remain together throughout the year, except during breeding season.

The covey members feed, rest and roost together. Just before dark, they form a circle of 10 to 15 birds with their heads pointed outward, tails pointed upward and bodies touching to conserve heat (photo below left).

Like a circle of covered wagons, they have 360 degrees of protection. If threatened, they flush in all directions, minimizing their losses and maximizing the challenge to predators.

Good communication helps keep the covey together. They talk to one another in low, conversational notes. If they get separated, they use their louder assembly call, "ka-loi-kee, ka-loi-kee," to get back together.

Coveys break up in April and May with the start of breeding season. Though very simple structures, bobwhite nests are well hidden and camouflaged.

Growing Up Fast

To build their homes, bobwhites use an impression in the ground, line it with grasses and other vegetation and then weave an arch over the cup. The birds leave an opening on the side that they use to enter and leave.

Quail are precocious birds. The chicks leave within hours after hatching, never to return to the nest. Families join others in late summer and form coveys that remain together until the next breeding season.

Though bobwhite populations have declined over the past few decades, they still hold a prominent spot in southern states.

Back at Roland's tree stand, he's not seeing any deer, but he doesn't seem to mind. The sound of the bobwhite echoes in the air. And he gladly returns the call.

Larry Ditto/KAC Productions

At a Glance

Size: Bobwhites are 9-3/4 inches with a wingspan of 13 inches.
ID Tips: This small, round-shaped bird has a short tail and neck. It is reddish overall with gray feathers. You almost always find it on the ground.
Voice: You can easily recognize the "bob-bob-white" whistle of the male. Members of the covey communicate with a "ka-loi-kee" call or a soft clucking noise.
Nest: Birds build a nest on the ground, usually in a tussock of grasses. They conceal it with weeds woven into an arch. Females lay 14 to 16 pure-white and pointed eggs. Both parents incubate them for 22 to 24 days until hatching. Chicks leave the nest within hours of hatching and follow their parents. Two broods a year is common.
Diet: Natural foods are weed seeds, wild fruits, legumes, small insects and spiders.
Fun Facts: Bobwhite chicks immediately learn the covey behavior. At less than 14 days, young start to fly, and then by 21 days, they join other families to form a covey.
Backyard Favorites: These lovable little quail will often wander into backyards and gardens in search of food. Offer wild birdseed mix or cracked corn on the ground to attract coveys all winter long.

Eastern Phoebe

Roland Jordahl

These friendly insect eaters are a pleasure to have in your yard.

By George Harrison
Contributing Editor

Imagine having voracious insect eaters working overtime in your yard, keeping the garden free of pesky bugs.

The eastern phoebe is just such an insect eater. As members of the flycatcher family, their diets consist almost entirely of insects. You won't be able to attract these birds with a feeder, but anyone who can lure a pair of these helpful and friendly fliers to nest under the eaves of their house should consider themselves lucky.

The phoebe's friendly personality more than compensates for its plain and drab olive-brown appearance. These birds seem to like people, and people certainly like them.

The two traits that distinguish a phoebe are its constant bobbing tail, and the insistent and rapid repeating of its name with its call, "fee-bee, fee-bee, fee-bee."

This is the sound I heard one day last spring when my neighbor Jean Smith called me over to her backyard to look at a bird nest. I noticed that it was a well-built structure under the eaves of her roof, and a bird was sitting on it incubating eggs. I was happy to inform her that it was an eastern phoebe.

About 10 days later, I returned to the Smith house with my camera and photographed the parent phoebes feeding their nestlings. Like all phoebes, the adults favored a nearby landing perch where they stopped before flying to the nest to feed the young.

The one here was just a post about 5 feet high and 20 feet from the nest. I was delighted when I was able to get photos of both parents on the staging perch, their bills stuffed with food.

Meeting a Legend

When I think of eastern phoebes, I remember the day I met the legendary father of modern bird-watching, Roger Tory Peterson, at a youth camp in West Virginia. I was outside photographing a phoebe's nest on an electric meter.

Peterson seemed interested that a 13-year-old boy with a huge Speed Graphic Press camera was taking black-and-white pictures of phoebes feeding their nestlings. We talked more about photography that day in 1949 than about birds, which surprised me. But that trend continued virtually every time we were together in the decades that followed.

It's not strange to see a phoebe's nest on top of an electric meter because these birds nest in some of the most unusual locations. Before people built

Photos this page: Rolf Nussbaumer

A PLACE TO CALL HOME. Eastern phoebes are known for building their nests in unusual places that are often near people. Above, a group of young birds fill a nest wedged on top of a light fixture. At left, phoebes often stop at a landing perch with food before taking it to their nestlings.

structures, phoebes constructed their nests in cliffs and in the entrances to caves. Today, they favor ledges on man-made structures.

When I was a boy, my dad showed me multiple eastern phoebe nests. One was to the entrance to an old coal mine in western Pennsylvania. The other one he showed me was on a beam under a small bridge crossing Standing Stone Creek in central Pennsylvania.

The Point of Return

I've also seen nests along the curves of downspouts and the tops of cabin bells. If you see a phoebe nest, there's a good chance you could see it again. When they are successful at a nesting site, they usually return to the same spot, year after year.

While visiting Tom and Ann Paugh at their cottage near the Blue Ridge Parkway in Virginia, I noticed a phoebe darting in and out from under their deck as we sat outside.

"Yeah, they nest there every year," Tom said.

To get an even closer look at the nest, we got down on our hands and knees on the deck, and peered down through a crack in the floor to see five white eggs delicately sitting there in a lovely cup of moss.

Eastern phoebes are not likely to visit bird feeders, though they will frequent backyards where there are birdbaths, ponds and a ledge or two on buildings. If you are lucky, a pair will bring joy and entertainment to you as they spend their days catching insects on the wing.

BIRD-WATCHER'S SECRET

Do you have phoebes in your area? You'll know you've got a phoebe in your backyard if you hear it call its own name. They sing a song that sounds like "fee-bee, fee-bee, fee-bee."

Eastern phoebes nest under eaves or beams of buildings. They are especially attracted to buildings that are near water. So keep your eye out. You might be surprised to find these birds in your neighborhood, maybe even nesting on your own house or garage.

At a Glance

Size: Eastern phoebes are 7 inches long with a 10-1/2-inch wingspan.
ID Tips: They are dark olive on top with a slightly darker head and white underparts. Males and females look alike.
Voice: Birds call their own name with a distinct "fee-bee, fee-bee" repeated over and over again.
Nest: You'll see nests on a shelflike projection over windows, on rafters or on bridge girders. They build a 4-1/2-inch nest of weeds, grasses, plant fibers and mud. Females incubate the four to five white eggs for 15 to 16 days. Young leave the nest 2 to 3 weeks later. They typically raise two broods each year.
Diet: These birds eat almost entirely insects, usually caught in flight like other members of the flycatcher family.
Fun Facts: Phoebes often sit upright, flipping their tails to create a wagging effect. In the early 1800s, John James Audubon conducted the first known bird banding on eastern phoebes. He banded them by tying strings around their legs and discovered that they returned to the same nesting spot year after year.
How to Attract: Attach a shelf under the eaves or beams of a building near water to persuade phoebes to settle down in your yard.

Bill Carter

Meadowlark

Listen carefully to recognize the difference between this eastern and western flier.

By George Harrison
Contributing Editor

Dad and I were on a mission. It was a sunny spring day in the 1970s, and we were out searching for an eastern meadowlark nest to photograph in central Wisconsin. Dad needed a photo for a field guide he was working on about eastern birds' nests.

"Take one end of this," Dad said, handing me a long rope.

A male eastern meadowlark was singing on a fence post nearby. This meant that a female was likely sitting on a nest in the field in front of us, so Dad and I were using the rope to flush it out. We gently pulled the rope through the long grass.

"There she goes!" I shouted to Dad as a female meadowlark flew out of the field.

We dropped the rope and rushed over to the

SPRING SONGSTERS. The eastern and western meadowlarks are indistinguishable (above left is an eastern; the other two pictured are western), until they open their bills and sing.

Though the two birds have tunes that are distinctly different, both are musical candy to the ears. In the East, the "spring o' the year" tune is as welcome as spring itself. In the West, once you hear the flutelike reverie of the western meadowlark, you find yourself longing to hear it again and again.

BIRD-WATCHER'S SECRET

You won't find meadowlarks searching your backyard feeders for food. They prefer prairie-like habitats like large, unmowed lawns and grassy fields. There, they'll scrounge for insects and nesting sites, which they build in depressions in the ground. Meadowlarks are known for gathering food in fields by walking, not hopping like most birds.

spot where the bird had emerged. Though it wasn't easy to see under a dome of grass, we eventually found the nest with four spotted white eggs.

As Dad set up his camera, we heard a different meadowlark singing from a nearby utility wire. We couldn't believe our ears.

This bird wasn't singing the usual "spring o' the year" song we had been hearing from the eastern male. Instead, it was a flutelike song, ending in a jumble of sweet notes.

"That's a western meadowlark!" I said.

Look-alike Birds

From appearance alone, this would have been impossible to confirm. Eastern and western meadowlarks look exactly the same. They even share behaviors–they both build similar nests, eat insects, lay identical eggs and neither male goes to the nest until the eggs hatch. The only differences between the two are their songs and ranges.

Breeding territories overlap in some areas for eastern and western meadowlarks. This is why Dad and I heard both birds that day.

Popular Songs

The mellifluous songs of the meadowlarks have also been featured in movie musical scores. The movies sometimes get the species mixed up, though. I remember watching a movie that was set in the Florida Keys, and it featured the song of a western meadowlark. Then there was a John Wayne Western that had the eastern meadowlark belting out its tune.

Sadly, meadowlark populations are declining, especially in the East, as their grassy field habitats are shrinking or getting mowed.

When I purchased my Wisconsin home in 1970, eastern meadowlarks, bobolinks, dickcissels and grasshopper sparrows nested in the grassy field across the road. Unfortunately, the farmer who owned that field needed to cut it for hay at the peak of nesting season. Year after year, more and more meadowlark nests were destroyed. Eventually, the meadowlarks and other birds disappeared from that field. I'm sure this pattern is similar for countless other hayfields across the country as well.

If you ever get a chance to see or hear either of the meadowlarks, consider it a red-letter day. Take a moment to enjoy the beauty of their striking yellow breasts, emblazoned with a black "V." And, of course, soak up their uniquely beautiful songs. May it be music to your ears!

At a Glance

Common names: Eastern and western meadowlark.

Size: Length, 9-1/2 inches; wingspan, 14 to 14-1/2 inches.

ID Tips: Western and eastern appear identical. Both have chunky bodies, short tails and long bills with a black "V" from their throats onto their bright-yellow breasts. Males and females look alike.

Voice: The best way to separate these two species is by their different songs. The western has the more complicated, liquid and flutelike song, starting with several whistles, followed by a jumble of sounds. The eastern's song is a simple, clear and slurred, "spring o' the year." Both sound a sharp "pluk" or "zitt" alarm note or call.

Nest: Female uses grasses to build a ground depression in a grassy field. She incubates three to five spotted white eggs for 13 to 15 days. Both parents feed the young, which leave after 2 weeks.

Diet: Their natural food consists mostly of insects but includes some grains.

Fun Facts: The birds gather food in grassy fields by walking, not hopping.

Backyard Favorites: Both of these striking birds live in prairie-like habitats; therefore, large, unmowed lawns and grassy fields may attract meadowlarks searching for nesting sites and food.

Red-Tailed Hawk

Raptor frequents backyards throughout North America.

By David Shaw, Fairbanks, Alaska

At a Glance

Size: Measures 19 inches long with a wingspan of 49 inches.

ID Tips: Most adults have red tails; colorings and markings can vary by regions, as there are several subspecies.

Voice: Rasping, scraping scream of "cheeeeeewv." Juveniles whistle "pweee, pweee."

Nest: Large and bulky 2 to 3 feet across, made of sticks; often in the tallest tree near the edge of a forest.

Francis and Janice Bergquist

Shortly before I sat down to write this, I watched a pair of red-tailed hawks sail in for the season on a spring wind. These were the dark Harlan's red-tails that breed in the boreal forest surrounding my home in Fairbanks, Alaska.

Watching the pair reminded me of the last red-tails I had seen back in January. I was leading a birding tour at the time in the far southern edge of the species' wintering distribution, high in the mountains of western Panama.

There, I watched a stunning adult hanging nearly still in a stiff breeze rising up the forested slope. Without warning, the hawk folded its wings and fell from the blue sky.

A medium-sized bird fled across a clearing toward the safety of the nearby forest. The prey reached the forest edge at the last possible moment, forcing the red-tail to flare its wings and pitch high into the air. From 100 yards away, I could hear the wind tear through its feathers.

It occurs to me how much these two observations say about this most abundant of North American hawks. From the northern extent of the boreal forest to the tropical forests of Panama, red-tailed hawks live in an incredible range of locations. They occupy almost every conceivable habitat and eat about anything into which they can sink their talons.

Some red-tails are migratory, while others are not. Around my home in interior Alaska, the red-tails arrive in April and depart for their wintering grounds in the lower 48 by late September. In other more temperate parts of the continent, they stick around all year.

In the far south of their range, red-tails are winter visitors. For example, the hawk in Panama hunts the cloud forests and coffee plantations only during the cold northern winter. Come spring, that bird will turn its tail to the tropics and fly back north.

ALL IN TIME. Juvenile red-tails (below) don't have the adults' coloration. First-year red-tails lack the red-colored tail. Instead, their tail is brown and striped.

At left, Maslowski Wildlife; below, Skip Moody/Dembinsky Photo Associates

When it comes to food, red-tails are the consummate generalist, consuming just about everything that walks, creeps, crawls, hops, slithers or flies. They don't care what it is.

I've observed them carrying dead bull snakes to nestlings in Oklahoma, eating a drake mallard duck in Washington and enjoying snowshoe hares here in Alaska. In short, red-tailed hawks will eat whatever is available, be it furred, feathered or even scaled.

Personally, this species holds special significance. My first bird book was *Peterson's Field Guide to Hawks.* I received it as a gift when I was about 10, and for years, it never left my side. Long before my interests spread to other birds, I loved the red-tail, and now, many years later, I still do.

There are few things that make me happier than watching a pair of freshly arrived migrant red-tails spread their wings and spiral away out of sight.

NESTING NOTES

With 14 recognized subspecies, the red-tailed hawk is also incredibly diverse. The northern subspecies, Harlan's hawks, are dark and don't look much like other red-tails. On the other end of the spectrum, the Krider's red-tail, a breeder of the northern Great Plains, is very pale.

Red-tails have a wingspan of 3 to 4 feet, and the birds weigh more than 2 pounds.

Diet: These hawks feed on anything from mice and birds to frogs and snakes.

Fun Facts: Hawks hover high in the air. They have amazing binocular eyesight and can spot prey from hundreds of feet away.

Backyard Favorites: These birds love trees and will also stop by birdbaths.

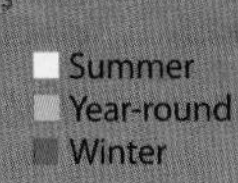

53
73
58
56
68

Chapter 2

No. 1 Green Thumb

47

44

50

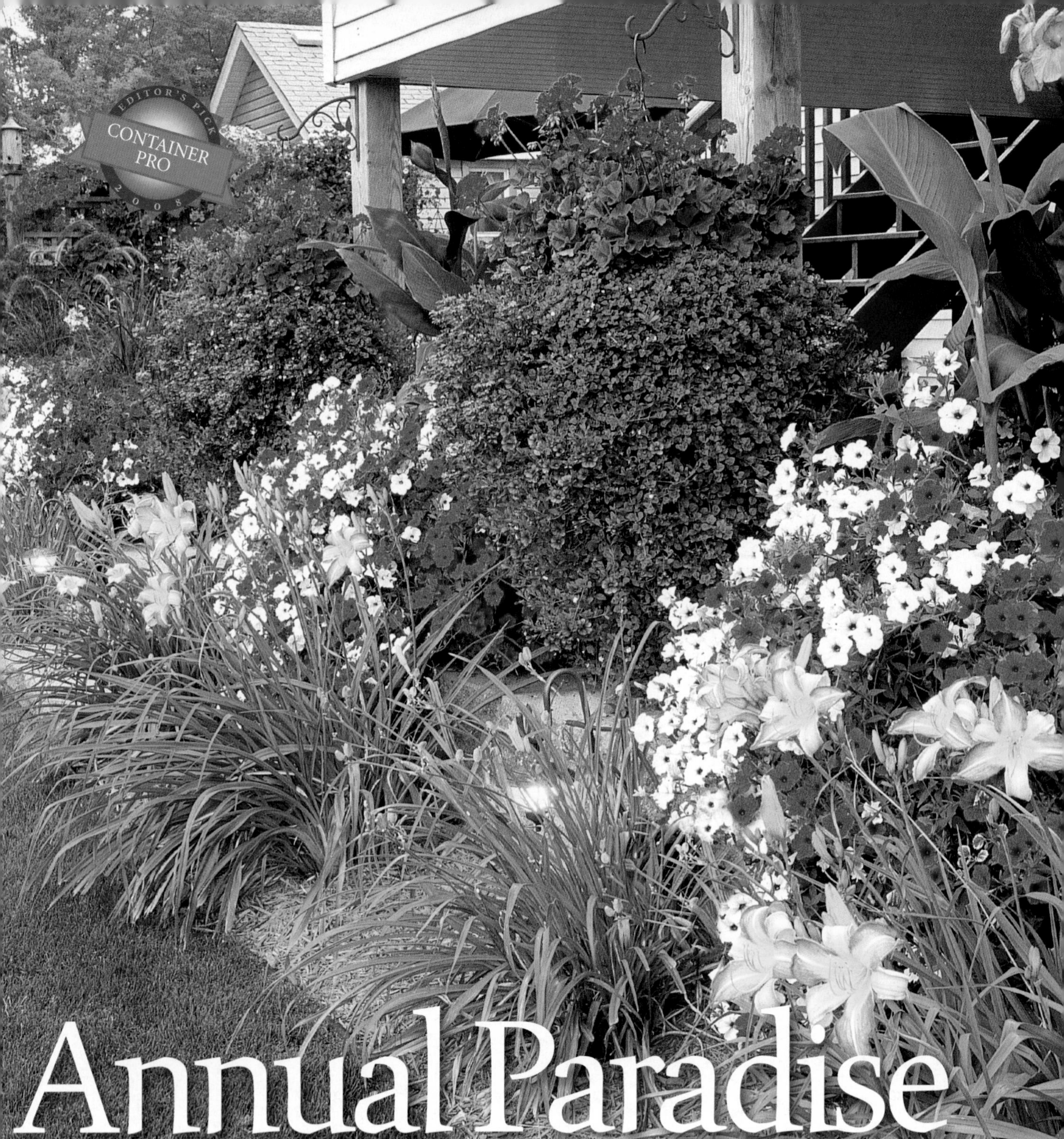

Annual Paradise

Bold and colorful flowers won this reader over at a young age.

By Brenda Kari
Scandia, Minnesota

My love for gardening started when I was 5. My mom was an avid gardener, and she always took me with her on trips to the greenhouse.

I remember looking around at the flower displays with wide eyes and a big smile. Everything was gorgeous! It was like my own little secret getaway.

My favorite part of the trip was when Mom would turn to me and ask me what I wanted. She always let me pick out a couple of plants, and I had a weakness for bright colors.

As I got older, my love for gardening faded a little bit. I was busy with other things in life, and didn't have much time to plant and tend a flower garden. But then, just as I was about to get married, this all changed.

At my bridal shower, one of my friends gave me some potting soil, plant containers and flowers. It was a perfect gift, and from that day forward, I was hooked...again.

Color Doesn't Fade

Now, I'll admit that I'm not a gardening expert. Even though I've been gardening for several years, I'm still not great about knowing the names of plants. But one thing hasn't changed since my childhood—I still love using bright, flashy flowers in my backyard near St. Paul.

Wave petunias are my favorites by far, which you'll easily see by taking a stroll through my yard. I use them just about everywhere, from my hanging baskets and trellis to the many containers scattered about my backyard. I love the bold purple and fuchsia blooms spilling over the top by the dozens.

I absolutely love annuals. It's fun to start with something small in spring and then watch how much it grows throughout summer. Annuals are perfect for making a big impact, no matter the size of your yard.

To save time (and space) with the many annuals in my garden, I take my hanging baskets to one of the local greenhouses in fall. They plant the blooms for me in early spring and keep them there to grow and flourish. Come May, I simply pick up my baskets from the greenhouse, hang up the gorgeous displays and enjoy!

RIDING THE WAVES. Brenda's favorite flowers are Wave petunias (above). She uses them in containers and many flower beds throughout her garden.

Change Is Good

Each year, I try to do something new with the color scheme in my backyard. Mixing different colors throughout the garden really adds a lot of visual interest. My favorite color is yellow, and I'm secretly hoping they'll figure out a way to grow yellow Wave petunias. That would be the best of both worlds!

Though my garden is planted almost entirely in annuals, I do sprinkle in some perennials, such

Q&A with Brenda

What's the one thing you'd change about your yard if you could?
I would make it bigger.

What's your best green-thumb tip for the garden?
Water in the morning before the sun comes up.

If you could have only one flower in your garden, what would it be?
Wave petunias.

If there were no weeding or gardening chores to do, how would you spend your day in the garden?
I would probably just lie down and soak up the sun.

What plant do you think is overrated?
Daylily.

What plant do you think is underrated?
Purple fountain grass.

What garden tool can you not live without?
I can't do without my miniature spade.

What's your best money-saving secret?
With containers, I reuse some of my potting soil in pest-free containers. It saves money and time!

CRAYON COLORS. Brenda (above left) loves boldly colored flowers and uses them wherever she can, including around her pond (above).

GREEN THUMB TIP

I plant mostly annuals, but I like to sprinkle in a few perennials. Clematis, daylilies, Karl Forester feather reed grass and hostas all create attractive combinations when planted with annuals.
—Brenda Kari, Scandia, Minnesota

as clematis, daylilies, Karl Forester feather reed grass and hostas. The plants create attractive combinations.

People see my colorful yard from the road as they're driving by, and they sometimes stop in for a closer look. I love to share my garden with guests!

Gardening Routines

I find gardening very therapeutic. During the growing season, I go out in the early morning and water before I go to work. I find this is the perfect time of day to clear my mind, and it's also beneficial to my plants.

If I water at night, I've found that the plants tend to get moldy. But after a morning watering, the flowers seem to soak up the energy throughout the day while the sun shines.

Not everything is as easy, though. One of my greatest garden goofs happened a few years ago when I accidentally burned my plants.

It was a sunny day, and I was out watering my plants. I like to use one of those convenient fertilizer jugs where you just add the powder and then hook it up to your garden hose.

Unfortunately, too much fertilizer flowed out at once. Plus, it was really hot that day. This combination burned my flowers, and I eventually had to throw many of them away.

Now I have my fertilizer routine down perfectly. I got some great tips from a local greenhouse, and my plants stay looking good much longer these days.

Passing It on

Today I am a mother myself. I have twins—a boy and a girl—who are 1. It will probably be a couple of years before they can really dig in and help with the garden, but I do hope it's something they will want to be involved with.

Gardening is definitely a part of who I am, and I want my kids to be a part of that. It's such a good way to spend time outside and enjoy nature.

I'm sure they'll pluck some blooms along the way and my flower beds won't be perfect, but it will be fun. Pretty soon, I'll be the one taking my kids to the greenhouse.

Photos by John Rockwood

Getting into Shape

Gardener brings backyard to life with creative plantings.

By Sue Rockwood
Auburn,
New Hampshire

Steve Smith plants everything in his yard with a purpose.

From his colorful layered beds to animal-shaped topiaries featuring the Loch Ness Monster, every little detail counts.

"I like to find something new to do every year in my garden," Steve says. "I love creating new designs and keeping them shaped with plants and flowers."

You can't help but feel childish delight when you're in his Tewksbury, Massachusetts backyard. Around every corner is a surprise and feast for the eyes.

The idea for Steve's garden began 24 years ago because he wanted to connect the three-tier waterfall around his pool to his ponds farther up the hill. He started with the trees, cutting down a few and adding several new varieties throughout the yard.

After he planted those, Steve started filling in the areas with plants. Pretty soon, there were beautiful flower gardens around the trees, pool and the rest of the yard.

The Family Gardener

"I've worked with flowers since I was 14," Steve says. "I did the gardening at my family's home where my father had his doctor's practice. His patients loved spending time in my gardens while

COLORFUL MASTERPIECES. Steve Smith's yard is bursting with color. His robust containers (above right), flower beds and topiaries (like this seal with a blue ball above) bring his yard to life.

GREEN THUMB TIP

Steve recommends turning the soil around plants as you're weeding. Soil is one of the most important components of a successful and healthy garden. It's best to keep the soil loose and air flowing to the roots.

waiting for their appointments."

Those early years with flowers made quite an impression on Steve. He loved the fact that he could make so many people happy with plants. After that, gardening became a permanent part of his life.

"I love sharing my garden," Steve says.

"I often have visitors from a nearby assisted living center. They bring their box lunches with them and just love spending time in my garden."

Add Life to the Garden

Steve's garden is all about balance and contrast of colors. The different types of trees he has planted stage the background for his flower gardens.

"I love having different shades of greens and yellows, so I get my trees from various nurseries for the best variety," he says.

Steve's secret for achieving the eye-catching symmetry of his gardens goes back to their shapes.

"I trim most of my trees to get them to grow in fuller," he says. "Anything can benefit from the right shape."

Throughout Steve's garden, unique topiaries abound. One of his favorites is a seal (above left) that sits near the pool. The seal is balancing a blue glass ball on its nose. And the Loch Ness Monster can't help but impress you with its green and burgundy serpentine body winding through the yard.

"Topiaries can take a long time to fill in, so you need some patience, but they're worth it," Steve says. "My seal took almost 4 years to complete, but my Loch Ness Monster was a bit faster."

Steve arranges his garden to have plenty of contrast so onlookers can appreciate every planting individually.

"The whole yard is like a painting," Steve says. "I arrange my garden with the idea in mind to have open space. Everything looks better if you have a little green in between."

Shape It with Flowers

Each year, Steve illuminates his garden with new colors. But instead of adding rows of flowers, he likes planting in rounded shapes or creating interesting designs. "You can easily accomplish any shape you want with annuals," Steve says. "Some of my favorite flowers to use for shaping beds are dahlias, ageratum, coleus and tree roses."

Steve's best tip for keeping an overall healthy garden is to take care of your soil.

"Once you plant something, it's always a good idea to turn the soil when you're weeding," he says. "The flowers grow better if you give more air to the roots and keep the soil loose. For container gardening, I recommend using a soil mix. Adding time-release fertilizer can also make a real difference in plant growth."

It's clear to see that Steve's bliss is in his garden. He puts a lot of tender, loving care and long hours into it, and it shows. From his topiary masterpieces to his bursting flower beds, all the shapes and angles come together perfectly.

Rural Charm

By Carl J. Klompien
Sioux Center, Iowa

You'll feel right at home among the flowers and trinkets in this central Iowa garden.

As a retired pastor, I always look forward to the beauty God has waiting around the corner. You never know what you'll find next. A couple of years ago, that beauty came to me in the form of a gorgeous garden near a little town in central Iowa.

Some 20 years ago, I was the pastor of a large rural church near Sully, Iowa. I still go back to visit old friends and preach in the church. During one of those visits, my wife, Ellen, and I had the privilege of staying near our friends Bob and Jan Pothoven in Kellogg.

We were both amazed by Jan's magnificent yard and gardens. Everywhere you looked, blooms seemed to light up the corners of her property. Now, anytime I'm in the area, I have to stop and take a stroll through Jan's backyard.

TEAMWORK MAKES IT WORK. Jan and Bob Pothoven are a great gardening duo. She supplies the vision, and he helps bring it to life.

Time to Play

Jan and Bob (below left) moved into their house more than 40 years ago. During the first 25 years, they spent a lot of time working on the inside of the house and growing vegetables on the outside.

Once their two children left for college, Jan finally found the time she had always wanted to garden. You see, Jan used to work in a bank, and her garden was the perfect escape. Today, it still helps her get away from the stresses of everyday life.

Some of Jan's favorite things in the garden come from the "art" she picks up from antique stores or garage sales. She loves to find ordinary pieces, and then Bob helps make her vision come alive.

"I can't always explain very well what I want to do, but fortunately Bob is very good at coming up with a way to accomplish my mission," Jan says.

Jan was at a craft sale one day when she found a pole with hearts that said "Garden of Love." This single item inspired her to make a flower garden in honor of her son, Scott.

"It really became a tribute to Scott," Jan said. "I included the bike he used to ride from our home to his grandparents' house (above right). I also added an old basketball rim, depicting his passion for playing basketball in high school and college. And now that he loves golf, I included an old golf bag with clubs."

SCOTT'S GARDEN. Above, Jan created this garden to honor her son, Scott. His old bicycle and basketball hoop are among the blooms.

It's All About Presentation

Not only does Jan know how to create new beauty in her yard, but she also knows how to hide the not-so-beautiful things.

They have a gas tank right in the middle of their yard, so Jan had Bob make a fence from old barn boards. With a few flowers, a walkway and a bench, she turned an eyesore into an eye-pleasing focal point.

Containers share equal space with the flower beds in Jan's yard. She says they add color to the

Q&A with Jan

If money and time weren't factors, what feature would you add to your garden?
I'd love to add a pond with a waterfall.

What's your best green-thumb tip for the garden?
Take the time to practice good weed prevention. For me, adding mulch works the best. It takes a little work, but it saves a lot of time and effort in the long run.

If you could only have one flower in your garden, what would it be?
Geraniums. When a geranium is in full bloom, it's beautiful. A close second would be hibiscus.

What's one thing you'd change about your yard if you could?
I would add more trees. We've had some really bad ice storms over the past few years, and we've lost a lot of trees.

What's your idea of a dream garden?
Garden sculptures and other yard art, surrounded by perennials. I love mixing objects throughout the garden.

If there were no weeding or gardening chores to do, how would you spend your day in the garden?
I would sit, relax and prune the flowers, which isn't a chore to me.

What plant do you think is overrated?
I think roses are overrated.

What plant do you think is underrated?
Impatiens. What would we do without them? They add marvelous color to a garden.

MIX AND MATCH. Jan often uses interesting objects she finds at garage sales or antique stores as focal points in her many flower beds. Everything is fair game to Jan, from an old red wagon wheel (above) to a weathered rooster statue (below).

yard and they're easy to move. For the containers, Jan mixes soil from their farm along with potting soil and a small bucket of corn gluten. It's a byproduct of corn that Bob feeds to their cattle, and it really seems to improve the soil.

Another trick Jan uses is to plant her flower beds on a gradual curve.

GREEN THUMB TIP

Recycled items from garage sales and craft sales are a great way to turn an eyesore into a beautiful focal point in the backyard. Adding pieces of garden art is a no-fail way to add interest.
—Jan Pothoven, Kellogg, Iowa

"I've never had anyone make a diagram of my garden for me. I just do it as I go," Jan says. "I like planting on curves because I like the look, and it makes it easier to mow!"

When Jan starts a new area, she begins by placing at least three similar plants in one area or row. Then she adds a little garden art.

"I'll use just about any object," Jan says. "Iron sculptures, rocks, birdhouses—these items and more do wonders to make the garden more interesting."

The Perfect View

While there's beauty from every angle, one of the best views of Jan's garden is inside, from the kitchen window.

"I'm married to a farmer, so I spend a lot of time in my kitchen," Jan says. "I still wanted to enjoy my garden from as I look outside, so I made sure all my flower beds are in full view from the window."

The Unfinished Garden

This backyard has come a long way, but it won't be complete anytime soon.

I don't know that my flower beds will ever be finished. In my mind, they're starting to look good. One day, they might even look great. But right now, they're still in the building stage.

My husband, Arik, and I bought our 2-acre lot 10 years ago after we got married. At the time, all that was here were three sedum plants, about five lilies and a huge mass of weeds, stone, glass, and everything else you can imagine. We intentionally bought a fixer-upper, and I couldn't wait to get started.

My first project was to tackle the area under some evergreens. Here, there was an old, half-buried stone fence surrounded with weeds. After trimming the trees, overgrown shrubs and much weeding, I finally started planting. Now, more than 20 sedum plants later, it seems to be progressing well.

Many people told me I wouldn't get anything to grow under evergreens, but I've grown sedum, lilies, columbine, hens and chicks, hostas, gaillardia, yarrow and coneflowers. The plants don't get as tall as they usually would, but they still look great!

Sowing the Seed Takes Time

When I first started gardening, I thought it would be cheaper to plant seeds, so that's all that I bought. Some worked while others didn't, and it

By Judy Schema
Kiel, Wisconsin

"IT GREW ON ME." Autumn Joy sedum (above) was one of the only plants around when Judy and Arik moved into their home. It's now one of her favorites.

ended up taking a lot longer than I'd expected to get results. I've learned from that experience, though. Now, I always start with plants. It's a lot easier, and I have much better success overall.

My knowledge of plants started out small, and then quickly grew as I read catalogs and books. Early on, I only knew about a couple of plants, but now I feel like I have a small botanical encyclopedia in my head.

One of my favorite areas in the yard is my sun garden. It started because Arik wanted to get rid of a box elder tree near our house. I immediately got out a piece of paper and started drawing a picture of what I wanted the area to look like. I loved organizing the plants by color, shape, height and bloom time.

Then Arik suggested I add a pond into the picture. I was thrilled, and quickly redrew my design. As soon as we got the pond in place, I was planting, placing stone and organizing my new flower bed.

Planning Is Half the Fun

It was such an accomplishment to see it come together from beginning to end. Some of the sun-loving plants in that area include yarrow, Asiatic lilies and black-eyed Susans.

As every gardener knows, sometimes plants just don't work in certain areas. Along the way, I've learned what works and what doesn't in my own backyard. Every mistake and new discovery encourages me to plant more. Arik always knows when I'm starting a new garden because I start moving stones and roughing out the new area in the yard.

Over the years, I've learned that there are two main types of gardeners—those who like form and then those who don't. For example, some people like to have their gardens perfectly balanced, while others will plant all different kinds of flowers in one area.

I like to do a little bit of both. I grow plenty of different varieties, but at the same time, I like to group blooms. For example, I use a 4-foot rule

UP, UP AND AWAY. When Judy and Arik first moved into their home, this mock orange shrub (above) was only 6 feet. Now, it's more than 12 feet tall and looks great next to this flower bed.

Q&A with Judy

If money and time weren't factors, what feature would you add to your garden?
I'd love to have a gazebo or pergola. I use arches now, but one day I'd like to have something bigger.

What's your idea of a dream garden?
I like an organized flower bed with a good symmetrical balance. I don't want a lot of clutter among my flowers.

What's your best money-saving secret for the garden?
I like to divide and relocate plants. It's an inexpensive way to add to your garden. Plus, you can exchange with your friends, too.

If you could only have one flower in your garden, what would it be?
Gaillardia (blanket flower). It's easy to grow, has great color, and there are a lot of unique varieties to choose from.

What's your most treasured piece of garden art?
The lighthouse from my mother. She passed away last year. She collected lighthouses, and I have the one from her garden.

If there were no weeding or chores to do, how would you spend a day in the garden?
I would just walk around and enjoy the sights and sounds of my garden, like those from the butterflies and birds.

What plant is overrated?
Tulips. I can't seem to get them to last for more than a year or two.

What plant is underrated?
Yarrows. People often think they're invasive, but if you grow the right ones and care for them correctly, they're great.

Do you remember the first plant you ever grew?
The first plant I grew here was Autumn Joy sedum. It was one of the only plants here when we moved into our home. I didn't know what it was at first, but it quickly became one of my favorites.

with my plantings. I plant several varieties to fill a 4-foot area, so when they're in bloom, they create a bigger impact.

Another element that adds impact to my garden is lighting. I now know why this has become such a popular trend. I love the way the lights look at night, and how they light up the movement of the flags and spinners scattered throughout the area. We now enjoy relaxing in our garden from day into night.

What's Mine Is Yours

My gardens are always open to people who want to come and see them. I often offer visitors a plant to take home so they can expand their own garden with a piece from my own.

Sharing is the best part of gardening, and it's fun to build your flower beds using other gardeners' favorites.

So, as you can see, my gardens are always a work-in-progress. I wouldn't have it any other way, though. To me, it's all part of the fun. I'm constantly adding new plants, garden art and more to my space.

My backyard may never be finished, but I'm definitely going to enjoy myself along the way.

Backyard Rescue

By David Hynds
Orlando, Florida

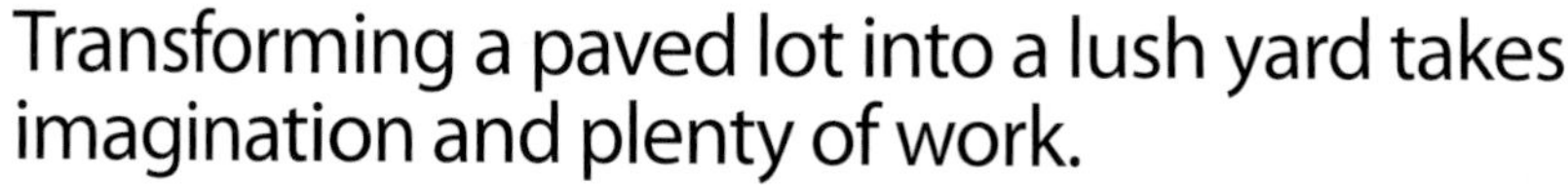
Transforming a paved lot into a lush yard takes imagination and plenty of work.

Fifteen years ago, I bought a 1930s home near downtown Orlando that had once been a two-family rental property. The yard was paved with concrete and used as a parking lot by the tenants. After I moved in, I'd drive into my parking lot and dream of a yard full of flowers and wildlife. I knew there was a lot of work ahead of me.

Little by little, I planted my garden. I imagined creating an escape from everyday life, a little piece of green heaven where I could sit, relax and listen to the birds. The more I planted, the more encouraged I became.

I put bricks recycled from old Chicago buildings right onto the concrete to create a beautiful courtyard. Then I cut holes in the concrete to plant five trees. Finally, I built a deck for lounging and dreaming. At last, it became the perfect place to have garden parties.

As any gardener knows, it's hard to stop once you start. Pretty soon, I was dreaming of more elements to add to my backyard. Since one of my favorite plants is wisteria, I knew I wanted to find a way to incorporate it into the garden. To do this, I built an arbor where it could grow freely (right).

After the wisteria was in place, I turned my attention to building a pond. It wasn't long before I had built a two-tiered waterfall from scratch with river rocks.

Somewhere along the way, I found the time to get married. Now my wife, Laura Lee, enjoys the garden as much as I do. She adds a few personal touches by planting great container gardens.

Our 3-year-old son, Alex, even gets involved. He has his own flower garden. I love working in

the garden while Laura Lee and Alex are outside at the same time, laughing, digging for worms, running through the sprinkler or playing hide-and-seek. The backyard truly is an outdoor getaway that the whole family enjoys.

Our yard is finally the beautiful, peaceful haven I dreamed it would be, and the National Wildlife Federation has certified it as a Backyard Wildlife Habitat. We have dragonflies, frogs, goldfish, birds, raccoons, lizards, opossums, bees, butterflies and, of course, mosquitoes.

I think back to the days when this was a parking lot and reflect on what all these creatures were missing. When we sit on the deck and watch the baby birds being fed by their parents, the butterflies laying eggs, and the bees enjoying the flowers, I am reminded that I did something good in my life.

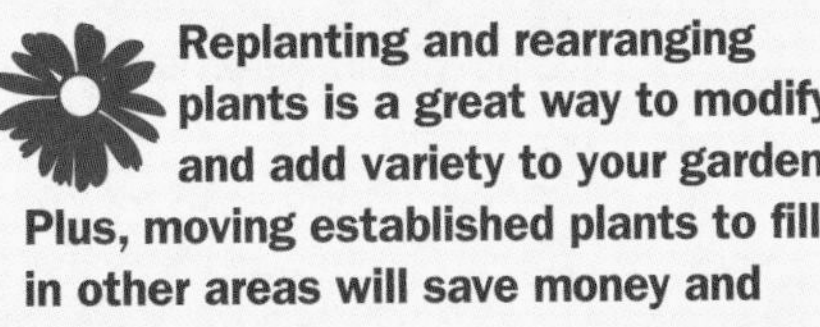

GREEN THUMB TIP

Replanting and rearranging plants is a great way to modify and add variety to your garden. Plus, moving established plants to fill in other areas will save money and time.

—David Hynds, Orlando, Florida

Q&A with David

If time and money weren't factors, what feature would you add to your garden?
A bigger waterfall and a stream.

What's your best money-saving secret for the garden?
Rearranging and replanting established plants to fill in other areas.

What garden tool can't you live without?
Hand trimmers.

If you could only have one flower in your garden, what would it be?
Wisteria.

What's your idea of a dream garden?
One with water features and hidden spaces.

What's your favorite fragrant flower?
Gardenia.

What's one of your gardening disasters?
A tiny handmade pond that turned into a raccoon bidet!

If you didn't have any chores to do, how would you spend a day in the garden?
Reading books, listening to the birds and dreaming by the waterfall.

Is there a plant you think is overrated?
Hibiscus.

What plant is underrated?
Wisteria.

Bird Paradise

This gardener always keeps her feathered friends in mind.

By Sharon Coyle, Mukwonago, Wisconsin

Blue jay

Red-bellied woodpecker

Baltimore oriole

Bird photos: Terry Molter

When Susan Bergmann wants a little slice of heaven, she just steps outside. She loves sitting on her deck (above) with a cup of tea, overlooking the shaded bird sanctuary and flower wonderland in her Mukwonago, Wisconsin backyard.

This avid bird-watcher and nature lover delights in any bird that stops by for a bite to eat. She has 18 different feeders and offers her feathered friends everything from birdseed and nuts to huge quantities of grape jelly for the Baltimore orioles.

"The orioles go through grape jelly so quickly that I've adapted several hanging feeders made from Cool Whip cartons," Susan says. "I fill the cartons up to the top with jelly, but then it's gone in no time."

Feeding an Interest in Birds

Susan's interest in birds started out small, when

COMBINING TWO LOVES. Susan had been gardening for years when she first started birding. Now she combines the two hobbies by designing her garden for the birds.

she put out a few feeders. Once the birds started coming, she wanted to identify them and her interest grew.

"Pretty soon, my son Geoffrey and I joined a birding group, and we were discovering all kinds of new birds," Susan says. "After one spring migration, I was hooked."

Susan knew if she wanted to attract as many birds as possible, then she would need the right mix in her backyard. She was already an avid gardener, so she got to work adding a water feature and even more shrubs and plants that she knew the birds would love.

Cozy Nooks and Big Spaces

Susan's 1-acre yard is a mix of shade and sun. Evergreen trees border the yard, and flower gardens add to the peaceful beauty.

She has a small pond nestled in a cozy spot within the yard. It includes lava rock with a waterfall that attracts all kinds of birds, especially warblers in spring. In winter, she keeps a heater in the pond so the birds can still enjoy a drink.

The birds are always on Susan's mind when she plants her garden. Bee balm and trumpet vines are her favorite flowers to use for attracting hummingbirds. When the growing season is over, Susan doesn't let that stop her from attracting birds. She leaves the heads on her coneflowers and black-eyed Susans to feed finches in winter. She also plants highbush cranberries, serviceberries and chokeberries, which are also a great food source in winter.

According to Susan, anytime of year is a good time to watch birds. She especially loves spring when the migratory birds are passing through. Summer has its perks because that's when she enjoys watching adult birds feed their young. And autumn and winter bring in the berry eaters.

Gardening has always been important to Susan, but now she has something to garden for. Birds dash in and out of her yard, and she wouldn't have it any other way.

Q&A with Susan

What gardening chore do you dislike?
I hate removing invasive species like garlic mustard and buckthorn. You just can't keep up with it.

What's your best money-saving secret for the garden?
You can save a lot of money by splitting up plants and nursing along seedlings. I also love getting plants from friends.

What garden tool can you not live without?
I have a spade that is incredibly small but strong. I can do heavy digging with it to remove invasive species.

If you could only have one flower in your garden, what would it be?
My garden is really shaded, and I love Corydalis lutea. It's a fernlike plant that reminds me of a bleeding heart in texture, but it has yellow blooms. It has wonderful dainty flowers, and it self-seeds.

If there were no weeding or chores to do, how would you spend a day in the garden?
I would sit out on my deck with binoculars and a book. I rarely just get to sit outside and watch.

Do you remember the first plant you ever grew?
I remember growing marigolds as a Brownie project.

What plants never fail you?
Hostas. They only way they fail me is when the deer come and eat them!

What bird is most entertaining in your garden?
For me, it's the black-capped chickadee (right) because they have so much personality. It's almost like they're bouncing around with happiness.

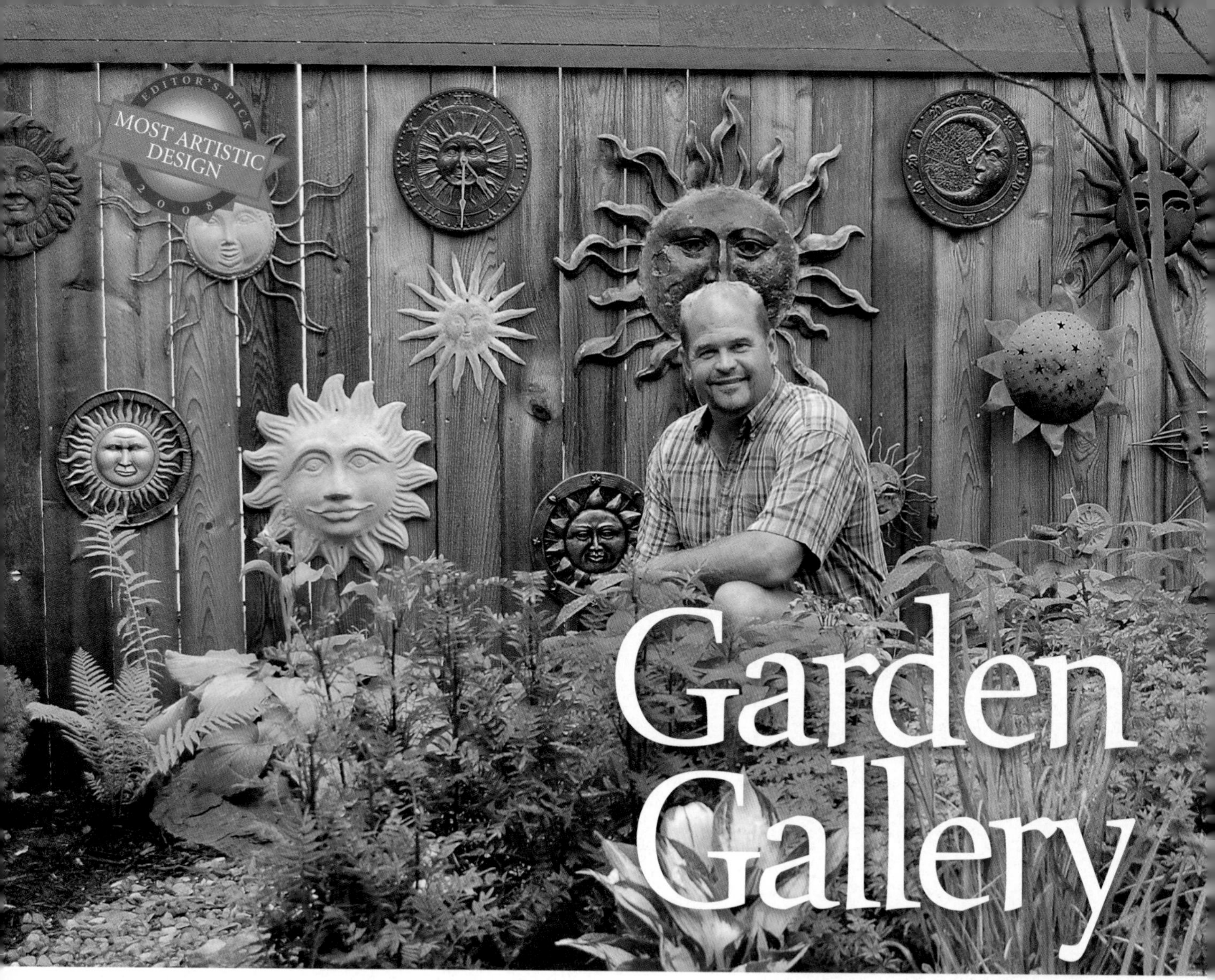

EDITOR'S PICK
MOST ARTISTIC DESIGN
2008

Garden Gallery

A home owner mixes art with flowers to make his backyard come alive.

By Karen L. Kirsch
Louisville, Ohio

When artist Russ Hench moved into his home 3 years ago, it was similar to all the others in the area. It was stately and handsome, with mature trees and a manicured lawn, but there was very little in the way of flowers and color.

As a professional landscape designer for more than 25 years, Russ was eager to work on his own yard for a change. In just 2 years, he transformed his ho-hum expanse of grass and overgrown plantings into a series of dramatic outside rooms.

"I wanted to bring the indoors outside," Russ says. "I designed my backyard to be a place where people can relax and feel at home."

Russ' neighborhood in Canton, Ohio is known for its elegant Tudor-style homes built in the 1920s and '30s, each with its own unique character. Unfortunately, the landscaping didn't match the house, so Russ set out to give the space the elegance it deserved.

To kick things off, Russ removed most of the existing shrubbery around the house. He knew it would be better to start from scratch than work

with existing plants.

"Fifty years ago, we didn't have the variety of plants we have today," Russ says. "People used to plant rhododendrons that grew 20 feet high or more. Now, we have plants that are much more manageable."

After he started getting the plants in place, Russ moved on to the bigger picture. He needed to de-

sign a pergola for a local home and garden show, so he offered to pay for the materials so he could keep it for his own yard. Following the show, he dismantled the piece and reinstalled it at his home.

"It was a win-win arrangement," Russ says.

GREEN THUMB TIP

Just because certain items aren't intended to be in the garden, doesn't mean they shouldn't be. I especially love using old windows. Recycling is a huge money-saver.

—Russ Hench, Canton, Ohio

"The pergola made my patio complete, and then I planted silver lace vine to cover the area and provide some shade. Silver lace was the perfect choice. It's a wonderfully rampant vine without being destructive."

The Right Accessories

Russ enjoys incorporating his artistic side into his garden. One of the most impressive areas in his garden is a wall just beyond the patio filled with artful metal suns (far left), some of which he created himself.

Above the pergola are hand-blown glass globes suspended over a table (above), adding whimsical tranquility to the area.

Pathways of brick and gravel meander through the entire garden, which Russ ties together

COMPLEMENTARY COLORS. To make an impact in his garden, Russ added colorful art elements like suspended glass globes in the pergola (above) and bold sun sculptures (far left).

Q&A with Russ

If time weren't a factor, what would you add to your garden?
Outdoor lighting. I haven't done that yet and would like to give it a try.

What gardening chore do you hate?
Planting bulbs.

What's your best money-saving secret?
I like using things that others don't intend to use in the garden. For instance, I love using old windows.

What's your most essential garden tool?
A wheelbarrow.

If you could only have one plant in your garden, what would it be?
Coleus. I know it's not exotic, but there's nothing like them, especially the larger varieties.

What's your idea of a dream garden?
To me, it's one that's not too large and overwhelming to maintain. I like the idea of going out for a few hours or on a weekend, and then I'm done.

If there were no weeding or chores to do, how would you spend a day in the garden?
I do a lot of entertaining, and I love to share my garden with others.

Do you think any plants are overrated?
Yes, rhododendrons and azaleas. They tend to be very fickle.

What plant is underrated?
Arborvitae. People think they're just tall and skinny, but they don't often use them to their full potential. These great plants require almost zero maintenance.

What's the first plant you ever grew?
When I just started gardening, I remember growing Christmas roses. I only have one left now, and I'm always looking for good varieties of these.

through repeated colors and textures. For instance, a cedar fence flows naturally from the weathered cedar wood shingles of the house.

While plants like shrub roses, black-eyed Susans, viburnums and sweet potato vines are common elements found throughout Russ' garden, it's the rare and exotic artwork that makes the space unique.

Formal with a Twist

"It's the theme of my garden from front to back," Russ says. "It's important for me to have artwork on the outside as well as inside at my home. My backyard has a sense of formality, but with a twist."

Russ mostly uses common plants, especially annuals, to make a statement in his own garden. So what accounts for his showy results?

"I'm not one of those less-is-more people," Russ says. "I like abundance. I may use ordinary flowers, but I use a lot of them, and the results speak for themselves."

Rise Above It All

He overcame the poor soil in his yard with raised beds—more than 20 in all!

By Joe Dyer
Pembroke, Massachusetts

You don't have to have great soil in your backyard to have a great garden.

Take my yard for example. Half the soil is clay and the other half sand—you want neither of which if you are a gardener. But this doesn't stop me from growing hundreds of gorgeous flowers.

So what's my secret? Raised beds.

With raised beds, it doesn't matter what kind of soil you already have. You can easily isolate an area by bringing in new or modifying existing soil.

I built my first raised bed more than 15 years ago when my wife and I moved into our home. The backyard was pretty sparse. It had a single pine tree and virtually no lawn.

We added a deck right away, but I still didn't have any plants to look at, so I put in a large raised bed. I filled it with mostly perennials, and it looked so good that I made another. Once I got going on this process, I couldn't stop!

Every week I was going to the nursery and

A MATTER OF PERSPECTIVE. Joe Dyer doesn't have great soil in his backyard, but that doesn't stop him from creating a beautiful landscape. With raised beds and unique planters (like the one above), his garden is always in bloom.

transplanting flowers into new raised beds. I must have hauled hundreds of yards of loam in with my wheelbarrow to fill those beds. And with each one, I added aged cow manure that I picked up from a nearby farm.

The Secret's in the Mixture

Now I combine manure and loam for all my raised beds and plantings. It seems to be the perfect mix, too, because people are always asking me how I got my flowers to look so good.

Not all of my plants are in raised beds, though. I have some great vines, like wisteria and grapevine, that grow great on arbors and trellises. The hummingbirds love my honeysuckle vine.

I have plenty of great trees and shrubs, too. Some of my favorites include mountain ash, flowering plum, mimosa, lion's head Japanese maple,

BACKYARD FAVORITES. Joe loves his mountain ash tree (left) because it provides berries for the birds. And wisteria (above) is one of his favorite plants.

Japanese stewartia, umbrella pine and Kousa dogwood.

After I got several of my raised beds in place, I started thinking of other ways to add life around our garden. When I was a kid, I used to visit a neighbor's house. She had a pond with fish in her backyard, and I remember thinking, *I'm going to have fish like that one day.*

My first pond was about 14 by 12 feet, and I filled it with koi. I couldn't stop with just one pond, though. I soon put in four more small ones and filled them with goldfish. I enjoy my fish year-round because I bring them indoors during winter to a large tank in my basement.

In addition to fish, we also have six laying hens and three Pygmy goats that stay in pens I built among the raised beds. Plenty of wildlife visit our backyard, too.

Every year around St. Patrick's Day, a pair of ducks land in my yard. I also attract a variety of birds with my nearly 15 birdhouses and several feeders. This year, we even had wild turkeys come through the yard.

GREEN THUMB TIP

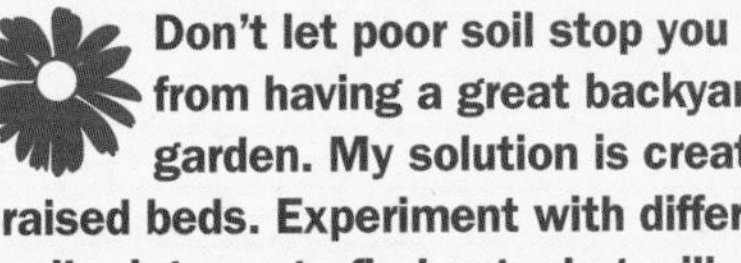

Don't let poor soil stop you from having a great backyard garden. My solution is creating raised beds. Experiment with different soil mixtures to find out what will work best in your yard.

—Joe Dyer, Pembroke, Massachusetts

So Much for Poor Soil

Today, we have 20 trees, 13 vines, 100 shrubs and 24 raised beds filled with flowers, berries and vegetables. The view from my deck couldn't be better. There's never a dull moment, thanks to the goats, chickens and other wildlife.

Our backyard entertains us year-round. Even when we put the beds away for fall, there's always something new around the corner. I put a heated birdbath on our deck in winter, and we always keep our feeders stocked with seed, nuts and suet.

During the colder months, I tie tree and pine branches to my railings with plastic ties. This helps give the birds some protection from the hawks.

I never imagined my backyard with poor soil would be filled with flowers and wildlife, but it's been one of my greatest accomplishments over the years.

My yard proves that you don't need perfect soil to create a great garden getaway. Now that I'm retired, I'll have even more time to spend in it!

Q&A with Joe

If time and money weren't factors, what feature would you add to your garden?
I would put an irrigation center in my yard. I have a well right now, and I have to water by hand.

What's your best garden tip for others?
Find the right fertilizer mix for your garden. I use cow manure, and it works great for my plants. If you can find the right fit for your garden, it can do wonders.

If you could only have one flower in your garden, what would it be?
I have to choose two—hibiscus and dahlias. I love plants with big flowers.

What's one of your gardening disasters?
Roses. I've spent a lot of money on them without success.

If you didn't have any chores to do, how would you spend a day in the garden?
I would sit on my deck with a glass of wine.

Is there a plant you think is overrated?
Chinese lantern and obedient plant. They are invasive, so I don't like to see anyone encourage them.

What plant is underrated?
Wisteria.

Planting Partners

They create loads of color in their farmyard from spring well into fall.

You'll immediately feel welcome as you step into Calvin and Shirley Nordberg's South Haven, Minnesota yard. Spilling over with impatiens and petunias, the flower-packed containers that dangle from their driveway-side posts offer guests a preview of the riotous gardens the couple cultivates around their 100-year-old farmhouse.

Century Masterpiece

Calvin and Shirley happily reside on a farm that's been in Calvin's family for more than a century. The couple married in 1950 and have been gardening together ever since. They tended sweeping vegetable gardens during their dairy-farming years.

As their four children grew older, Shirley downsized her produce production and turned her artistic eye to flower gardening. Meanwhile, Calvin built trellises, erected large, freestanding plant stands, and fashioned other structures that support Shirley's love of blossoms.

"His help really encourages me to do more things," Shirley says. "He does a lot of building for me. He built arches and trellises where our barn—taken by a tornado—once stood. With his help, I've been able to do so many things in the garden."

The most striking of Shirley's gardens encircles a pond that Calvin installed behind their home. He framed the preformed pond basin with boards and stones to give it a natural appearance. Then he planted water lilies that protect his ever-expanding families of goldfish.

The Perfect Mix

The pond border is a work in progress that is likely to look different from year to year. Perennials, such as lilies, blue salvia and purple coneflowers, are the stalwarts that return year after year. But the annual plants shift along with Shirley's springtime planting mood. One year, petunias may ring the pond; the next year, flame-hued marigolds may take the stage.

"I like plants that make it through our winters and do well each year—plants that reliably return," Shirley says. "I have a good mix of perennials, but I use a lot of annuals to fill in. As holes appear, I try to add something that's new to me and different."

Shirley ensures there is loads of color from spring to fall. Early-spring tulips give way to bearded irises, perennial geraniums and columbine. A few weeks later, stands of tiger lilies bloom along with clumps of daylilies, masses of daisies and hardy hibiscus (left). Toward summer's end, Autumn Joy sedum flowers alongside still-trucking zinnias, cleome and marigolds that carry the gardens to and through frost.

More Is Better

In addition to the pond garden, Shirley tends a modest vegetable garden, smaller flower beds and chromatic container groupings displayed on a freestanding 27-pot plant stand (right).

Shirley's a frugal gardener who saves seeds from her favorite plants, and starts flats of impatiens, petunias, and other annuals and perennials in a basement growing center.

"My advice to gardeners is to choose plants that please you and to enjoy what you're doing," Shirley says. "I really enjoy what I have and love to work with the things I've planted."

Q&A with Shirley

If you could only have one flower in your garden, what would it be?
Roses. Although they take a bit of work this far north, you just can't beat a rose when it blooms.

What plant is overrated?
The biggest disappointment for me has been butterfly bush. I started some from seed and planted them in the rocks around the pond. They grew beautifully for a couple of years, and then after a severe winter, they died.

I've tried to plant more, but I never seem to be able to keep them going.

What plants are underrated?
Impatiens and lilies. I love impatiens because they have so many uses, and lilies because they are reliable.

What plants never fail you?
Irises, lilies and daylilies come up every year.

What's your idea of a dream garden?
I think I already have it!

If money and time weren't factors, what feature would you add to your garden?
Calvin has been talking about enlarging the pond or adding a second one to accommodate our many, many fish.

What's your best money-saving secret for the garden?
I save seeds, dry them on paper plates on top of the fridge, store them in plastic bags and then start them in early April so I have plants for the pots and gardens. Saving and starting seeds has saved us quite a bit of money over the years.

What bird is most entertaining in your garden?
The pileated woodpeckers are always interesting. It's fun to watch them adjust their large bodies so they can get at our suet feeders.

What's your favorite bird?
Northern cardinals (below). They are the prettiest of the birds that visit our gardens. You really notice them when they're around.

Jerry Acton

Back to Their Roots

After years of dreaming, this gardener finally got what she wanted by mixing gardening with horses.

By Ellen Sousa
Spencer, Massachusetts

From a distance, our house looks like a typical Cape Cod surrounded by a sea of woods. However, as you get closer, you're likely to find yourself in an unexpected sanctuary filled with flower beds, birdhouses and, of course, horses.

Our sunny porch invites visitors to sit and take in the view across the stream near the horse barn. A grassy hill sweeps up from our small lawn toward stone walls and a green pasture where our two beloved horses graze.

Large plantings of trees, shrubs, perennials, ferns and grasses fuse together the various areas of the farm. At the same time, they also provide an attractive habitat for the many birds, butterflies and other wildlife that share our little corner of the world.

Things weren't always like this. When my husband, Robert, and I first moved in, invasive plants had nearly taken over the yard.

We fell in love with this property the moment we saw it. We had been looking for a horse farm to fulfill my lifelong dream of keeping horses at my home. And since I'm also a passionate gardener, this land immediately appealed to us.

It's located on 4 acres of wooded river valley, complete with a pond, several streams and a pasture. It really was my dream come true!

Building on the Framework

The previous owners had already established wonderful garden areas by installing stone retaining walls and planting dozens of ornamental trees and shrubs. They even had fences put up to prevent the horses from munching on nearby plants.

Unfortunately, many of the plants on the property were invasive. We had to remove several plants like Oriental bittersweet, variegated bishop's weed, Japanese barberry, burning bush, autumn olive, multiflora rose and wintercreeper.

After removing the invasive plants, I immediately started planting flowers, trees and shrubs that would be good nectar sources for butterflies and birds. I also added seed-producing plants to provide food for birds and other small mammals.

Flowers Bring Wildlife

It didn't take long to see the results. During our first summer, we saw hummingbirds and butterflies visiting every day. The first winter, we hung

LURING IN WILDLIFE. Ellen chose plants specifically for wildlife. Middle, purple liatris grows in her garden near the elderberry bush along her fence. Above, a swallowtail caterpillar feeds on dill, and red salvia grows strong (top left).

bird feeders and kept them filled, and put up birdhouses to encourage feathered friends to nest in our yard later that year.

Sure enough, that summer, a pair of tree swallows nested in a birdhouse we placed at the edge of our horse pasture, and our barn eaves hosted a family of eastern phoebes. During that season, a bat house also attracted roosting bats that eat the mosquitoes and bugs that bother our horses.

To keep the pond clean and free of invasive weeds, once a year we draw the water level down. Then we go out in waders and kayaks to pull any aggressive aquatic plants that might take over the pond.

I love creating beneficial patio pots and window boxes that contain plants that are highly attractive to birds, hummingbirds and butterflies. This allows us to view our flying visitors up close from our patio and porch.

Some of my favorite blooms to use in pots include petunias, phlox, fuchsia, ornamental grasses, zinnias and milkweeds.

A Helping Hand

Robert helps me create new garden areas by using his tractor to dump loads of composted manure onto thick layers of newspapers. Within the first year, worms and other beneficial soil dwellers break down the area into wonderful soil for planting.

As we created all these new flower beds, I realized I needed an inexpensive way to acquire a large number of plants. I learned about plant propagation by taking classes at the New England Wild Flower Society. Many of our New England plants require a stratification period of cold weather before they germinate.

Preserving What You Have

Each winter, I sow the seeds in potting soil in clear, plastic containers. I leave them outside with ventilation and drainage holes. Come spring, most of them germinate, and I get four to 10 hardy seedlings from each container. I plant these in my garden, and in no time, I have a large bed of thriving plants.

As we identify and remove the invasive plants and replace them with lovely natives, our little horse farm is slowly but surely becoming a valuable sanctuary for wildlife. We try our best to be good stewards of our beautiful New England landscape. After all, local wildlife may depend on it!

Hillside Haven

She created a bird sanctuary in her large, sloping backyard.

By Patty Duncan, Eugene, Oregon

"Bird Sanctuary"—this sign at the edge of Karen and Ken Cruickshank's home tells you all you need to know about this family's gardening intentions. If you take a stroll around their Sheridan, Oregon yard, you'll find vibrant, exotic flowers and inviting feeders that welcome countless varieties of birds to their hillside haven.

Karen pulls out all the stops to attract and protect a diverse array of feathered friends. Most years, she uses more than 100 pounds of nyjer and sunflower seeds in half a dozen feeders. And she has at least 20 nest boxes for wrens, swallows and many other species.

Evening grosbeaks, house finches, juncos, mourning doves, robins, towhees and bluebirds frequent the yard. But it wasn't always this way. The creation of this charming bird refuge has unfolded one step at a time.

From the Ground Up

Eight years ago, the Cruickshanks fulfilled Ken's boyhood dream by building a home on the hillside overlooking the family's western Oregon grass seed farm. The soil is rich and deep in the front where the hill slopes, providing the perfect breeding ground for lush flower growth.

Ken planted the lawn with his own seed and provided ample water from the farm's irrigation system. Then he turned the yard over to Karen for

A PARADISE FOR BIRDS. When Karen adds a new feature or plant to her yard, she always has her feathered friends in mind. Birds frequent her home year-round, but summers with hummingbirds (below right) are her favorite time.

her flower gardening. Initially, there was little rhyme or reason to her plant selection.

"At the beginning, I just planted things that caught my eye," Karen says. "I had no plan, only a deep desire for a great garden."

A year later, she had the good fortune to start work as manager of the garden department at a local farm and feed store.

"A whole world opened up to me," Karen says. "I read everything I could on plants, took classes and asked questions. I ordered unfamiliar varieties to the store, figuring if they appealed to me, they would no doubt appeal to other flower fanciers.

"The garden department grew like crazy, and I brought home one of everything."

Since she worked full-time, Karen had limited time for gardening, but she still did what she could.

"I just stuck plants in the ground where they seemed to fit," she says. "I moved them later, if necessary. The plants grew and bloomed, giving me a great deal of delight."

GREEN THUMB TIP

My insect control method is simple. My goal is to attract enough good bugs into my garden to take care of the bad ones. So far, this method has worked. I haven't had to resort to chemicals.

—Karen Cruickshank, Sheridan, Oregon

An Organic Approach

Karen plugged away at her garden, little by little. Before long, the lawn started shrinking as a result of her ever-widening flower beds.

"Several years after Ken planted the front lawn," she says with a laugh, "he commented that it sure wasn't as wide as it had been. I just smiled."

Ken didn't sit back and watch, though. Soon,

Q&A with Karen

If money and time weren't factors, what feature would you add to your garden?
Definitely water. A small pond and some fountains would keep the frogs and birds happy.

What gardening chore do you hate?
Gosh, can you use the word "hate" and "garden" in the same sentence? I don't enjoy cleaning up the mess when I have a pruning and weeding frenzy.

What's your best money-saving secret for the garden?
Use plants that will reseed, and then sit back to enjoy the surprises. Columbine are really awesome at this.

What plant is underrated?
Natives. They can be so easy to care for. One of my favorites is Ribes sanguineum, the red flowering currant. It's just gorgeous.

What's your favorite bird?
Hummingbirds, no question. Swallows are a close second.

What plant is underrated?
Caladium. It has vivid colors and contrast.

What plants never fail you?
Hosta and hydrangeas.

SHARING SPACE. Above, American goldfinches' bright-yellow plumage stands out at this feeding station in Karen's yard. At left, roses grow large and vibrant.

he installed two arbors, while Karen masterminded the design of rest of the area. While creating the garden, Karen imagined the area filled with birds, butterflies and bees, as well as other critters like snakes, lizards and frogs.

Since birds and other critters were important for Karen's yard, she started taking an organic approach to fertilizing and pest control. She now mixes her own organic fertilizer. As for insect control, her method is simple: She tries to attract enough good bugs to take care of the bad ones.

"It's worked so far," Karen says. "Even my pet duck helps out, wandering through the yard and eating slugs."

Aesthetically Appealing

For nesting birds, Karen planted a wide variety of trees, including maple, Japanese snowbell, forest pansy, native cascara and vine maple. Then she began filling the flower beds, placing tall plants in back and low ones in front.

Besides birds, Karen lures bees and butterflies to her garden. She cultivates showy milkweed for monarchs, though she sees the majestic butterflies infrequently. More often, she finds pale tiger swallowtails working the blooms of the Sunrise coneflower, providing a nearly perfect match of colors.

Karen calls her charming yard "a cottage garden gone wild." Her planting list seems to evolve eternally.

Another sign tucked into a flower bed provides a fitting disclaimer for this Oregon garden. It reads, "I don't remember planting this."

Retirement Is Bliss

A couple's new backyard is just what they needed to ease into retirement.

By John Dunzelman
Barnegat, New Jersey

Ah...retirement. When the time finally came for this wonderful life change, my wife, Barbara, and I moved into our new home and looked forward to spending some time relaxing and taking it easy. That was 6 years ago, and I'm still anticipating the "relaxing" part. Instead, we discovered a hobby, which became a passion that we don't think we'll be retiring from anytime soon—gardening.

Humble Beginnings—Big Dreams

A major bonus in building our dream home was that we had the opportunity to landscape the backyard from scratch, too. That first summer, we built our cottage shed and picked out our foundation plantings.

Since we are only 3 miles from the Atlantic Ocean and 114 feet above sea level, we chose river rock, evergreens and azaleas, with some red barberry and daylilies as well. Our backyard was off to a great start for future plantings, and we were hooked.

Every summer following, we chose another area of our property to landscape. One year it was the barren area along the driveway; another year,

STARTING FROM SCRATCH. John and Barbara enjoyed creating their backyard from a blank slate. Among their favorite items are a cottage-style garden shed (top) and a koi pond (above).

the flower bed around the flag pole. And in 2003, we decided to start our largest project of all—a koi pond.

Our backyard has a beautiful wooded area only about 30 feet from our sunroom—the perfect place for a pond with a viewing area to watch the wildlife it would surely attract. The towering pine and oak trees would give the pond protection from birds of prey and the sun, since koi like cooler water and it would be less susceptible to algae.

GREEN THUMB TIP

Transforming your yard will seem less overwhelming if you do it in sections. Each summer since we've been living in our new house, we've chosen a different area to landscape.

—John Dunzelman, Barnegat, New Jersey

A Place for Friends

After a local contractor dug the hole, we wasted no time. Within a few months, we had a 12- by 14-foot pond with two waterfalls flowing into it. There was one area that received a bit of afternoon sun, so it gave us the opportunity to experiment with a number of different sun- and shade-loving plants. Sixteen varieties of hosta, rhododendron, viburnum, Japanese painted fern, holly and Henry's Garnet are a few of the plants gracing our pond, bringing some color and texture into the area.

With so many visitors to our garden pond, we decided to construct a cobblestone walkway so they could meander from the pond to the other areas of the yard. We also doubled the garden area by clearing out the wild berry underbrush between the trees.

Here, we planted more than 35 perennial shrubs, plants and trees, including hydrangea, andromeda, daylilies, rose of Sharon, butterfly bush, coral bells, astilbe and many more. We also added

Q&A with John

What gardening chore do you hate?
Fall and spring cleanup. Our garden is in a wooded area with pine and oak trees.

What's your best money-saving secret for the garden?
Some annual flowers will return in the spring if you stop deadheading them in late fall.

If you could only have one flower in your garden, what would it be?
Dragonwing begonia.

What's your idea of a dream garden?
A garden without moles and voles!

What plant do you think is overrated?
Roses—they can be beautiful—and they can turn ugly!

What plant is underrated?
Caladium. It has vivid colors and contrast.

What plants never fail you?
Hosta and hydrangeas.

WELCOME WALKWAY. After John and Barbara filled their front and backyard with plants, they added a cobblestone path (top) that meanders though different areas of their yard.

more cobblestone paths around the new plantings and garden areas. Recently, we added a new water feature with a water wheel that I built in my wood shop.

The pond and plants also invited another group of friends—birds! They love the water feature and plants that we've added. Since we've moved, I've built more than 30 birdhouses to keep our feathered friends around.

Our tenants are usually sparrows, finches or bluebirds, but many of the houses are also used as shelter for the birds that stay during winter. By creating shelter, a water fountain, the waterfalls, stream and koi pond, we have attracted over 25 species of birds, including woodpeckers, nuthatches, titmice, wrens, bluebirds, juncos, hawks and even ducks. We record the sightings of our frequent visitors in our bird guest book.

With our backyard retreat almost complete, we're thinking we might reward ourselves with some down time to sit in the sunroom, enjoy our visitors and really "retire." But then again, maybe it's time to start on our second pond.

98
95
84
92
78

Backyard Bird Haven

Chapter 3

Photos: cedar waxwing, Tracy Laqua; aster, Rick Wetherbee; grapes, Rick Wetherbee; holly, Rick Wetherbee; chickadee, TomVezo.com.

Dining on Daisies

Aster

Members of the daisy family are among the prettiest flowers in the garden. When it comes to attracting birds and butterflies, they are also one of the most versatile.

By Kris Wetherbee
Oakland, Oregon

Daisies have always been welcome in my garden. I love their versatility. They can be quite sophisticated and showy at times, yet there's something uniquely simple and uncomplicated about their beauty.

Perhaps it's that attraction that has made daisies one of my favorite flowers. Daisies were even the focal feature of my bridal bouquet when I married my husband, Rick, many years ago. What I didn't realize back then was that daisies, and daisy-like flowers, also are a focal feature for many birds and butterflies.

Mention the word "daisy" and thoughts of chrysanthemums, English daisies or Shasta daises often come to mind. But daisy is more of a generic term that actually refers to thousands of different species of flowers belonging to the aster family.

Most share the classic daisy shape—a starlike arrangement of petals circling a prominent center.

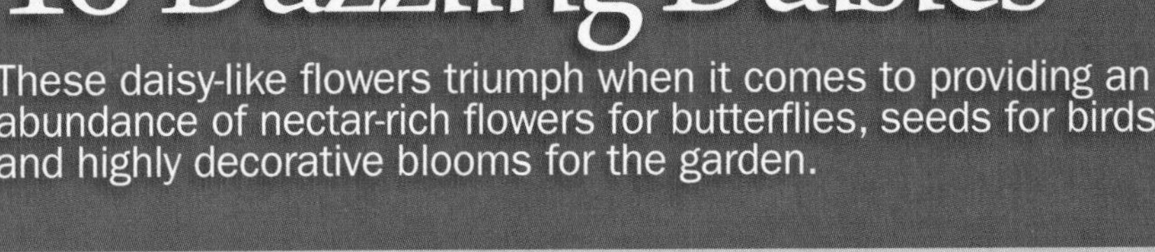

10 Dazzling Daisies

These daisy-like flowers triumph when it comes to providing an abundance of nectar-rich flowers for butterflies, seeds for birds and highly decorative blooms for the garden.

Purple coneflower

Annuals

BACHELOR'S BUTTONS
(Centaurea cyanus): Flowers in late spring to midsummer in shades of violet to blue. Grows up to 3 feet tall in full sun and light, well-drained soil.

CALENDULA
(Calendula species*)*: Long-blooming flowers in orange and bright yellow along with shades of apricot, cream and soft yellow—many with double blooms. Flowers in spring to midsummer in cooler climates, and late fall through spring in milder climates. Grows from 12 to 30 inches tall in full sun and well-drained soil.

COSMOS
(Cosmos bipinnatus): Showy flowers with feathery leaves; blooms from summer to fall in a spectrum of colors and forms. Grows from 1 to 6 feet tall in full sun and well-drained soil.

SUNFLOWER
(Helianthus annuus): Flowers from summer to early fall in vibrant yellows, reds, oranges and browns. Heights range from compact, 12-inch dwarfs to 12-foot giants. Best in full sun and well-drained soil. Provides high-energy seeds for birds.

ZINNIA
(Zinnia species*)*: Flowers from summer to fall in a diversity of shapes and sizes in shades of white, yellow, orange, red, purple and lilac. Heat-loving plants grow from 6 inches to 3 feet tall in full sun and fertile, well-drained soil.

Perennials

ASTER
(Aster species*)*: Profusion of flowers in white and varying shades of blue, red, pink or purple, with most flowering in late summer through fall. Plants grow from 6-inch, compact mounds, to tall, spreading plants up to 6 feet. Caterpillar host plant for crescents and painted ladies. Zones 3 to 8.

COREOPSIS
(Coreopsis): Flowers late spring through summer on a drought-tolerant plant. Blooms in yellow, orange, maroon, red and pink. Plants are 8 inches to 4 feet, and require full sun and well-drained soil. Zones 3 to 11.

PURPLE CONEFLOWER
(Echinacea purpurea): Flowers from summer to autumn in shades of pink to lavender and rose, as well as yellow, orange and white. Decorative seedheads in late autumn and winter. Sturdy, branching and heat-tolerant plants grow from 1 to 5 feet tall in full sun to light shade. Zones 3 to 9.

RUDBECKIA
(Rudbeckia species*)*: Flowers in summer and autumn in varying shades of yellow, orange, russet and mahogany. Grows from 12 inches to over 6 feet tall, depending on the variety. Black-eyed Susans (*Rudbeckia hirta* and *Rudbeckia fulgida*) are a familiar favorite. Best in full sun and moderately moist soil. Decorative seedheads resemble brown cones. Zones 3 to 9.

SHASTA DAISY
(Chrysanthemum x superbum): The classic daisy with a white ray of petals around a yellow center. Blooms from early summer to fall, with plants 10 inches to 3 feet tall. Zones 4 to 8.

All photos: Rick Wetherbee

Cosmos

This pollen-laden center also dishes up a smorgasbord of good eats for birds, with each tiny floret capable of producing seed. That's why the flowers will bring in a large variety of seed-eating birds, such as finches, towhees, cardinals, sparrows and chickadees.

Not Just for the Birds

Birds aren't the only fliers going after what daisies have to offer. Butterflies seek out daises as well. The plants' typically flat flowers make nice landing platforms, and the flowers' nectar is easily accessible.

With so many different colors and sizes to choose from, daisies will fit any style of garden, from casual to formal, or in just about any landscape situation—whether mixed in beds and borders, framing a walkway or featured in container plantings, window boxes or hanging baskets.

Make a place for daisies in your garden, and it's bound to become a more welcoming place.

Setting the Table

Our best reader tips to transform your yard into a bird haven.

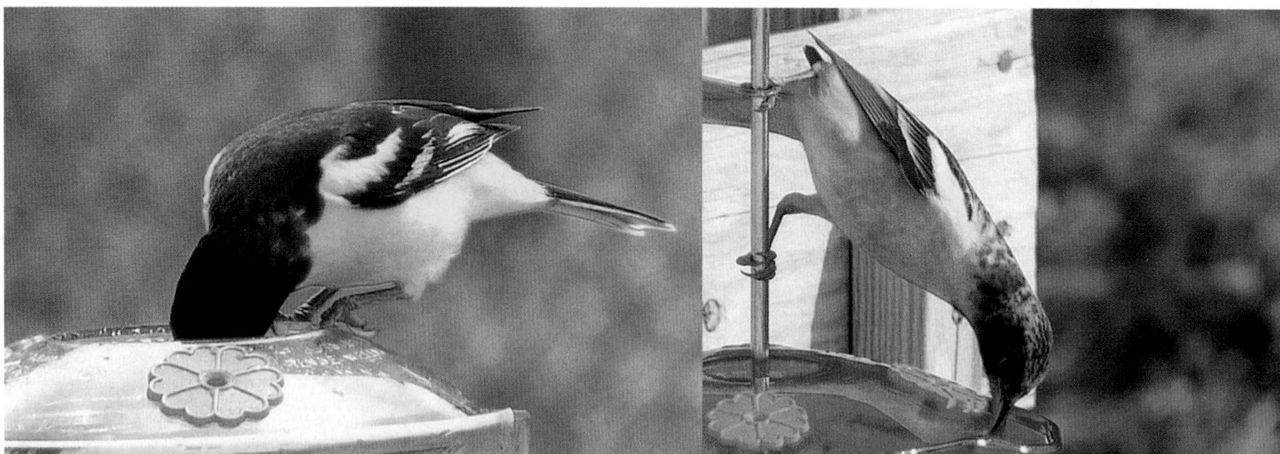

Modify and Conquer

I always put out an oriole feeder and oranges in spring, but these gorgeous orange birds seemed to favor our hummingbird feeders instead.

I figured I shouldn't fight it, so I decided to devise a feeder specifically for them. First, I took one of those round, flat hummingbird feeders and put it on a pole. Then I took the center section out and filled it with hummingbird nectar.

It's a huge hit (photos above)! The orioles and hummingbirds are constantly at this feeder. They even buzz around me when I'm sitting out on the deck. They're not afraid of me. They just want to get at that sugar water!

—Ann Ponzek, Plymouth, Massachusetts

Have a Seat

I was watching my feathered friends try to hang onto a standard suet feeder when I decided they would have an easier time eating if they had a perch. That's when I hit on an idea.

I pushed two 8-inch dowel rods through the bottom corner of the suet feeders, and then I wired two more rods across those to create a perch on each of the four sides.

I know woodpeckers don't *need* the perches to eat, but it sure has increased the traffic at my suet feeders. Juncos, Carolina wrens and even downy woodpeckers seem to appreciate my "sit-down" lunch counter.

—Alvon Abbott, Warsaw, Indiana

Dose of Fat

When we have really cold spells, I set out a few pieces of bread overnight to dry. The next day, I spread peanut butter on both sides and dip them in birdseed. I lay these pieces on the ground around my bird feeder, and the birds go nuts! It's a good fat-filled treat that helps keep them warm.

I'll also dip slices in loose field corn to put around my squirrel feeder. Those critters will run off with whole slices!

—Jo Rinard, New Haven, Indiana

Out of the Shell

Every morning when I feed the birds at my feeder, I also put out shelled peanuts on the deck railing. The squirrels, blue jays and tufted titmice love the treat!

If I'm late, the birds stare in my glass doors while patiently waiting on the railing for their breakfast. Once I feed them, they all have different dining styles.

The squirrels eat one at a time until they are bulging. The jays gather as many peanuts as they can in their bills before flying off to stash them. The tufted titmice take one at a time, and then fly away to a nearby branch to eat it.

So, the next time you fill your bird feeders, consider putting out some shelled peanuts. It could bring you some amusing new animal friends.

—Louise Moseley, Roanoke Rapids, North Carolina

Stay Safe

I used to have trouble with birds flying into my window, but not anymore. I came up with a simple solution: I placed a feeder close to the window. Now, even if birds do fly into the window, they are too close to get hurt.

—Paul McAfee, Fort Wayne, Indiana

Put a Top on It

In *Birds & Blooms*, readers have asked for ideas for keeping starlings, grackles and other bully birds from hogging all the suet from their hanging feeders. I have a simple solution.

I took a 7-inch funnel and put it on the top of a suet basket (right). This makes it harder for larger birds to latch onto the basket.

I have several woodpeckers that visit, as well as titmice, chickadees and nuthatches. But the starlings, grackles and others haven't been back. It's such an easy solution. I hope it works for others.

—*David Sabol, Topeka, Kansas*

Tilt-a-Squirrel

When squirrels were constantly emptying one of my bird feeders, I fought back in a way that still makes me chuckle. I drilled a hole through the middle of a square piece of plywood and threaded it onto the clothesline in between the pole and feeder.

Our family enjoyed the hilarious antics of all the squirrels that tried to cross the clothesline. They would hop on the 'squirrel-a-whirl', spin off and fall to the ground. One squirrel finally managed to hang on and reach the food, but by that time, we felt he deserved a treat for his perseverance.

—*Ellen Hustings, Leavenworth, Kansas*

Jim Crosiar

Add Some Color

Years ago, we moved to an acreage just 1-1/2 miles out of town. I saw American goldfinches everywhere (like the ones above), so I put up several feeders and tried all kinds of seed. They never came. I attracted some sparrows and a few red-winged blackbirds, but no goldfinches.

Then one day, my coworker found an old yellow bird feeder and offered it to me. I was willing to give anything a try, so I brought it home, cleaned in up, and in less than 10 minutes, I had goldfinches fighting for a port.

Eventually, they moved on to my other feeders, but it took several days. Later that year, my aunt and uncle were visiting and couldn't believe all the goldfinches at our feeders. They said they had tried to attract goldfinches as well, but nothing worked. They just couldn't get them to come to their yard.

On a whim, I told them they should try a yellow feeder instead. It seemed to work for me, so I figured it was worth a try. They went right out and bought one. That same afternoon, they called to tell me it had worked! Adding a yellow feeder lured goldfinches to their yard, too.

I don't know whether it's a coincidence, but if you're trying to attract goldfinches, it might be worth it to add a yellow feeder!

—*Cindie Mead, Correctionville, Iowa*

No-Melt Suet

Because of the heat here in Oklahoma, suet can become a real mess during summer. Luckily, I've found a no-melt suet recipe that allows me to serve this treat all year long. Here's what you'll need:

2 cups quick-cooking oats
2 cups cornmeal
1 cup flour
1/2 cup sugar
1 cup lard
1 cup crunchy peanut butter

Combine the oats, cornmeal, flour and sugar in a large bowl. Melt the lard and peanut butter (I use my microwave oven) and add to the dry ingredients. Mix well. Pour the suet into a square pan about 2 inches deep, or spread it directly on tree limbs.

—*Virginia Barnard, Okmulgee, Oklahoma*

Squeaky Clean

I had trouble cleaning our large cedar bird feeder because it would not fit in our sink. My husband suggested I take it to a self-serve car wash. The high-pressure washer did the trick. It removed every trace of seed and dirt easily.

—*Sheryl Miller, Fogo, Newfoundland*

Miracle Recipe

Aside from mealworms, we've found that the bluebirds in our yard also like this creation we like to call Miracle Meal. Here's the recipe:

1 cup lard or melted beef suet
1 teaspoon corn oil
4 cups yellow cornmeal
1 cup all-purpose flour

Melt the suet and then stir in the other ingredients. Add anything else you think the bluebirds might like, including raisins and sunflower hearts.

After the mixture sets, cut it into chunks and serve as suet. To make the bluebirds really happy, try adding some mealworms as well. We offer this Miracle Meal every morning and evening, and the bluebirds always come back for more.

—Eva Every, Elsie, Michigan

Bring It to Life

I have lots of trees in my backyard, but very few have low branches. I priced some pole feeders, but then I came up with a better plan. Since I live in the woods, there are plenty of branches lying around on the ground. I found a big red cedar and stuck it in the ground outside my patio.

I call this my giving tree. It might be a dead branch, but it's alive with dozens of bird species. My feathered friends have plenty of perches to choose from, as well as five different feeders.

I enjoy decorating my giving tree in winter, and then in summer, I plant a vine at its base.

—Nancy Rosson, Columbia, Missouri

Increase Bird Traffic with Flowers

When we moved into our home 6 years ago, the backyard was open and uninteresting. Then I decided to create a "bird island" by placing a birdhouse on either side of a tree. I added a dish feeder and a birdbath as well.

Once those were in place, I planted petunias, marigolds, daylilies and vincas. Then I put in a few hanging baskets near the birdhouses.

We now have so many birds that enjoy the sanctuary. I never realized how much of a difference it would make to have the birdhouse, feeder and bath alongside the plants.

—Mary Lou Rosemont, Darien, Illinois

Squirrel Wok

After 15 years of fighting pesky critters, I finally found a way to squirrel-proof a bird feeder. I loosely attached a wok frying pan facedown above the feeder so that it hung over like a roof. It sways easily side-to-side, so when squirrels jump on it to try and get to the feeder, the roof swings away and the squirrel falls to the ground. Since I put this on my feeder, not one squirrel has had a meal from it!

—Lee Hodges, Grants Pass, Oregon

Do the Dishes

Our heavy concrete birdbath was nearly impossible to clean, until I discovered a simple remedy. I set a glass pie dish inside it. It's clear, so it doesn't detract from the bath's beauty. I just wash the dish in the dishwasher.

—Dee Fannin, Santa Rosa, California

Sunflower Roost

At harvest time, I cut down my sunflowers and remove the seed heads. Then I use the leftover stalks to create 'tepees' for birds to roost in during cold nights.

It's easy to do. Just gather the tops of the stalks with rope and spread the bottoms for stability. The birds will eat the leftover seeds and will roost in the stalks.

—Wilbur Jensen, Onalaska, Wisconsin

Worm Alternative

I love bluebirds, but I've learned that it's not particularly easy to attract them with food. Sure, they love insects and mealworms, but these aren't good options for me.

I keep hoping they will want to try some seed from my feeder, but they never do. Then, a couple of springs ago, I found an alternative that works.

I had a pair of bluebirds nesting in my backyard, and to my surprise, they started eating suet from my nearby feeding station. The suet had lots of ground peanuts. The parents would eat it themselves and take some to their fledglings.

I'm glad I found a way to attract bluebirds without using mealworms. I just hope the peanut suet keeps them coming back!

—Robert Dilworth, Knoxville, Tennessee

Orange Look-alike

We love to attract orioles in spring and then watch them all summer long. We wanted a feeder that would attract as many of these birds as possible, so I came up with a plan.

First, I took two orange plastic bowls. Then I placed a 1/2-inch piece of round plywood inside with a 3-inch hole to accommodate a fruit cup for holding jelly. I added three dowels to hold the top and bottom together. The orioles lock their long toes around these spindles to balance while they're eating.

I devised the entire thing to look like an orange (above). It works—the orioles stick around my yard all summer.

—Ray Wigern, Blue Earth, Minnesota

Cherry Picking

One year, I tried a wild birdseed blend that included dried cherries. Soon after, I noticed eastern bluebirds stopping at our feeder. Bluebirds don't normally eat seeds, so I grabbed my binoculars for a better look.

The birds were plucking the dried cherries from the mixture. Now I always throw a couple handfuls of dried cherries or raisins into the seed when I refill the feeder.

—Mrs. Dallas Walker, Milan, Georgia

Warm Welcome

To help bluebirds get accustomed to my enclosed mealworm feeder, I prop open the hinged top with a stick. After they've entered the box a few times through its side entrances, I remove the stick. Once they've found this reliable source of mealworms, they'll keep coming back for more.

—Patti Farnum, Nashville, Michigan

Breakfast for the Birds

We always feed the birds through our cold and snowy Pennsylvania winters. One favorite treat of our feathered friends is this recipe I call Bird Breakfast. When I put it in my suet feeders, the activity at our feeders immediately increases. Here's the recipe:

1-1/2 cups quick-cooking oats (not instant)
2 cups boiling water
1/2 cup chunky peanut butter
3/4 cup suet (or vegetable shortening)
1/2 cup birdseed
1 cup yellow cornmeal
1 cup Cream of Wheat cereal (not instant)
1/3 cup dry cranberries, chopped

Cook rolled oats in boiling water in a large saucepan for about 2 minutes, stirring constantly until very thick. Remove from heat. Stir in peanut butter and suet until melted. Stir in remaining four ingredients. Cool and shape as desired.

I often make a double batch of this mixture. I also use trail mix, nuts, berries and even peanuts if I have them on hand because the birds love it. You can store this in the freezer and use as needed. As you can see by this tufted titmouse and downy woodpecker (below), this is a very popular treat!

—Debbi Barate, Seward, Pennsylvania

A Bird in the Hand is Worth Two at the Feeder

By A. Antonow
St. John's, Newfoundland

Black-capped chickadees are one of the friendliest birds. around. They have a round shape, a cheerful "chick-a-dee-dee-dee" call and are common in most urban backyards.

Visitors at the Ontario Royal Botanical Gardens are often amazed at the bold behavior of black-capped chickadees in the area. People are used to seeing these fliers quietly at bird feeders, not swooping down near hikers and walkers like they do here.

What's the secret? The chickadees here are hand-fed, so they see most people as a potential food source. Here, if you hold out a few sunflower seeds in your hand, there will be a bird snatching it up in no time!

You don't have to travel to Ontario to try your hand at hand-feeding birds. Most chickadees throughout North America will gladly eat right out of your hand. All you need is a little patience.

Setting the Stage

First off, it's best to do this in winter when natural sources of food are not as abundant. The ideal spot is a quiet backyard or an empty hiking trail. You want an area with little traffic so noise or movement won't scare the birds away.

I've noticed that it helps to wear neutral colors. It's also a good idea to dress warmly since you could be standing there for a while.

I like to look for a tree or spot where there already is a chickadee or two. Then I simply pour some sunflower seeds into my hand and hold it out so the birds can see. Finally, the most important part of success is this—stand very still!

Usually, after several minutes, one of the chickadees will get curious and hop onto a lower branch. If you keep perfectly still, one of the braver birds will land on your hand, snap up a seed and fly away.

The Buffet's Open!

Pretty soon, chickadees will materialize seemingly out of nowhere and will take turns swooping down for a treat. They will retreat to the tree to open and eat their snack, though some might elect to enjoy a more leisurely lunch on a hand. They'll glance at the person feeding them and pick over the seeds to find the best morsel.

Enjoy your close encounter with your feathered friends. And remember, one bird in the hand is worth two, three and even a dozen at the feeder!

More Trees, Please

Discover why they're at the root of any plan to attract birds and butterflies.

Trees can add elegant stature, unique character or beautiful blooms to the landscape. But trees make yards lively in other ways, too.

By Kris Wetherbee
Oakland, Oregon

As a group, trees have the potential to be the most valuable resource in your yard for attracting birds and butterflies. Trees offer multipurpose appeal as cover from the elements and predators, and offer places for birds and butterflies to perch, rest and produce offspring.

Trees also can provide edibles in the form of fruit, seeds, nuts, nectar, pollen, insects or sap.

Take a Look Around

If you don't have many trees in your yard, or if they're not helping you attract the birds and butterflies you'd like, I have some suggestions that will give you a good start.

As with any project, it's best to take stock of what you have first. Make note of the trees in your yard. Do they vary in structure, height, bloom season and vegetation?

Tracy Laqua

Tom Allen

Greg Jarboe

THE NEED FOR TREES. Birds and butterflies use trees for nourishment, nesting and more. Above, a juniper hairstreak uses red cedar as a host plant...a juvenile cedar waxwing fills up on crabapple berries....an American robin feeds its nestlings.

Are there any that produce fruit, nectar, nuts, seeds or sap? Are there food sources available throughout the year? Does your yard include evergreens for winter shelter? Where are the trees located? What about suitable nesting sites?

Decide which existing trees provide shelter, breeding sites and food for birds, and then remove any that don't make the grade—especially if the tree is unhealthy, unsightly or unsuitable for your backyard.

Next, determine which wildlife attributes are still lacking and what types of trees will help fill those needs in your yard. The number of trees will vary according to your space, but a good rule of thumb for an average-sized yard is one or two large trees, at least one grouping of smaller trees and shrubs, and one clump of conifers for winter shelter.

Branching Out

The first step in selecting trees is to pick species that are compatible with your climate, specific soil type and light conditions. Also check what size the trees will be when fully grown, and make sure they will not overwhelm the allotted space.

Not all trees flower or produce food at the same time of year, so the more types of trees you have, the more enticing your yard will be. Keep the buffet coming by offering both evergreen and deciduous trees with overlapping blooming and fruiting cycles.

For example, in spring, dogwood offers insects and buds for birds to eat, and is a host for many butterflies in the blues family. Serviceberries (*Amelanchier*) provide June fruit, while mountain ash (*Sorbus*), fringe tree and magnolia follow with fall fruit offerings. Hollies and hawthorns bear fruit in fall that persists into winter and often through early spring.

Serviceberry

RDA

Birds like finches, juncos and nuthatches favor seeds. Seed-producing trees include redbuds and maples, along with the seed-filled cones of spruce, fir, pine and hemlock.

Even sap from trees like oak, birch and maple can be a feast for some winged wildlife, especially butterflies like mourning cloaks, anglewings and wood nymphs. And any insects attracted to the sap may become a meal for nuthatches and other insect-eaters that search nooks and crannies for grubs, ants and other bugs.

Natural Winners

Trees with multitasking abilities are naturally more valuable. Maples, for instance, offer summer shelter, food for birds and nesting sites. Others, like willows and tulip poplars, offer those benefits, plus serve as caterpillar hosts for mourning cloaks and tiger swallowtails, respectively.

When you broaden the appeal by growing a variety of trees, the result will be a backyard sanctuary that appeals to you and your family, as well as your winged friends.

Variegated dogwood

Tempting Trees

Seven picks that offer food, shelter and other attributes for birds and butterflies…plus beauty for you.

Redbud

ARBORVITAE (*Thuja* species): Evergreen conifers with a wide array of sizes and forms.
Wildlife benefits: Seeds, cones, insects, four-season shelter and nesting sites.
Landscape attributes: Evergreen, textured bark and minimal pruning to maintain shape. Zones 2 to 10.

BEECH (*Fagus* species): Medium to large deciduous trees.
Wildlife benefits: Fruit (nuts), seeds, insects, nesting sites, shelter and caterpillar host plant.
Landscape attributes: Spring flowers, contrasting gray bark, coppery-red fall foliage, textural fruit and dense shade. Zones 4 to 9.

DOGWOOD (*Cornus* species): Ornamental deciduous trees.
Wildlife benefits: Fruit, flowers (nectar), insects, nesting sites, seasonal shelter and caterpillar host plant.
Landscape attributes: Beautiful spring blooms, colorful fall foliage, and some have colorful or attractive horizontal branching patterns. Zones 2 to 9.

FIR (*Abies* species): Large group of coniferous trees.
Wildlife benefits: Seeds, cones, insects, four-season shelter and nesting sites.
Landscape attributes: Evergreen appeal, colorful upright cones and woodsy fragrance. Zones 3 to 10.

FRINGE TREE (*Chionanthus* species): Deciduous flowering trees.
Wildlife benefits: Nectar flowers, fruit, nesting material and summer shelter.
Landscape attributes: Fragrant, lacy clusters of snowy-white flowers, and colorful fall fruit and foliage. Zones 4 to 10.

MAGNOLIA (*Magnolia* species): Evergreen and deciduous trees.
Wildlife benefits: Flowers (nectar), seeds, shelter.
Landscape attributes: Some of these beautiful trees have fragrant flowers from winter to summer, but it varies with species and location; has large, glossy leaves and showy cone-like clusters of bright-red seeds. Zones 4 to 11.

Magnolia

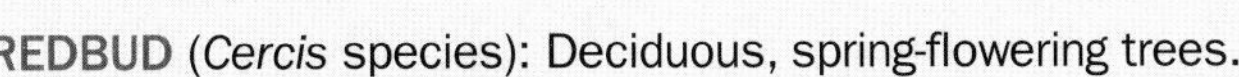

REDBUD (*Cercis* species): Deciduous, spring-flowering trees.
Wildlife benefits: Flowers (nectar), seeds, insects, summer shelter and nesting sites, nesting materials and caterpillar host plant.
Landscape attributes: Spectacular spring flowers, attractive foliage with three seasons of color (reddish purple in spring, blue-green in summer, yellow in autumn), beanlike seedpods. Zones 4 to 9.

Photos this page: Rick Wetherbee

Home Tweet Home

Readers share their best birdhouse creations.

Double Duty

"My son Jason Keel built this lovely birdhouse for me," writes Beverly Ann Keel of Louisville, Kentucky. "In addition to being a birdhouse (the opening is above the front door), it's also a bird feeder. Jason designed the house with two feeders on the sides. It's a perfect place for the birds to stay and play."

Everything but the Tracks

"I love trains and enjoy making birdhouses and feeders," writes Gurney Cox of Archdale, North Carolina. "I bought a model train engine and cut it to make a birdhouse. It's battery operated, so the headlight glows, the smokestack smokes and the whistle blows."

Looking for an Adventure

"My son Scott is always building birdhouses in his spare time," writes Brenda Johnson from Auburn, Georgia. "He puts them together, and I add the finishing touches with paint and miniature details. This hunting and fishing cottage is perfect for our adventurous feathered friends."

Decorative Detail

"My husband built this beautiful ornamental birdhouse stand (right) for our front porch," says Jeanie Payne of Markle, Indiana. "It's 52 inches tall and has 17 birdhouses on it.

I painted vines, trees, flowers and shrubs on the houses to add more details. It's quite an eye-catcher!"

Ready for Liftoff

"I made this birdhouse out of scrap pieces of PVC pipe," writes John Jackson of Marble Falls, Texas. "The only thing I bought were the three plastic funnels for the top cones."

Off the Ice

"My dad, George O'Neil, of Portage la Prairie, Manitoba, retired a few years ago and took up woodworking as a hobby," writes Dianne Russell of Lacombe, Alberta. "Someone gave him several broken hockey sticks, and he turned them into birdhouses!"

Salvage Team

"My husband, Danny, and I are always looking for old barn boards and salvage materials to create primitive crafts," says Connie Lunning of Mt. Pleasant, Iowa. "One afternoon, he created this elaborate birdhouse. It just kept getting bigger and better. Now, he has made several unique birdhouses similar to this one."

Tiki Hut

"Even though I didn't have any plans, I was determined to build my own tiki hut for the birds," writes Warren Hankins of Humboldt, Iowa. "I mitered 20 individual pieces of wood to create the roof's scalloped edge. Then I cut and painted each of the 32 vertical boards separately. Several birds have been checking it out, and I can't wait to meet my new tenants this spring."

Guitar Vacancy

"An old guitar that no one played inspired me to work on my own version of a musical motel," writes Sharon Colley of Dayton, Nevada. "It's now finally ready for occupancy. The sound of new chicks in the spring will be music to my ears!"

Trash to Treasure

"This creation all began with a single gourd I found in a compost pile at my friend's house," says Candice Bella of Mountain Top, Pennsylvania. "My friend said I could have it, and the next thing I knew, my husband was drilling a hole and I was preparing to paint it. We enjoyed making it so much that now we want to plant more gourd seeds."

Come One, Come All

"While visiting Colonial Williamsburg, Virginia nearly 30 years ago, my wife and I saw a 48-hole birdhouse for pigeons and stopped to take photo," writes Terry Mattive of Penns Creek, Pennsylvania. "Recently, my 81-year-old uncle, Tim Farver (right), used the photo as a model and built one like it, but it has 288 holes!"

First Try-umph

"My husband saw a birdhouse at a local gift shop for $130," writes Jody Crandall of Dowagiac, Michigan. "Instead of buying one, he decided to try to make his own. This colorful, pretty house isn't bad for a first-timer."

Spared for the Birds

"Phil Sturgeon of Mt. Zion, Illinois is a big Kentucky Wildcat fan," writes Debbie Younger of Decatur, Illinois. "His brother George made him a Kentucky Wildcat-themed mailbox. He thought it was too big, so he converted it into a birdhouse. Since Phil loves bowling, he recycled bowling balls into a birdhouse pole. It stands 16 feet tall!"

New Construction

"My husband, Jack, makes all kinds of beautiful things for our yard, but I like his birdhouses the best," writes Janet Petzler of Richmond, Indiana. "We enjoy seeing how long it takes the birds to discover a new one."

Fairy-Tale Castle

"I built this castle birdhouse so that each side has an entrance to a separate apartment," writes Richard Adamus of Penfield, New York. "The drawbridge and the roof serve as feeders. The castle is mounted on the pole that supports our trumpet vine."

grapevines for all

Treat your family and feathered friends to homegrown seedless grapes.

By Kris Wetherbee
Oakland, Oregon

Photos by Rick Wetherbee

If you enjoy eating grapes, then you're in for a triple treat. By planting your own seedless varieties, you not only get to enjoy great fruit, but you'll also attract a new group of feathered friends.

More than 100 bird species eat grapes. This includes backyard favorites like cardinals, orioles, waxwings, bluebirds and towhees. While native wild grapes are popular with birds, especially in winter, you can also plant a wide range of seedless varieties to bring in summer and fall visitors.

But it's not just fruit that makes grapevines appealing. This backyard favorite has its looks, too!

Grapevines provide ornamental attraction as well as excellent summer shade. They also bring added interest to the spring and summer landscape with their boldly textured leaves and colorful fruit in shades of green, white, red, pink, blue or black. The fall color is also fantastic, with foliage in varying shades of yellow, orange, red and purple.

The beauty of this versatile fruit is that the fast-growing, ornamental vine is easily trained along an arbor, trellis or fence. You can also use it to decorate a gazebo or pergola. Vigorous vines climb by winding their tendrils around any nearby structures, so you may need to tuck a few in here and there.

Seedless grapes, which are self-pollinating like those with seeds, can survive in many parts of the country. Most varieties do well in Zones 5 to 9, with some even growing to Zone 4.

The vines are easy to grow as they can survive in a wide range of soil types and conditions. But if optimum growth and fruit production are what you're after, they thrive best in a sunny location with good air circulation and well-drained, slightly acidic soil.

To establish grapevines, pruning is critical early on in the growing process. Once your vines take off, it's also important to keep up your pruning to ensure good fruit production.

Plant bareroot grapevines in late winter or early spring before the buds begin to swell. You can put container-grown grapevines into the ground anytime from spring to late fall.

Space plants about 6 to 10 feet apart. For faster coverage on a structure such as an arbor or gazebo, 5-foot spacing works best. Just be sure to install a trellis or other sturdy support before planting the vines.

Once the vines are established, a yearly mulch of quality compost should provide all the fertility you need to grow healthy plants and flavorful fruit. When the harvest starts, you can reach out and savor the fruit right off the vine.

And since a well-tended vine can produce 30 to 50 pounds of fruit each season, there will always be plenty to share with the birds.

10 best seedless grapes

CANADICE
Tight clusters of red fruit with deliciously sweet, slightly spicy flavor; one of the best winter-hardy varieties.

CONCORD SEEDLESS
Similar color, flavor and texture as the popular Concord variety with seeds, but with smaller berries and clusters.

EINSET
Bright-red, medium-sized berries with a unique strawberry-like flavor.

GLENORA
Huge clusters of medium-sized, midnight-blue grapes with a deliciously sweet blend of blueberry and Concord flavors. Save some for jam, jelly, juice and pies.

HIMROD
Small- to medium-sized golden-amber berries with a slightly spicy, crisp and sweet honey-like flavor.

INTERLAKEN
Large clusters of small greenish-amber fruit with crispy flesh and excellent flavor. Birds love it, so watch your harvest!

RELIANCE
Large clusters of medium-sized, rosy-pink fruit with tender skin and melting flesh that reveals a seductively sweet and fruity flavor. This hardy variety is good for colder zones.

SWEET SEDUCTION
Beautiful golden-amber berries with sweet, deliciously rich muscat flavor.

VANESSA
Medium-sized red berries on well-filled clusters with firm texture and sweet, fruity flavor.

VENUS
Huge clusters of medium- to large-sized, blue grapes with a rich, fruity and earthy flavor.

RELIANCE PINK

How to Keep Your Harvest

Gardeners who grow grapes know that birds will devour their crop, if given the chance. To keep a few grapes for yourself, you can either plant extra, so you'll have plenty to share, or use protective coverings on the grapes you want to harvest for yourself.

The 2-Minute Feeder

It doesn't take long to make this simple feeder with a recycled soda bottle.

By Albe Zakes, New Hope, Pennsylvania

I'm an employee of the eco-friendly company TerraCycle, and people are always asking me how we make our products. One of the items that I often get questions about is our recycled bird feeder made from a 2-liter soda bottle.

We make these feeders for retailers, but you can re-create the feeder yourself at home. Anyone from families to do-it-yourselfers can do it. So go ahead and dig a bottle out of the recycling bin, and let's get started!

Here's What You'll Need:

- **Empty, clean 2-liter bottle**
- **Up to 4 pounds of your favorite birdseed**
- **Two picture hanger triangles with screws**
- **Bird feeder base (at craft stores or through the TerraCycle Web site)**
- **Screwdriver**
- **4-1/2 feet of string**
- **Funnel or piece of paper**

Let's Start Building:

1. Make sure bottle is empty, clean and free of labels. Use scissors to take the label off if you have trouble tearing it.
2. Screw the picture eyelets into the base of the bottle using the accompanying screws.
3. Take a 6-inch piece of string and loop it through each eyelet knot in the center to create a small loop that connects both eyelets.
4. Take the other 4 feet of string and loop it through to connect the eyelets. Tie off the string to make a 2-foot loop. Now you'll be able to hang your feeder from any branch or hook.
5. Turn over the bottle and remove the cap.
6. Use a funnel or roll up a piece of paper into a cone.
7. Fill with your favorite birdseed until the bottle is full.
8. Take the bird feeder base and screw it onto the bottle.
9. Turn it over and hang your feeder!

Fantastic Feeders

These creative feeders offer birds fine dining year-round.

Pine Pavilion

"I've recently constructed a gazebo bird feeder as an anniversary gift for my sister and brother-in-law," says Steve Krajewski of Quaker Hill, Connecticut. "It's made from 1x12 unfinished rough-cut pine that will weather to a beautiful silver-brown color. I bought the wooden finial in the drapery department. And the feeder has a base that slides over the top of a 4x4 post top."

Crafting for the Birds

"Kaitlyn, our 11-year-old, made this bird feeder using jumbo ice-pop sticks and a glue gun as part of her bird-watching badge for Girl Guides of Canada," writes Kristi Dease-Waluchow of Point Edward, Ontario. "Red-breasted nuthatches were the first birds to feed, followed by black-capped chickadees (like the one above), house finches and even a rose-breasted grosbeak."

First-Class Service

"My father, Joe Reljac, built this high-flying feeder as a gift for my husband, Paul, and me because we are both pilots," says Rebecca Mihalcik of Pittsburgh, Pennsylvania. "Our backyard birds perch on the feeder, patiently waiting for their turn to walk onto the wing for a tasty treat."

Log Cabin Cozy

"My brother, Francis Wallace, made this sturdy log cabin bird feeder," writes Rhoda Hreha of Alexandria, Ohio. "Each log is individually cut to size. He added a stack of wood, a hatchet, some trees and a sawhorse on the outside of the house for decoration. The birds love the protection the roof gives them."

Satisfied Customers

"My father, Steven Arnoczky, made a fast-food birdhouse for my wife, Brenda, and me," writes Steven Arnoczky of East Lansing, Michigan. "The birds love this 'take-out window.' They come and go as they please."

Happy Holly Days

From small-scale shrubs to large trees, these plants benefit landscapes and backyard birds alike.

By Kris Wetherbee
Oakland, Oregon

Chinese holly

Richard Day/Daybreak Imagery

Anytime I can accomplish two things at once, it brightens my day. One way to do this in your garden is to include plants that bring in more birds by offering most of the essentials they need for survival. Hollies do that and more.

"Berry" Attractive

With over 400 species of fruit-bearing trees and shrubs, hollies (*Ilex* species) are one of the most valuable and versatile resources in any backyard bird garden. For starters, most are evergreen and therefore serve as excellent shelter sites, especially in winter when other deciduous plants are left leafless and barren.

Hollies range in size from trees that tower up to 100 feet tall to creeping shrubs less than 1 foot in height, providing a range of options to suit different species of birds. The evergreen canopy is without a doubt an attraction, but many birds also build nests in the densely covered branches.

Hollies have the additional bonus of rewarding both birds and people with brightly colored berries. Red, yellow, orange, white or black berries ripen in fall and, in some species, last until early spring.

The berries not only enliven the wintry scene, but the nutritious fruit also is consumed by a variety of songbirds, including northern cardinals, waxwings, jays, northern mockingbirds, American robins, chickadees and woodpeckers.

Hollies in the Landscape

Hollies hold a lot of appeal for birds, but another asset lies in the ornamental beauty they bring to the landscape. The versatility in style, range of heights, diversity of form and long-lasting berry display make hollies a must any garden.

Hollies can be rounded, spherical, pyramidal or columnar in form. Leaf shape and size run the gamut, too—from smooth to spiny, narrow to

Narrowleaf English holly

English holly

Photos this page: Rick Wetherbee

SHAPELY VARIETIES. No matter which type of holly you choose, all of the varieties have shapely, unique leaves.

English holly 'Bacciflava'

English holly 'Zelta's Elite'

BIRD-WATCHER'S SECRET

Not only do hollies provide plenty of food for the birds in winter, they serve as shelter. They don't shed their leaves during the cold months like other deciduous plants.

broad, and quite tiny to rather large. Most are dark green to glossy green in color, but blue types exist and variegated forms are quite striking.

Types to Try

English holly (*Ilex aquifolium*) has the classic "Christmas" appearance of glossy, green leaves and red (or yellow or orange) berries. American holly (*Ilex opaca*) looks similar, though it is more cold tolerant and withstands hot, dry summers a bit better.

The low, smooth-leaved Japanese species (*Ilex crenata*) works well to line a path, or try a taller evergreen variety as a backdrop to beds and borders. Columnar varieties like 'Sky Pencil' can serve as sculptural points of interest, especially in areas where you wish to draw attention.

Hollies also make an effective foil for other colors. For example, the lustrous Meserve or "blue" hollies (*Ilex* x *meserveae*) feature blue-green leaves that heighten the beauty of plants with yellow or pink flowers.

Most hollies thrive in Zones 5 to 9, with some even growing to Zone 4. Holly plants are either male or female, with the female plants producing fruit as long as a male plant of the same species is growing nearby.

Many of the Chinese hollies (*Ilex cornuta*) are partially self-fruitful and will produce some berries without a male variety. In most areas, hollies produce the best berry crops when planted in full sun, but many adapt well to partial shade, especially where summers are hot.

Most hollies grow best in well-drained, slightly acid soil enriched with organic matter. Regular fertilization based upon soil test results helps keep foliage healthy and fruit abundant. I also find that a thick mulch of pine needles or other woody material applied each year helps maintain the soil's acidity and keep roots cool and moist.

Few plants rival the attraction that hollies bring to birds and the landscape. Hollies may be the classic symbol of the winter season, but they also offer a multitude of benefits for both birds and people year-round.

Watanabeana Japanese holly

Best of Bird Tales

Amazing bird encounters from the past year.

Hawaii Surprise

You never know what you'll find on vacation. We were getting into our car at Sunset Beach in Oahu, Hawaii when this beautiful bird landed on the car next to us. The bird seemed to be taking advantage of the mirror to admire its plumage—we certainly were.

We soon learned that this bird is a red-crested cardinal, though Hawaiians often refer to them as Brazilian cardinals. This gorgeous bird is a native of South America and was introduced to the Hawaiian Islands in the 1930s. This photo is one of our favorites from the trip, and continues to bring us great memories.

—Marjorie Romero, Corrales, New Mexico

Shower Power

Last summer was very hot and dry, but the chore of watering my pine tree turned out to be a delight when a few sparrows discovered the benefit of the frequent showers.

It started with one brave bird checking out the water that must have seemed to come out of nowhere. Soon, it flew off and returned with other sparrows. All of them jumped from limb to limb as the water dripped over them.

This routine went on for 2 weeks. Then, one day, I came out and found all the birds waiting in the pine tree for the mysterious water source to appear.

As the summer cooled down, I began to see fewer of the sparrows on my sprinkling days. But they're always welcome whenever they want to cool off.

—Lorraine Buskey, Anchorage, Alaska

Taking Turns

Outside my window, there's a crabapple tree loaded with bird feeders and suet holders. On cold, rainy days, I love to sit with a cup of coffee or hot chocolate and watch the birds.

One dreary day, after watching downy woodpeckers, finches, nuthatches, chickadees and a titmouse, I decided that the birds were due for a special treat, and I filled a hanging dish with roasted peanuts.

It wasn't long before I noticed that the chickadees had organized an assembly line of sorts. One chickadee would be at the hanging dish and one at the tube feeder. As soon as the chickadee left the hanging dish, the bird on the tube feeder would move over to the dish, and another chickadee would appear at the tube feeder. They never missed a beat.

—Susan Shattuck, Falconer, New York

Open Wide

Last summer, my wife, Marie, and I noticed a pair of birds spending a lot of time perched at the top of the pine trees in our front yard. We couldn't ID them right away, but after some research, we discovered that they were eastern kingbirds.

To our delight, the pair built a nest and began to raise a family. After about 5 days, I was able to get this photo (right) of one of the babies waiting for a bite to eat.

We watched each day as the babies grew amazingly fast. They left the nest, but we love it when they come back to visit us.

—Marlin Diskerud, Huntley, Illinois

She Flew the Coop

My mom bought me a small feeder so I could enjoy watching birds from my kitchen window. One morning, I did a double take after spotting the biggest bird I had ever seen at the feeder. It turned out to be a chicken!

Nobody in the neighborhood has claimed her, but she seems to have claimed me because she's at my feeder every chance she gets.

—Jennifer Mrozek, Magna, Utah

That Sinking Feeling

I was watching a purple gallinule feeding on a large fireflag bush when it decided to dine on the seeds at the end of a thin branch that reached out over the water.

As it climbed toward the tip, its weight forced the end of the branch down, submerging the seeds. The bird then backed up, allowing the seeds to come to the surface where they remained out of reach. Again, the bird inched forward, only to have the branch dip below the surface again.

I enjoyed this show for at least 5 minutes before realizing that the bird's reflection in the water was a great photo opportunity. I stopped laughing long enough to get several shots of this pretty and shy Florida bird.

—George Forrest, Delray Beach, Florida

Cardinal Trio

On Mother's Day last year, I found this nest of northern cardinals (above) in a rhododendron bush near my home. The cardinals are in various states: one is hungry, one is asleep, and one is still "in progress" in its egg. Nine days later, all three were out of the nest but still under the watchful eyes of their parents.

—Bill Charles, Saltville, Virginia

Colorful Visitors

For the past 6 or 7 years, we've had painted buntings visit our lighthouse feeder (left) from mid-November until mid-April. The gorgeous males are multicolored, while the females are green.

The buntings stay at the feeder when northern cardinals feed, but they dash off when they see blue jays, red-bellied woodpeckers and mourning doves.

When they're not feeding, we often see them in our palmetto bushes. They add such a bright spot to our yard.

—Jim and Lois Hains
Port St. Lucie, Florida

Birdie at 18 Holes

One Saturday, my husband and I had the pleasure of watching this yellow-bellied sapsucker outside our basement window. He made 18 little holes in this tree and waited for the sap to run. Then he went from hole to hole, drinking sap from each one. We really enjoyed watching him. It was the first time we'd seen this bird.

—Sandra Weber, Mohnton, Pennsylvania

Thinking Outside the Box

We had tree swallows raising a family in a bluebird box on the side of our screen porch. The baby swallows were quite loud and often stuck their heads out of the house. They were quick, too! Whenever I was near with a camera, they disappeared back inside.

One evening at feeding time, I decided to try to take photos from inside, so I climbed on my kitchen countertop. (My husband calls me "Crouching Tiger, Hidden Dragon" for my photo efforts indoors and out.) One baby swallow poked its head out of the box, followed by another, until four heads peered out.

They were waiting for their dinner, and when a parent arrived with food, it was time for all the babies to open wide (above).

Yes, I got my perfect shot. What a way to end the day!

—Cindy Slopsema, Westfield, Indiana

Stretched to the Limit

It's great fun to watch American robins in my backyard. This particular bird had latched onto a worm, and it wasn't going to give up trying to get it out of the ground (above).

It's amazing just how far a worm can stretch when it's at the end of an eager robin's bill!

—Mona Doebler, Hinsdale, Montana

Morning Chatter

I live on the Gila River Indian Reservation in the Sonora Desert surrounded by saguaro cacti and a lot of desert critters. Roadrunners play in and around my yard on a daily basis.

One roadrunner—I named it "Rhoda"—has become very friendly (left). Rhoda often visits me as I sit on my patio in the early morning hours enjoying my coffee and watching the sun come up over the Santan Mountains.

One morning, Rhoda sat on my Bible for a long time. Then, as if the bird had a secret to share, Rhoda came right up on the table, got close to my face and started chattering up a storm. I really enjoy these visits.

—Brenda Rogers, Chandler, Arizona

Seize the Moment

I'm only 13, but I love taking nature photos, especially of birds. We live in a suburb, and I usually don't get special photo opportunities. But that all changed when a flock of cedar waxwings (above) came to visit.

My family and I have bird feeders in our yard, which attract birds and squirrels. But this waxwing didn't come for the seed. It wanted the berries from our bittersweet vines.

The flock of about five waxwings spent the entire morning in our yard, and I happily snapped away with my camera.

—Brian Magnier, Springfield, Massachusetts

Listening from the Heart

My mother lost her hearing by the time she was 50, but there were a few sounds she could still hear. For instance, bird songs and my pop's whistling were just the right frequency for her.

One day, I was working in the kitchen and had the radio playing loud enough to hear over the mixer and food processor. Mom walked into the kitchen and asked, "Is that a robin I hear?"

I turned everything off and looked out the window. Sure enough, in our maple tree there was an American robin singing its heart out to the world.

I turned back to Mom. Her expression puzzled me.

"You really had all those things on?" she asked.

Mom has said before that she doesn't care if she can only hear God's birds because they are most important to her. I guess she can because all she heard that day was the robin.

—Willa Fershee, Miamisburg, Ohio

High-wire Act

Last summer, on a hot and windy afternoon, I saw something fluttering on the telephone wire at the end of our lane. I looked closer and saw that it was an adult eastern bluebird.

It beat its wings, trying desperately to fly, but one leg was caught in the twisted cable.

I had no way to reach the bird. I called the telephone company, but the bird wasn't endangering anyone or anyone's service, so they wouldn't help. Then I called the Ministry of Natural Resources, but since it was the weekend, they couldn't help either.

Finally, my brother-in-law came to the rescue. Standing on his truck's roof and using a long aluminum pole, he untwisted the cable slightly.

The exhausted bird went to a nearby fence. When we slowly approached, it quickly flew away and perched nearby in a neighbor's tree. I'm sure this bluebird eventually recovered since we had several broods in our bluebird houses. Hopefully, we will not have another incident like that again.

—Melinda Marin, Barwick, Ontario

A Helping Hand

My son Eric Gowen and I know that sometimes birds accidentally fly into our window, which is what happened to the beautiful male purple finch we found.

Eric wanted to keep the bird out of harm's way, so I placed it on his finger, and it rested there for about 20 minutes (above). Fully recovered, the bird flew to a nearby tree and started to sing.

We're glad we were able to offer comfort to the little finch.

—Alice Villa, Terrace Bay, Ontario

Time for Dessert

When my wife, Marilyn, and I were visiting Katy, Texas for our granddaughter's high school graduation, we spotted a young northern mockingbird sitting near us on a garden fence. My daughter dug up a few worms to feed the little creature, and we immediately had a friend.

One afternoon a couple of days later, as I was enjoying dessert on the deck, my new friend decided to join me, landing first on my shoulder, then hopping onto my dish, and finally settling right on my cake and ice cream.

Watching this bold mockingbird go from eating our freshly dug worms a few days earlier to helping itself to my slice of cake was an amusing experience for all of us.

—Kenneth Sjogren, Lindsborg, Kansas

Eviction Notice

Every spring, the squirrels take over my flicker house. I knew the flickers wouldn't use the house for nesting while the squirrels had control, so I decided to do something about it. I purchased a screech-owl house instead with a nice large opening. I dubbed it Peanuts Place, and was happy to give the squirrels a place of their own to stay.

Late one afternoon in December, I saw something peering back at me from the box. I walked closer, holding held my breath. I was looking into the face of an owl.

After a few days of closer observation, I was able to confirm that my visitor was an eastern screech-owl. I never dreamed an actual owl would actually occupy the house, but there it was, roosting every night.

One evening when the owl didn't return, a squirrel seized the opportunity and started taking leaves inside the box. After 3 days, there was still no sign of the owl.

I wanted my feathered friend back, so I went out one morning and cleared the leaves while the squirrel watched me from high in the tree. How ironic that I was now evicting the critter for whom I had originally purchased the box!

But I was determined to keep the box vacant for the owl. I did not want to lose my new feathered friend. The next morning, I stood at the tree, clapping my hands and making noises to discourage the squirrel from returning.

There was no activity at Peanuts Place for the next 3 days. All I could do was watch and wait. On the fourth day, I saw a familiar face. The owl had returned!

—Christine Conroy, West Yarmouth, Massachusetts

Icy Escape

Last winter, I woke up to find that the lake we live on was partially frozen. Immediately, I thought of the two white ducks that are regulars on our lake.

I feed them every morning, but now they couldn't get across. I saw the birds swimming in a small circle of water near the bank on the opposite side of the lake. They would just have to wait for the water to thaw.

While we were enjoying our coffee, a bald eagle suddenly swooped down near our ducks. I could not believe my eyes. They were under attack. I had no idea that an eagle would go after such large birds.

My poor duck friends kept diving under the water to escape the eagle. White feathers were flying in the air, but the ducks' efforts seemed to be working. The eagle stayed for about 30 minutes. Each time it swooped down, the ducks frantically dove for safety into the icy water.

Finally, the eagle gave up and left for good. The ducks soon made their way out of the water and nestled under a bush near a woodpile. They stayed there for a few hours and then finally came to my backyard looking for their daily snack.

Thank goodness all was well and the ducks were fine. What an exciting morning on Sweetwater Lake!

—Karen Westfall, Nineveh, Indiana

Lucky Shot

I was lucky to be in the right place when this American goldfinch flew onto a rose of Sharon bush in my yard. I've seen photographs of goldfinches on roses, but never on a rose of Sharon.

—Carol A. Lewis, Newport News, Virginia

What's for Lunch?

Anywhere you find someone fishing around Charlotte Harbor, Florida, you're likely to find a heron, egret or pelican standing nearby. They're always carefully examining the bait bucket and the catch of the day.

Without permission, this snowy egret boarded our boat for a chance to steal a quick meal. It even posed for this picture...perhaps to better its chances for a handout.

Nice "hood ornament," don't you think?

—Hank Mendenhall, Punta Gorda, Florida

Patience Pays Off

I love photographing birds, but I have a hard time attracting northern cardinals. My mom usually has 15 to 20 at a time, so I sit at her house for hours trying to snap pictures of these gorgeous birds.

One morning, she called and told me to come right over because there was a funny-looking bird among her cardinals. It took me three trips before I finally saw and captured a photo of this beautiful bird.

After doing some research, I believe this is a leucistic northern cardinal. Unlike albinism, leucism is a reduction in all types of skin pigments. This photo is an amazing addition to my collection.

—Diane Scott, East Ellijay, Georgia

Celebrity Bluebirds

We keep a mealworm tray on our backyard patio. At feeding time, we make a calling noise, and within minutes a pair of adult eastern bluebirds shows up, followed by their fledglings (left). My husband took this photo during one of their "family meals."

We sent the photo to one of our TV stations, and it was shown on a morning broadcast. That day, the bluebirds won the hearts of our local newscasters and community. They had definitely already won ours.

—Richard and Vanessa Voisinet, The Woodlands, Texas

From House to Home

After retiring, I wondered what to do next. A friend suggested building birdhouses, so I got busy.

One day, during breakfast, my son looked out the kitchen window and said, "Look at the wren on the birdhouses!"

We watched as the tiny bird hopped from birdhouse to birdhouse, looking in and sometimes going all the way in. It finally pulled one of my price tags off and flew away. My son said, "He's probably going to show his wife that he's found a terrific buy!"

Soon, a pair of wrens set up a nest in a rustic wren house hanging on a post. One wren flew to a pile of weeds and selected choice pieces for the nest. It was priceless to be close to the nest building and egg laying, and to hear peeps of the young wrens.

—William V. Wilson, Indianapolis, Indiana

Rowdy Robins

I have lived in Minnesota for 33 years, and I have never before seen robins do such a curious thing. One fall, I was caring for the neighbors dogs when I heard a loud bird commotion.

Looking around, I was expecting to see a large flock of grackles or some other noisy birds making a scene. Instead, I found hundreds of robins filling the trees overhead! They must have been migrating south together in raucous waves.

The dogs got very excited and riled up as hundreds of robins flew by in a big wave above our heads. It was a surreal experience that I'll probably never see again. Now I look at fall migration in a new light, and I can only hope that the robins will fly by again next fall.

—Sandee Swanson, Stillwater, Minnesota

106

114

116

110

108

122

Chapter 4
Flying Flowers

Photos: western tiger swallowtail, Richard Shiell; common checkered skipper, Rolf Nussbaumer; American lady, Richard Day/Daybreak Imagery; little metalmark, Will Cook; variegated fritillary, Richard Day/Daybreak Imagery; silver-spotted skipper, Rick and Nora Bowers/KAC Productions; Io moth, Leroy Simon/David Liebman Stock; Malachite, Kathy Adams Clark/KAC Productions; dogface butterfly, Kathy Adams Clark/KAC Productions.

Western Tiger Swallowtail

Brilliantly hued butterflies bring sunny silhouettes to the West.

Richard Shiell

Richard Shell

Spotting a bright-yellow western tiger swallowtail soaring through the landscape is sure to brighten anyone's day. Happily, it's a common and lively visitor to western gardens, urban areas and parklands. It's also the swallowtail species people view in large numbers in Rocky Mountain regions.

You won't have trouble seeing this swallowtail with its large, graceful wings, painted with black tiger stripes and splashes of blue and orange. It will stand out as it glides through woodlands or flits through backyard flower borders.

A native of western North America, the western tiger swallowtail makes its home from British Columbia and Alberta south along the Pacific Coast to Baja California, and east through the Rocky Mountain states. It ranges into New Mexico, Arizona, central Texas, central Colorado and western South Dakota, occasionally drifting into Nebraska.

Along the eastern edge of their territory, western tiger swallowtails often mingle with their similarly marked cousins, eastern tiger swallowtails (*Papilio glaucus*). Large groups of the two species are likely to congregate around mud puddles and waterways in western canyons. The two species have also been known to interbreed.

In most regions, the western tiger swallowtail flies in June and July but remains active from February to November along the Pacific Coast and southern California. Swallowtails produce one generation in short-summer areas and three generations each year in warmer regions. Moist areas draw the brightly hued butterflies wherever host plants such as aspen, sycamore, cottonwood, ash and alder trees grow.

Females lay a single deep-green egg on the underside of the host plant leaf. In about 4 days, a small blackish caterpillar with a white saddle emerges from the egg. As it grows, it turns green with an enlarged thorax bearing conspicuous eyespots.

The caterpillars grow to nearly 2 inches before pupating. As they prepare to pupate, they build a protective structure of folded leaves that they line with silk.

The irregularly shaped chrysalis has a wood-like texture, and it's attached to a twig or bark in an upright fashion with a silken thread as a belt. Depending on the season, butterflies emerge in a couple weeks from the top of the chrysalis by splitting it open.

Adult butterflies are attracted to gardens outfitted with water sources for sipping, walkways for basking and flowering plants that supply nectar. The western tiger swallowtail often stops to sip at the blossoms of morning glory, agastache, salvia, sunflowers, thistle, California buckeye, zinnia, penstemon, milkweed, lobelia and butterfly bush.

One of the more active butterfly species, the western tiger swallowtail is generally on the move, which allows people to easily observe and enjoy it. Males soar through the air as they patrol for mates, and adults of both sexes glide above and flutter through plantings as they search for food.

When they finally alight upon a bloom, they settle in with wings spread, showing off their beautiful stripes and iridescent blue markings that glimmer in the sun. If you're lucky enough to spot one on a warm, sunny day, be sure to take a moment to enjoy its beauty.

BUTTERFLY BIT

Look for the western tiger swallowtail caterpillar on deciduous trees like sycamore, ash, cottonwood, aspen, willow, alder, plum and maple. Once it turns into a stunning butterfly, you'll see it gliding through your flower beds.

ON THE DEFENSIVE. Menacing eyespots help the caterpillar ward off predators. Later, its leaflike chrysalis (below) offers camouflage.

Caterpillar and chrysalis photos: Bob Jensen ©

Flying Flower Facts

Scientific Name: *Pterourus rutulus* or *Papilio rutulus*.
Family: Swallowtail.
Wingspan: Varies from 2-1/4 to 4 inches.
Distinctive Markings: Lemon-yellow wings with black tiger stripes and black margins; black margins are marked with yellow dots and blue lines. Hind wings have blue and orange dots near the black "tails." There's a continuous blue margin on the underside of the hind wing.
Distinctive Behavior: Glides slowly through gardens and trees, but moves rapidly when frightened. Males gather at mud puddles and streams for moisture and minerals.
Habitat: Commonly visits city and suburban areas and parks where sycamores grow. Generally opts for moist sites. Found in gardens, in canyons, near streams, amid sagebrush, on roadsides and trails, and on mesas with creeks.
Caterpillar: Growing to 2 inches in length, the blue-spotted light- to dark-green caterpillar boasts an enlarged head banded with yellow and black at the neck. Large yellow eyespots on the front of the head are marked with black and blue centers.
Host Plants: A wide array of deciduous trees, including sycamore, cottonwood, aspen, willow alder, ash, plum and maple.

Above, Kathy Adams Clark/KAC Productions; all other photos, Rick and Nora Bowers/KAC Productions

Dogface Butterfly

Fido-like features make these brightly colored fliers unique.

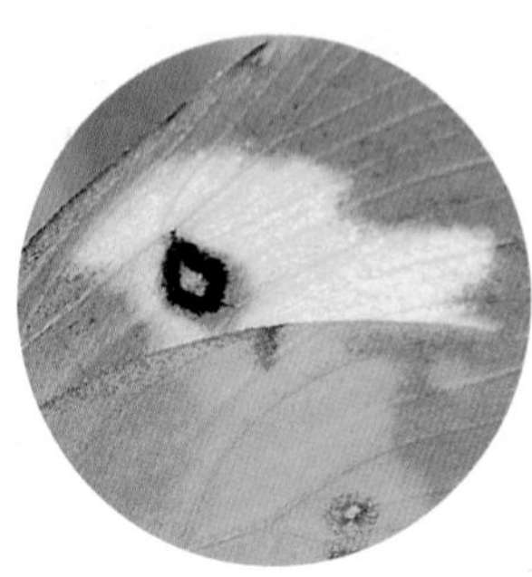

Of all the members of the sulfur family, dogface butterflies have some of the most distinctive features. Both the southern and California dogface butterflies boast a canine countenance.

Just look closely as these butterflies spread their wings, and you'll note two profiles of black-eyed pooches, outlined by black margins on each forewing. You can even see the profile from the underside of the wing (left). Some say it's a poodle's mug; others insist it's a hound's head.

Although the butterfly cousins share similar markings and dine on many of the same host plants, they boast subtle differences in appearance and range.

The tropical southern dogface (*Zerene cesonia*) is lighter yellow than its saffron-orange California

(*Zerene eurydice*) relative. They also showcase darker black markings. Meanwhile, the California dogface males boast a purple sheen across the poodle-like pattern on their forewings, which led to its "Flying Pansy" nickname. (Photos of the southern dogface are on this page; those of the California are on the opposite page.)

The undersides of each species also differ. The southern's yellow undersides appear to be mottled in rose, while the California's undersides are deep yellow or greenish yellow.

The southern dogface makes its home in the Deep South, and you can commonly find it in open areas from California to Florida.

The butterflies are irregular visitors to Mid-

LOOK AT THIS FACE. Take a close look at a dogface butterfly with its wings open (right). You'll see that it has two separate dog profiles, facing out, on each wing.

western states and may occasionally stray into Canada. Generally, these butterflies produce three broods throughout the summer in their southern territories and one brood farther north. Butterflies will likely hibernate or may overwinter as pupae. When they emerge from overwintering, they sport a remarkable magenta-flushed winter form.

The California dogface is a resident of the Golden State and soars through coastal woodlands from north-central California south to the Baja Peninsula. It may occasionally stray into western Arizona as well.

In 1973, the California legislature named this butterfly its state insect. Three years later, its vibrant image appeared on a U.S. postage stamp. This butterfly generally produces two broods from spring to autumn.

Since the two species inhabit such different areas, it's not likely you'll be able to compare them side by side. But if you're wandering through the San Bernardino Mountains at the right time, you may spot southern and California dogfaces flying together. Or you may see a hybrid of the two—the interesting result of the species intermixing.

Both butterflies are rapid fliers, with the California varieties soaring 20 feet above the ground and gliding through the treetops. The best time to observe the butterflies is when they dip down to sip nectar or dabble in mud puddles.

To draw the butterflies into your garden, cultivate dogface caterpillars' favorite host plant of false indigo and grow the adults' preferred nectar plants. California varieties will stop at roadside thistles or visit butterfly gardens planted with sages, lantana, California fuchsia and wooly blue curls. Southern dogfaces often stop by landscapes that have cottage-garden favorites, such as butterfly weed, asters, butterfly bush, coreopsis, verbena and scabiosa.

Keep your eye and camera aimed at the flowers, as these butterflies flit in and out quickly. If you're vigilant, you might see a dogface staring up at you.

BUTTERFLY BIT

Both the California and southern dogface butterflies are named for what looks like the face of a dog on each of the forewings. You can also spot the outline of a dog on the undersides of the wings. Take a look at the photos. What do you think?

Flying Flower Facts

CALIFORNIA DOGFACE (ABOVE)
Scientific Name: *Zerene eurydice.*
Family: Whites and sulfurs.
Wingspan: 2 to 2-1/2 inches.
Distinctive Markings: Males may boast a purplish-red iridescence across profile. Females have light or no black margins. Undersides are deep yellow or greenish yellow; silvery spots below on hind wing cell.
Distinctive Behavior: Rapid and high fliers, soaring up to 15 or 20 feet.
Habitat: Foothills, chaparral and oak or coniferous woodlands.
Caterpillar: Growing to 1 inch in length, the dull-green larvae boasts either orange-edged white side lines or thin, light cross bands.
Host Plants: Caterpillars feed on small-leaved plants in the pea family.

SOUTHERN DOGFACE (OPPOSITE PAGE)
Scientific Name: *Zerene cesonia.*
Family: Whites and sulfurs.
Wingspan: 1-7/8 to 2-1/2 inches.
Distinctive Markings: Curved, pointed yellow forewings with black margins and black eyespots. Undersides vary, but are mostly yellow with reddish-pink mottling.
Distinctive Behavior: Males patrol for mates and have a rapid flight.
Habitat: Open woodlands, oak scrub deserts, road edges, short-grass prairies and open woodlands.
Caterpillar: Growing to 1 inch in length, the green larvae vary in coloring. Some boast longitudinal black and yellow stripes; others may be cross-banded or plain.
Host Plants: Caterpillars feed on small-leaved plants in the pea family.

EDITOR'S PICK BLUE BEAUTY 2008

Common Checkered Skipper

Keep an eye out for these petite and lively butterflies as they flit from flower to flower in search of nectar.

Rolf Nussbaumer

Whether you've cultivated a cottage garden or planted a native prairie, you're likely to spot the common checkered skipper bouncing about your landscape. Lilliputian in stature and mothlike in form, common checkered skippers are drawn to sunny sites that abound with nectar-rich flowers.

Where to Find This Flier

The most common of the skippers, checkered skippers range across southern Canada, Mexico and most of the United States, with the exception of northwestern states and states north of Massachusetts. They reproduce all year in southern climes, but in northern areas, they produce broods only from April to October.

Members of the Hesperiidae, or skipper, family, the checkered skipper is just one of more than 200 skippers that make their home in North America. And like their cousins, they have the same rapid and somewhat jerky flight pattern when they're on the move.

Plantings They'll Love

You might spot these tiny fliers skipping between verbena, butterfly bush and lantana blooms or settling atop a sunflower or ironweed flower. Watch for activity near white composite-type flowers—the voracious feeders are especially fond of white-flowering asters, coneflowers, fleabane and zinnias. Include caterpillar hosts like hollyhock, hibiscus and mallow in your planting palette, and these full-of-zip butterflies may become permanent or seasonal residents.

Don't Forget the Caterpillar

Females lay small, greenish eggs singly on host plant leaf buds or leaves. Then, as the eggs age, their color shifts to creamy yellow.

Eggs give way to hairy, striped caterpillars, which construct nests from folded leaves and silk. The larvae morph into green-tipped, brownish chrysalises. These eventually release another round of checkered skippers to feed, flit, dash, dart and skip about the landscape.

> You might spot these tiny fliers skipping between verbena, butterfly bush and lantana blooms, or settling atop a sunflower or ironweed flower.

Did You Know?

Adult butterflies actively feed and mate in the afternoon. Males patrol and protect their self-assigned territories, about 100 feet in length, by aggressively flitting after any insect, avian and human invaders that pass by.

Unlike statuesque swallowtails or monarchs, the checkered skipper has an ungainly shape similar to a moth. Its large body is covered in long hairs, undersized wings and hooked antennae.

The chrysalis of the common checkered skipper starts off fairly light in color (like the one at right), but as it ages, it darkens to a brownish shade.

Rolf Nussbaumer

Caterpillar and chrysalis photos: Tom Allen

Kathy Adams Clark/KAC Productions

Eyed Brown

Look for this subtly hued flier in wetlands and prairies.

You may have to schedule a walk through native wetlands, saltwater marshes or moist open meadows to observe eyed brown butterflies. Although they occasionally stray into gardens, these butterflies are denizens of natural areas rich in moisture and sedges, their preferred host plant.

Delicate in looks and lazy in flight, the North American eyed brown butterfly commonly ranges from southeast Saskatchewan to the northeastern United States, with outlying populations in Nebraska, Colorado and northern Quebec.

Even though its range spans nearly one-quarter of the United States, the eyed brown is not easy for the butterfly watcher to spot. The 2-inch brownish-tan butterfly, with distinctive yellow-edged black eyespots, commonly weaves and bobs low amid sedge-rich meadows and wet prairies—neither of which are easily traversed by human spectators.

They perch low in the vegetation, infrequently fly above the foliage and rarely wander far from sedge-filled wetlands.

Just one of the satyr subgroup of brush-footed butterflies, the eyed brown is often confused with its darker-winged cousin, the Appalachian brown (*Satyrodes appalachia*). They share a preference for similar habitats, although the Appalachian brown mainly resides along woodland edges. It's not unusual for the sibling species to overlap territories, mingling together in areas where woodland paths wind near an open marshland.

Eyed browns produce one brood and are abundant from June through September. Adult females lay smooth, dome-shaped, light-green eggs singly on leaves of sedges and non-host plants. Light-green caterpillars

Mike Reese, www.wisconsinbutterflies.org

TEST YOUR VISION. Eyed browns are a bit reclusive. They stick close to the marshlands where their host plant, sedge, grows, and they even keep a low profile while flying. The small butterfly is a treat to see, however, with warm-brown coloring and prominent rows of yellow-edged black eyespots.

Flying Flower Facts

Common Name: Eyed brown.
Scientific Name: *Satyrodes eurydice.*
Family: Brush-footed.
Wingspan: 1-1/2 to 2-7/16 inches.
Distinctive Markings: Rounded wings are light to medium brown on top with black eyespots. Eyespots on undersides of forewings are linked, while those on the hindwings zigzag.
Distinctive Behavior: The eyed brown flies tentatively through low-growing grasses, and it stops often to perch amid low-growing vegetation. Males scout for females by flying through or perching on foliage.
Habitat: Open wet meadows, sedge marshes and wet areas in tallgrass prairies and along slow-moving streams.
Caterpillar: Slender and light green with lengthwise stripes of yellow and dark green, and red-tipped horns on head and tail.
Host Plants: Sedges (*Carex* species).

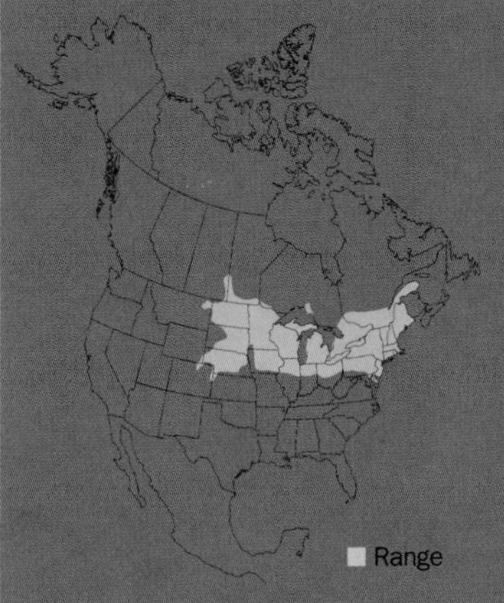

BUTTERFLY BIT

This species does not usually travel far from its preferred habitat of wet marshlands, making it difficult for humans to spot them in backyards. Eyed browns will rarely feed on flower nectar, choosing sap or bird droppings instead.

with lengthwise yellow and dark-green stripes, and red-tipped horns at head and tail emerge from the eggs.

The caterpillar's leaflike coloring effectively camouflages the caterpillar as it feeds on the grassy blades of nearby sedges. The caterpillar morphs into a green chrysalis with a hooked head, dorsal stripe and buff shadings.

Eyed browns generally overwinter in the third and fourth larval stages, with butterflies emerging the following June.

Adult butterflies feed on sap, bird droppings and, very occasionally, flower nectar. People have spotted them sipping at mud puddles and pausing to bask on sunlit walkways. Interestingly, as adults age and are battered by the elements, their wings become lighter in color and may appear to be white.

Gardeners may be able to lure this elusive native into their yards by re-creating their preferred habitats. Try planting an array of sedges in boggy, low-lying areas. The grass-like perennials—valued by gardeners for their tussock-like forms and tolerance for shade and damp—may just attract a flock of these unusually understated, but always interesting to observe, winged creatures.

Richard Day/Daybreak Imagery

American Lady

Watch for these common garden visitors in just about any yard!

You're sure to have American lady butterflies if you have a garden. These black-marked, rusty-orange fliers are common backyard visitors, refueling on nectar in flower beds from spring through fall.

Adults feed on more than 38 types of nectar-rich plants and are common visitors to yards and open areas from southern Canada south into Venezuela. The butterflies have a global presence as well. They stray as far north as Newfoundland and have established colonies in Europe and the West Indies.

In tropical and southern climes, the midsized butterfly flits about most of the year. Farther north, the butterflies generally appear from May through August. One of the hardiest of the *Vanessa* species of butterflies, the American lady is often confused with its similarly colored cousin, the painted lady (*Vanessa cardui*).

Both boast rusty-orange wings with black patches and borders and white dots (above right). It's the markings on the undersides of the hind

Above, Richard Day/Daybreak Imagery; right, Tom Allen

SOMETHING SWEET. American lady butterflies will feed from a variety of nectar-rich flowers, including verbena (above) and zinnia (opposite page).

Rick and Nora Bowers/KAC Productions

BUTTERFLY BIT

American lady butterflies sport two blue-ringed black eyespots on their hind wing undersides, a key to help identify them. Painted ladies, a close cousin to the American lady, look very similar except for these distinguishing spots.

wings that differentiate the two. The American lady displays two large blue-ringed black eyespots (above); the painted lady has five smaller eyespots.

In the spring, look for American ladies feeding on blooming shadbush and chokeberry shrubs. In summer, they sip from lantana, purple coneflower, yarrow, daisies, zinnia, borage, heliotrope, common milkweed and other familiar garden flowers. In autumn, they'll dine on asters, mums and goldenrods.

If you cultivate the caterpillar's preferred host plants, including sweet everlasting (*Gnaphalium obtusifolium*) and pearly everlasting (*Anaphalis margaritacea*), you'll take in up-close views of the egg-to-pupae metamorphosis. Adults lay single dome-shaped, yellowish-green eggs beneath the leaves' hairy covering.

Each egg produces a colorfully spotted and striped black caterpillar (left) that weaves its own silky nest amid the plants' flower heads. The solitary caterpillars often pupate in their larval nests, turning into dark-striped yellow chrysalises with two conical projections at the head (inset above).

American ladies are prolific breeders, producing up to four generations of caterpillars annually. An American lady's summer form is larger and more vibrant than that of a winter-emerging adult, which is smaller and drabber in hue.

While American ladies appear to have a wide range, they are primarily considered a southern species. In autumn, they fly south to overwinter in warmer areas. Come spring, they migrate northward all the way up to Canada.

In summer, they take up residence in backyard landscapes all across the country to feed, breed and delight observant gardeners.

Flying Flower Facts

Common Name: American lady.
Scientific Name: *Vanessa virginiensis.*
Family: Nymphalidae (Brush-footed butterflies).
Wingspan: 1-3/4 to 2-5/8 inches.
Distinctive Markings: Irregular brown, yellow and orange patterns on uppersides; forewings have a black patch, a white spot below the patch, and a white bar at the wing edge. Two large blue-ringed black eyespots on hind wing undersides distinguish the American lady from the painted lady, which has four small and one tiny eyespot.
Distinctive Behavior: American lady males look for mates by perching on low-growing plants in the afternoon. It flies rapidly and erratically, pausing to sip flower nectar with open wings while basking in the sun.
Habitat: Commonly visits gardens and open areas with low vegetation, such as coastal dunes, meadows, forest edges and roadsides.
Caterpillar: Red- and white-spotted black bodies with branched black spines separated by black and green stripes.
Host Plants: Sweet everlasting (*Gnaphalium obtusifolium*), pearly everlasting (*Anaphalis margaritacea*), pussy toes (*Antennaria species*), edelweiss (*Leontopodium alpinum*), wormwood (*Artemesia*), ironweed (*Vernonia*) and burdock (*Arctium*).

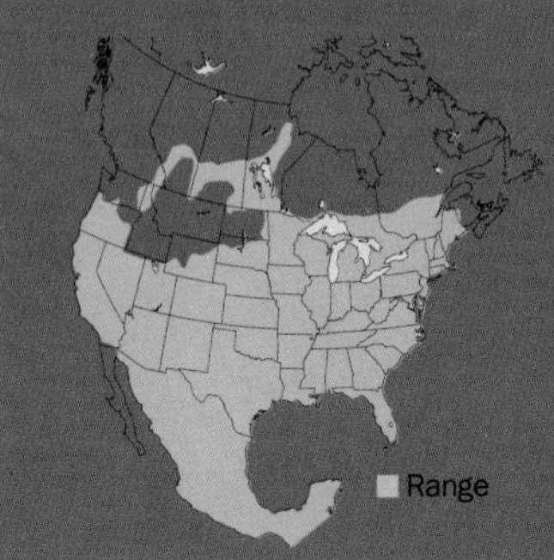

Delicate and lovely, these little butterflies shine like diamonds in the Southeast.

Little Metalmark

You'll think you've hit the mother lode if you're lucky enough to spot a little metalmark. These tiny, but mighty pretty, butterflies have a wingspan of less than an inch and generally fly under a human's radar.

Butterfly photos above and at right, Will Cook

Discover the Little Metalmark

Little metalmarks flit close to the earth. You rarely see them until they perch—either upright atop a flower or upside down beneath a leaf. Here, they will open their fringed, coppery-orange wings shimmering with gleaming, silvery-blue dots lined along dark bands.

The silver spots are a signature characteristic of metalmark (*Riodinidae*) butterflies—a category that encompasses 1,000 species, 24 of which make their home in North America.

Where to Find This Flier

The little metalmark ranges from Maryland and Virginia south to Florida and west along the Gulf Coast to Texas. It is the only metalmark residing along the Southeastern coast.

A stay-at-home species, these butterflies rarely roam far from areas that satisfy their feeding and procreating needs. Little metalmarks inhabit damp and sunny areas, such as sandy coastal fields and salt marsh meadows.

Yellow thistle plants host and feed developing larva, while flat-flowered plants like yarrow, lance-leaf coreopsis and blue mistflower satisfy adult butterflies' thirst for nectar.

Don't Forget the Caterpillar

Depending on the area, little metalmarks usually reproduce three to five times during the breeding season running from March through October.

Little metalmarks hatch from flat, turban-shaped eggs on the leaves of yellow thistle plants. Unlike many other larva, these caterpillars are likely to snooze amid leaves littering the ground during the day. They start foraging for food after dark on an overcast day.

Caterpillars transform into oval-shaped, bright-green chrysalises marked with black spots and covered with long and feathery clumps of hair. The chrysalises, which protect the pupae within, are generally attached via a silk strand to a host-plant leaf.

Derb Carter

"This butterfly is beautiful to see up close, especially when its metallic bands are glittering in the sunlight."—Will Cook, photographer

Did You Know?

Little metalmarks are common throughout Florida. Here, they will produce a new brood each month.

Long white hairs, or setae, cover the caterpillars (top photo, right) and the chrysalis (lower photo). The plumes protect them from predators since they blend with the hairs on their host plant and make them look inedible.

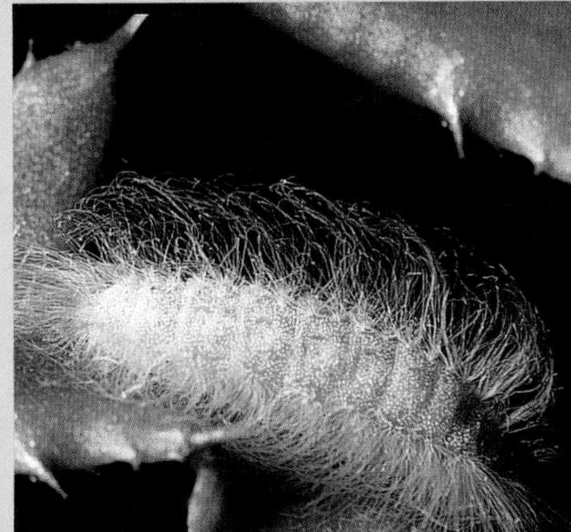

Above and below photos, Tom Allen

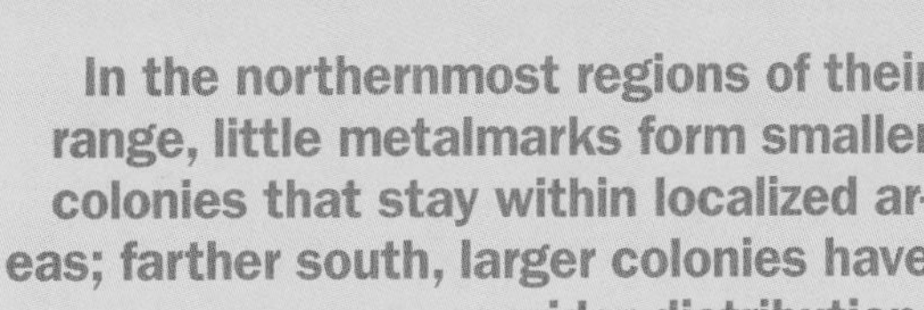

In the northernmost regions of their range, little metalmarks form smaller colonies that stay within localized areas; farther south, larger colonies have a wider distribution.

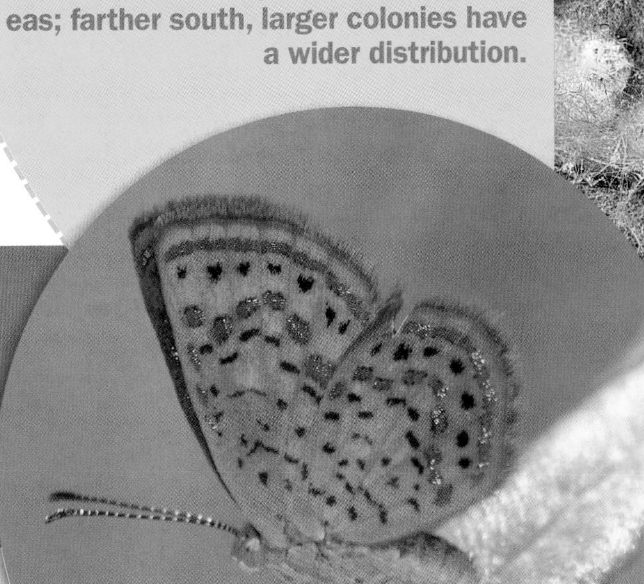

A RARE MOMENT. If you're fortunate enough to spot a little metalmark perched, then look quick! It's always on the move and doesn't stay in one spot for long.

Carolina Sphinx

& Five-Spotted Hawk Moth

Mark Werner/The Image Finders

These moths are fascinating, but you probably won't want the caterpillars on your tomatoes.

As the sun descends in the western sky, Carolina sphinx and five-spotted hawk moths emerge and dart out into gardens in search of nectar.

From a distance, the moths' hovering motions and the buzzing of their rapidly beating wings make them look a lot like hummingbirds.

If you've been fooled by this scenario, you're not alone. These fliers may look like hummingbirds in flight, but when you move in closer, you'll easily see the differences. Instead of a bill, you'll note a long proboscis that the moth uses to extract nectar. You'll also see that its elongated, brownish-grey wings and yellow-spotted abdomen are not birdlike at all.

Although you might be a little disappointed that your hummingbird sighting turned into an insect spotting, the moths' antics will soon enthrall you. After all, the Carolina sphinx and five-spotted hawk are a couple of very cool moths.

A Cousin Comparison

Both the Carolina sphinx (top) and five-spotted hawk moth (above) are members of the Sphingidae, or sphinx moth, family and are natives of North America. You can find them in most backyards around the country.

Although the two are similar in looks, the Carolina sphinx has more vibrantly white markings on its brownish-grey wings, which are slightly shorter than its hawk moth relative. The Carolina sphinx boasts a wingspan of about 4 inches, while

TOMATOES BEWARE! It's no wonder these caterpillars (right) have earned the name tomato hornworm. They devour tomato, potato and other plants in the nightshade family. If left alone, they can do a lot of damage to crops.

BUTTERFLY BIT

When these fliers are first spotted in backyards, they are usually mistaken for hummingbirds. They hover and feed from the same flowers as hummingbirds. But instead of extracting nectar with a bill, they use their proboscis.

the hawk moth's more understated wingspan ranges up to slightly more than 5 inches.

Furthermore, you can distinguish the two moths by counting the spots on their abdomens. The Carolina sphinx has six pairs of yellow spots; the hawk moth usually has five pairs.

Both moths are fast. Their narrow forewings are wider than their hind wings, which results in a streamlined form that allows them to hustle and hover as they navigate the landscape.

Adult Carolina sphinx and hawk moths both enjoy tubular blooms (like their hummingbird look-alikes). They are especially fond of sipping at petunias, flowering tobacco, phlox, honeysuckle and moonflower.

The Hungriest of Caterpillars

Unfortunately, these good-looking and interesting moths arise from two pesky and gluttonous caterpillars that strip leaves and fruit from tobacco crops, tomato vines, potatoes and plants in the nightshade family.

The larva of the Carolina sphinx goes by the name tobacco hornworm, while the hawk moth's larva earned the name tomato hornworm. The 4-inch, bright-green horned caterpillars are easy to spot when they're gnawing on leaves.

When disturbed, the caterpillars raise their head and thorax, striking a pose that looks like that of an Egyptian sphinx.

Interestingly, when the caterpillars are ready to pupate, they drop from host plant leaves to the soil. They burrow beneath the soil and form hard and shiny brown pupae. Once the moths emerge from the pupa, they tunnel to the surface, dry their wings, and resume their hummingbird-like antics amid the petunias.

Don't be fooled the next time you see these fliers in your yard. Take a closer look, and you'll see they are not hummingbirds, even though they will feed on similar flowers.

And as for the caterpillars, just beware. They are not easy on your vegetable crops, so keep an eye on those tomatoes!

Photos this page and moth photo below left: Judy Burris and Wayne and Christina Richards

Flying Flower Facts

CAROLINA SPHINX
Scientific Name: *Manduca sexta.*
Family: Sphinx moths.
Wingspan: 3-3/4 to 4-3/4 inches.
Distinctive Markings: Gray forewings with black-and-white markings; forewings and hind wings have white-spotted fringes; abdomens sport six pairs of yellow spots.
Distinctive Behavior: Adults begin flying at dusk and feed throughout the night.
Habitat: Tobacco fields, vegetable gardens, flower gardens and areas where plants in the nightshade family grow.
Caterpillar: Known as tobacco hornworms, the lime-green caterpillars grow to 4 inches in length and have seven diagonal white lines and a red-tipped horn at the tip of their abdomens.
Host Plants: Caterpillars feed on leaves and fruits of tobacco, potato and tomato plants, and plants in nightshade family, including petunias.
Range: Massachusetts west to central Colorado and northern California. South to Florida, through Texas, New Mexico, Arizona and southern California.

FIVE-SPOTTED HAWK MOTH
Scientific Name: *Manduca quinquemaculata.*
Family: Sphinx moths.
Wingspan: 3-1/2 to 5-1/3 inches.
Distinctive Markings: Forewings boast blurred brown-and-grey markings and plain grey fringes; brown-and-white-banded hind wings showcase two conspicuous black, zigzagged lines and white-spotted margins.
Distinctive Behavior: Adults begin flying at dusk and feed throughout night.
Habitat: Tobacco fields, vegetable gardens, flower gardens and areas where plants in the nightshade family grow.
Caterpillar: Known as tomato hornworms, the light-green caterpillars grow to 4 inches. Sports V-shaped markings and a black-edged horn at tip of abdomen.
Host Plants: Caterpillars feed on leaves and fruits of tobacco, potato and tomato plants, and plants in nightshade family, including petunias.
Range: Mexico north through the United States, occasionally strays into Canada, and is an uncommon visitor to southeastern and Great Plains states.

Red-Banded Hairstreak

Not a bit skittish, these pretty butterflies pause in flower borders to flaunt their wings.

Red-banded hairstreaks are always causing a scene in the garden. With scarlet-striped, gray wings splashed with blue, iridescent scales, they are easy to spot perching atop a blossom or sipping at a mud puddle.

Kathy Adams Clark/KAC Productions

Fooling Predators

Happily for butterfly watchers in the eastern U.S., red-banded hairstreaks are common garden visitors that take a show-off's stance, pausing to feed, rest and bask. Not easily ruffled, these tiny butterflies can easily be viewed as they hold their wings upright and move their hind wings up and down.

The butterfly's wings (a mere 7/8 to 1-1/4 inches wide) are a joy to watch. They work to fool potential predators. Their antennae-like tails and the eyespots on their hind wings create a head-like pattern. The twitching hind wings, which predators can tear without dire results, draw them to the butterfly's rear rather than its head.

Where to Find This Flier

Red-banded hairstreaks range from New York's Long Island, south through Florida and west into southeastern Kansas, eastern Oklahoma and eastern Texas. Occasionally, the butterflies will roam north into Nebraska, Illinois and Michigan.

You're likely to find them in open fields, woodland edges and landscapes where the caterpillars' host plants, sumacs, wax myrtles, crotons and oaks, thrive. The small butterflies have short proboscises, which makes it difficult to get nectar from deep, trumpeted blossoms.

You're more likely to see them feeding at plants with small, flat or fluffy flowers. These include blue mist shrubs, eupatorium, sedums, yarrow, sumac, common milkweed, tickseed, butterfly bush, garlic chives and rudbeckia.

The butterflies become very active around dusk and often feed in large numbers at a single plant. When they're not feeding, males perch on low branches to keep watch for potential mates.

In northern ranges, the butterflies produce two broods from May through October. Those in Florida produce offspring year-round.

Since red-banded hairstreaks have short proboscises, they can only get nectar from shallow blossoms like this sedum.

Did You Know?

Unlike many other butterfly larvae, the red-banded hairstreak caterpillar feeds primarily on dead host-plant leaves, not live ones. Females lay their tiny, creamy-white eggs singly on the undersides of leaves that have fallen to the ground below the host plant. The hairy, brown caterpillars emerge and feed on dried leaves or leaf litter, occasionally climbing up the host plant stems to munch on lower leaf buds.

Caterpillar and chrysalis photos: Tom Allen

The caterpillars morph into mottled, hairy and dark-colored chrysalises (right), and they may hibernate through winter in some regions.

When butterflies first emerge, they have bright, vibrant colors (like the one at right). As they age, they begin to lose their bright coloring and become slightly tattered (like the one at left).

John and Gloria Tveten/KAC Productions

Richard Day/Daybreak Imagery

Variegated Fritillary

This butterfly brightens wild and weedy landscapes.

A lover of sunny, wide-open spaces, variegated fritillaries feel most at home in tropical climes. But luckily for butterfly lovers, this midsized fritillary also is common throughout North America, except along the Pacific and the Pacific Northwest.

As members of the brush-footed family and longwing subfamily, these beauties have an extraordinary range, from Argentina to Central America and Mexico up to Maine.

Sometimes called "vari-frits," these butterflies are quite striking. They have dark zigzagged lines that create glass-like patterns atop their elongated, brownish-orange wings.

Meanwhile, variegated patterns of brown and orange dot their underwings. This mottling allows the variegated fritillary to blend in with the natural scene for protection from predators.

Unlike the gulf fritillary (*Agraulis vanillae*) and true fritillaries in the *Speyeria* genus, variegated fritillaries lack silvery spots on their undersides.

Also, they are far less picky about the host plants they choose for feeding and breeding. In fact, their larvae dine on more host plants than almost any other butterfly species. Only painted

Richard Day/Daybreak Imagery

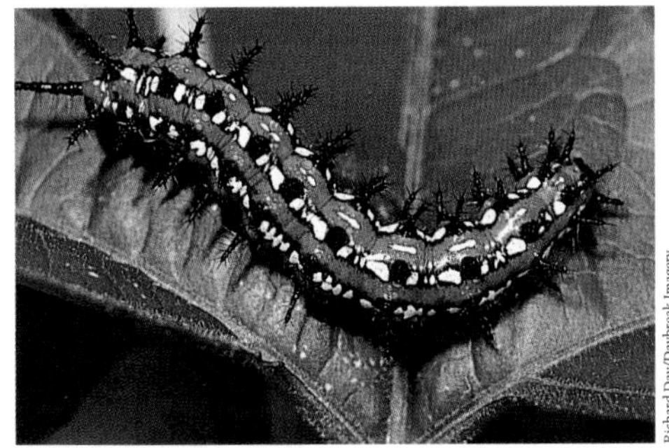

Richard Day/Daybreak Imagery

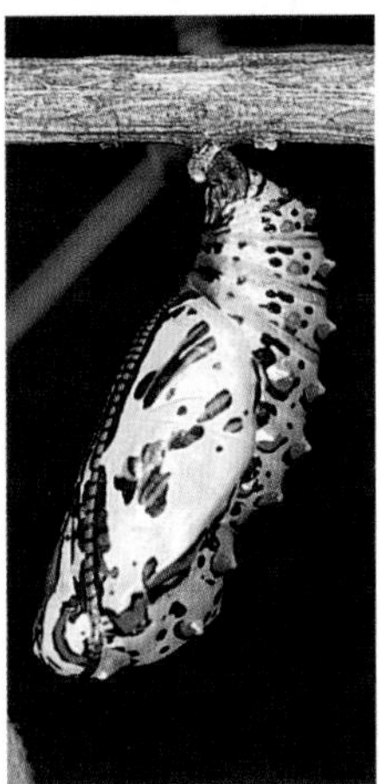

Tom Allen

GREAT DESIGNS. The caterpillar (above) and chrysalis (left) of the variegated fritillary butterfly sport gorgeous markings. These butterflies feed from a variety of plants, including milkweed (opposite page) and thistle (far left).

Flying Flower Facts

Scientific Name: *Euptoieta claudia.*
Family: Brush-footed.
Wingspan: 1-3/4 to 2-1/4 inches.
Distinctive Markings: Elongated, tawny-orange wings with dark zigzagged lines and black-dotted margins; hind wings are slightly scalloped and undersides of wings are mottled with whitish brown patterns and splashes of orange.
Distinctive Behavior: They fly in rapid darting patterns close to the ground and rest by perching on the ground or grass blades. Males looking for mates take short flights through open, dry areas. Adults tentatively flutter between blooms as they feed.
Habitat: Commonly visits gardens and sunny open areas such as grasslands, fields, meadows, roadsides and mountaintops, but avoids deeply forested spaces.
Caterpillar: Strikingly colored, the salmon-red caterpillar boasts bright-white stripes running the length of its body, rows of dark spines and knobby black horns at the head.
Host Plants: A wide array of plants, including passionflower, may apple, flax, violets, pansies, purslane, stonecrop, moonseed and plantain.

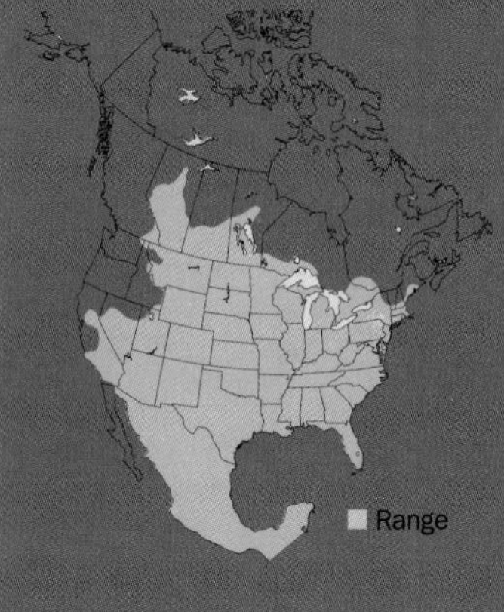

BUTTERFLY BIT

Variegated fritillaries are certainly not picky eaters. The caterpillars have more host plants than almost any other butterfly. As adult butterflies, they feed on a wide variety of nectar-producing flowers, as well as dung and carrion.

lady, spring azure and gray hairstreak butterflies consume a wider array of plants.

Metamorphosis Marvel

Egg-laying variegated fritillaries make beelines for wild and weedy areas where purslane, may apple, plantain and moonseed flourish. They also look for gardens planted with stonecrop, pansies, violets, flax and passionflower.

The butterfly's penchant for variety is a boon for butterfly watchers—experts point to its larva and pupa as two of the most eye-catching forms in the butterfly world. Adult variegated fritillaries lay single, creamy ribbed eggs on host plant leaves and stems. The eggs open to reveal dark caterpillars that measure slightly more than 1 inch in length.

The caterpillars eventually develop salmon-red bodies, which sport white longitudinal stripes, numerous black spikes and long, spiked black horns at the head.

These caterpillars, which munch on host plant leaves and flowers, have shimmering, opalescent white chrysalises, artistically detailed with yellow and black flecks and gold bumps.

Variegated fritillaries produce broods continuously from spring through late fall in the south where they overwinter. In northern zones, the butterflies begin appearing in summer and produce fewer broods than their southern relatives.

Adult variegated fritillaries are as unfussy as their larva when seeking nourishment. Tending to flit erratically when feeding, these butterflies sip nectar from an array of wildflowers and backyard plants. They also dine on dung and carrion.

Some of their favorite nectar plants—many of which are cultivated in butterfly gardens and natural prairie borders—include red clover, common milkweed, swamp milkweed, butterfly weed, tickseed and dogbane.

Worth the Effort

Although they may be understated in appearance and diminutive in form, it's well worth the effort to track variegated fritillaries through the landscape.

The adults are quite entertaining to watch as they flit timidly from flower to flower, and their caterpillar and chrysalis forms offer observers a truly memorable look at an amazingly beautiful metamorphosis.

Rick and Nora Bowers/KAC Productions

Silver-Spotted Skipper

These common guests may be flitting through your garden every day.

Picture a perfectly propelled stone skipping across a quiet pond. Now, envision that same stone outfitted with 1-inch white-splashed, brownish wings, and you'll have a good mental image of a silver-spotted skipper in flight.

Luckily, most of us don't have to imagine what a silver-spotted skipper looks like—they are one of the most common butterflies to visit summer gardens. It's thought to be the widest-ranging butterfly. You can find silver-spotted skippers from southern Canada through the continental United States (with the exception of the Great Basin and western Texas) to northern Mexico.

The smooth and rapid fliers breed in landscapes planted with the legume-producing plants preferred by their larvae. Locust and acacia trees, wisteria vines, clover, false indigo and green-bean plants host the feeding and nesting activities of the butterfly's pale green-and-yellow striped caterpillars, which hatch from green globular eggs laid singly on host plant leaves.

The brown-headed caterpillars create a protective tent-like nest of a single leaf and silk (opposite page, top right). As they mature and lengthen, the caterpillars add more leaves and silk to expand their nests.

Unlike most butterfly chrysalises, which often dangle from host plant leaves, the loosely wrapped brown pupa of the silver-spotted skipper develops, and sometimes overwinters, amid leaves cluttering the ground (opposite page, lower right).

Depending on the region, silver-spotted skip-

Richard Day/Daybreak Imagery

Remaining photos this page: Rick and Nora Bowers/KAC Productions

LIFE CYCLE. For camouflage, the silver-spotted skipper caterpillar (above left) hides in a leaf shelter (top right) before creating a chrysalis (above right) that blends in with leaves on the ground.

pers produce one to four broods during a season. Butterflies flutter through flower borders in search of nectar and oftentimes feed on the flowers of their larval host plants.

Experts believe that adults bypass yellow blooms in favor of blossoms in shades of blue, red, pink, purple and occasionally white or cream.

Watch for their white wing patches as they alight on asters, everlasting, pea, common milkweed, red clover, salvia, verbena, blazing star, thistle and ironweed blooms. Easily startled by unexpected motion when feeding, the silver-spotted skipper will speed off, and then quickly return a few moments later.

People have observed these busy-as-a-bee butterflies chasing after dragonflies and other insects that invade their territories. They will also occasionally settle on resting humans to sip from a sweaty arm or brow.

Keep an eye out throughout your backyard for these fliers. Silver-spotted skippers sip at puddles and from shallow birdbaths in the daytime. And then at night and on hot, sunny days, adults take shelter by perching upside down beneath a commodious leaf.

Whether in flight or at rest, silver-spotted skippers always are a welcome sight. Once you identify them, they are sure to become familiar faces in gardens big and small.

BUTTERFLY BIT

The silver-spotted skipper is thought to be the widest-ranging butterfly. Chances are, this flier is already a common visitor to your flower garden. They have even been known to make a stop for a quick drink in shallow backyard birdbaths.

Flying Flower Facts

Common Name: Silver-spotted skipper.

Scientific Name: *Epargyreus clarus.*

Family: Skippers.

Wingspan: 1-3/4 to 2-5/8 inches.

Distinctive Markings: Elongated, brownish-black wings marked with glassy yellowish-gold, squared-off spots on upper forewings, and silvery-white patches and metallic-silver margins on undersides of lobed hind wings. Thick-ended and hooked antennae.

Distinctive Behavior: They fly erratically and quickly through the garden. Males search for mates by sitting atop tall grasses and low branches.

Habitat: Commonly visits gardens, woodlands, waterways, roadsides, parks and meadows.

Caterpillar: Growing to 2 inches in length, the larvae boast light yellow-and-green striped, spindle-shaped bodies and large, reddish-brown heads with two orange eyespots.

Host Plants: Caterpillars feed on the leaves of an array of woody legumes, including mossy locust, black locust, false indigo, hog-peanut, American potato-bean, common honey-locust and wisteria.

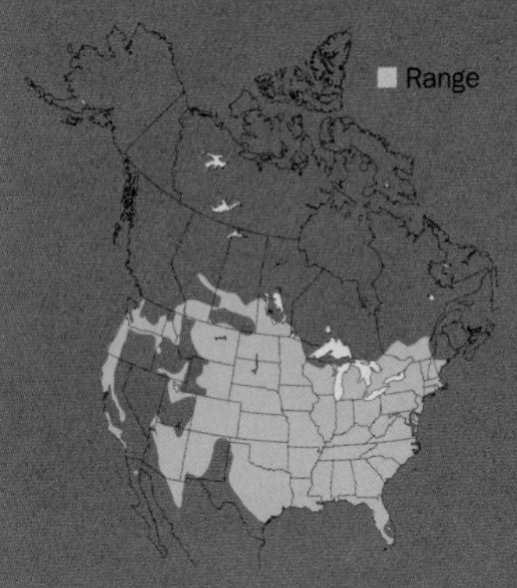

Io Moth

Colorful moths come and go in just a few days.

Io moths don't linger around the way some other moths or butterflies do. Adult Io moths do not have digestive tracts or functioning mouthparts, so they can't eat. They live less than a week, surviving on stored fat. In just a few days, they emerge, mate and reproduce.

Leroy Simon/David Liebman Stock

Discover the Beauty of the Io

Commonly dubbed the bulls' eye moth, the Io moth has large, white-splashed blue and black eyespots on its hind wings that catch the eye and ward off predators.

The wingspan of these beauties usually ranges from 2 to 3-1/4 inches. Males' forewings are golden yellow, while females' forewings are browner with a purplish or orange cast.

Adults emerge from cocoons in late morning or early afternoon. Females perch on plants until mating and then take to the air. In late evening, males fly in search of mates.

Lure This Moth to Your Yard

The Io moth is found in much of the eastern and central U.S. and southeastern Canada. It frequents habitats from woodlands to scrub to suburban areas.

Females lay clusters of small white eggs on more than 100 different host plants. The eggs then produce tiny, muted-orange larva that feed as a group, following each other in a train-like parade. Some of their host plants include farm crops, grasses, clover, raspberry plants and deciduous trees, such as alder, ash, birch, cherry, elm, pear and sassafras.

Don't Forget the Caterpillar

Growing to 2-1/2 inches in length, mature caterpillars are yellowish green to green. The color depends on the colors in the host plant leaves. They have white linear stripes with thinner red bands. They also have spines along their backs that can give you a sting!

BUTTERFLY BIT

Female Io moths lay eggs on more than 100 different host plants, including farm crops, grasses, clover, raspberry plants and deciduous trees. Eventually, the eggs turn to caterpillars that will sting you if you touch them. Be careful!

"The Io is one of my favorite moths," says butterfly expert Tom Allen. "It's one of the smaller Saturn moths, but it is also one of the most colorful."

Did You Know?

Io moth caterpillars wrap themselves in leaves and pupate on the tree or in the leaf litter on the ground. They spin a loose cocoon and winter this way.

The Io moth was named after a Greek mythological maiden that was romanced by Zeus.

If you see the Io caterpillar, don't touch! They release a painful stinging venom.

David Liebman

Bottom photos: Leroy Simon/David Liebman Stock

PINK OR BLUE? Io moths have telltale colors. The males' wings are golden (right), while females have brownish wings with an orange or purple tinge (left).

Tropical Beauties

Butterfly houses bring amazing species close to home.

By Ann Wilson
Geneva, Illinois

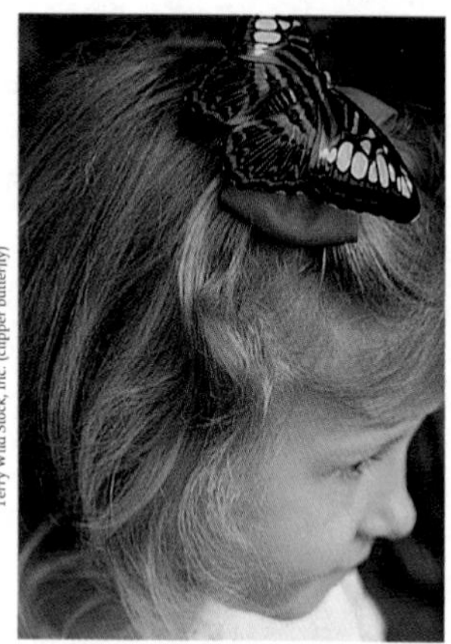

Terry Wild Stock, Inc. (clipper butterfly)

In winter, landscapes can be a little bleak. But there's a simple way to lift your spirits—visit a butterfly house, where vibrant species sail amid tropical plants. Here, meet a few of the butterflies that are common to many butterfly houses.

Postman

Boasting striking, elongated black wings with brilliant reddish-orange stripes, Postman butterflies are easy to spot. Both adults and caterpillars rely on passionflower vines for nourishment. They build immunity to its toxins as caterpillars. The adults live longer than other butterflies, thanks to the passionflower's protein-rich pollen and nectar.

Scientific Name: *Heliconius melpomene.*

Family: Brush-footed.
Wingspan: 2-1/2 to 3-1/4 inches.
Distinctive Markings: Elongated black wings with a reddish-orange stripe on forewings.
Distinctive Behavior: Adults and larva both feed on passionflower vines; caterpillars feed on the lower leaves and adults visit the flowers for pollen and nectar.
Native Habitat: Forests, jungles and river edges and streams.

Rolf Nussbaumer

judywhite/GardenPhotos.com

Owl

Found in South American and Central American rain forests, the large-winged yellow and purple butterfly dines primarily on rotting fruit, but their larvae are partial to banana leaves. In fact, banana growers consider these caterpillars a pest.

Scientific Name: *Caligo atreus.*
Family: Brush-footed.
Wingspan: 5 to 6 inches.
Distinctive Markings: Strong yellow and purple markings on upper wings; eyespots that resemble an owl's eyes on chocolate-brown undersides.
Distinctive Behavior: Adults primarily fly at dawn and dusk; caterpillars feed as groups on host plants.
Native Habitat: Dense rain forests.

E.R. Degginger/Dembinsky Photo Associates

NOT IN YOUR BACKYARD. Although it's unlikely you'll ever see one of these butterflies in your garden, you could spot one at a butterfly house near you. The seven species on these pages are just a few of the large and vibrant butterflies at these exhibits, which are growing in popularity.

Thoas Swallowtail

The Thoas swallowtail often is confused with its cousin, the giant swallowtail. This species, which ranges from Brazil north through southern Texas, boasts large, black wings marked with diagonal stripes made up of bright-yellow squares. It sips nectar by hovering like a hummingbird above blossoms.

Scientific Name: *Papilio thoas.*
Family: Swallowtail.
Wingspan: 4 to 5 inches.
Distinctive Markings: Black wings with diagonal lines of bright-yellow squares.
Distinctive Behavior: When visiting flowers for nectar, adults don't land, but hover while they sip.
Native Habitat: Mid-elevation tropical forests and lowland edges.

Blue Morpho

This large, brilliant-blue butterfly makes its home in South America and Central America and some parts of Mexico. At night, they fold up their wings to display the dark side of their wings, which allows them to go unnoticed by predators. During the day, they slowly beat their wings as they fly, producing an iridescent blue flash.

Scientific Name: *Morpho menelaus.*
Family: Brush-footed.
Wingspan: 5 to 7 inches.
Distinctive Markings: Iridescent-blue upper wings; bronze eyespots on brown undersides. Females have less-colorful wings with white-dotted brown encircling a blue area.
Distinctive Behavior: Adults drink juice from rotting or fermenting fruit with their long, straw-like proboscis.
Native Habitat: Rain forest canopies.

Thoas swallowtail
David Liebman

Blue morpho
Jim Battles/Dembinsky Photo Associates

Kathy Adams Clark/KAC Productions
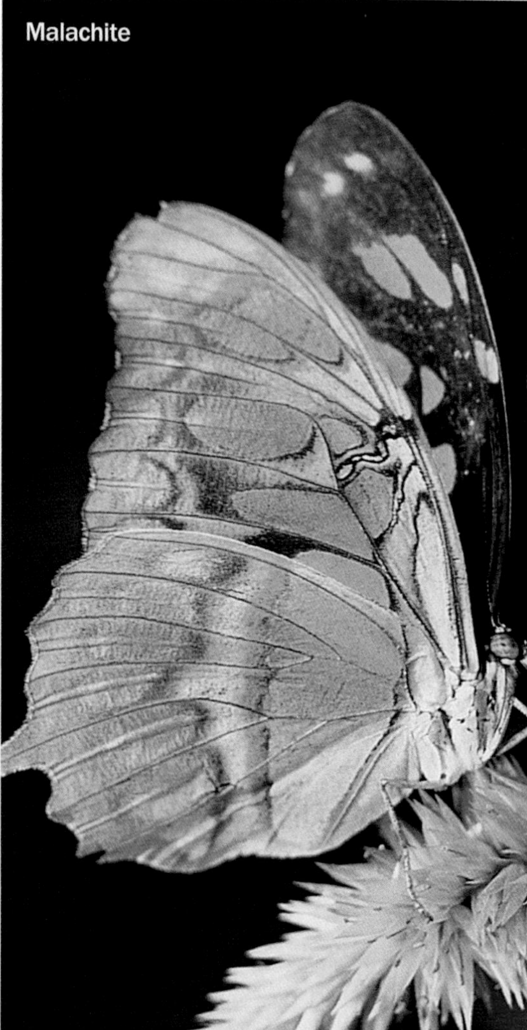
Malachite

Malachite

Native to Brazil through Central America and into Mexico, southern Texas, southern Florida and Cuba, the malachite boasts dark-brown to black wings marked with translucent whitish-green or yellow patches. Generally, adults eat rotting fruit, but sometimes feed on flower nectar or bird droppings.

Scientific Name: *Siproeta stelenes.*
Family: Brush-footed.
Wingspan: 3-1/4 to 4 inches.
Distinctive Markings: Whitish-green or yellow patches on dark to black upper sides; greenish patches on orange undersides.
Distinctive Behavior: Males float slowly as they seek mates; adults rest as a group on leaves of low-growing shrubs.
Native Habitat: Florida citrus and avocado orchards; subtropical evergreen and semi-deciduous forests.

Giant Wood Nymph

A Southeast-Asian cousin of the monarch, this species also is commonly called a paper kite or rice paper butterfly. The "kite" moniker aptly describes its flight pattern. It slowly, but continually glides in a circular pattern high in the trees. Like the monarch, the giant wood nymph has an articulated head, which allows it to turn its head from side to side and look upward.

Scientific Name: *Idea leuconoe.*
Family: Milkweed.
Wingspan: 6 inches.
Distinctive Markings: Tissue-like, transparent white wings with yellow shadings and black markings.
Distinctive Behavior: Slowly glides like a kite in circular patterns.
Native Habitat: Mangrove swamps and surrounding areas.

Julia

Julia butterflies make their home in subtropical clearings and woodland margins from Brazil north to southern Texas and Florida. They're also found in Mexico and the West Indies. Occasionally, the orange-winged butterflies stray as far north as Nebraska. Julias feed on the nectar of firebush, lantana, porterweed and Spanish needles.

Scientific Name: *Dryas Julia.*
Family: Brush-footed.
Wingspan: 3-1/4 to 3-5/8 inches.
Distinctive Markings: Elongated, bright-orange wings with black margins; females have paler wings with patchy black markings.
Distinctive Behavior: A quick and agile flier that forages along a set route of nectar sources each day.
Native Habitat: Subtropical clearings, paths and woodland margins.

Giant wood nymph

David Cavagnaro

Julia

Paul Rezendes

158
154
162
146
156
143

Chapter 5

Blooming Beauty

Photos: geraniums, Donna and Tom Krischan; hydrangea, Richard Shiell; cannas, Richard Shiell; bee balm, Pam Spaulding/Positive Images; clematis, Donna and Tom Krischan; lungwort, Donna and Tom Krischan; bougainvillea, Richard Shiell; liatris, Richard Day/Daybreak Imagery; shasta daisy, Frank Moegling/The Image Finders.

Geraniums

Perky annuals pump up yards from spring until frost.

By Ann Wilson
Geneva, Illinois

Nothing signals summer like the sight of scarlet geraniums spilling from window boxes or marshaled in tidy rows in public gardens. This look-at-me plant demands, and deserves, attention.

Generally treated as an annual, geraniums (*Pelargonium* x *hortorum*) bring season-long color to borders and containers. They're inexpensive to buy, easy to grow and simple to propagate. As an added bonus, you can bring them inside to overwinter as houseplants until next spring.

The free-flowering plants put forth showy, spherical clusters of blooms in colors ranging from pastel pink and crisp white to vivid red and fiery orange. Geraniums boast thick, branching stems and lush foliage in varying hues.

Possibly America's favorite bedding plant, geraniums have been continually hybridized to create a surprisingly wide selection of cultivars. This selection offers gardeners a geranium perfectly suited to their gardening needs.

The Plant of Many Flowers

Growers propagate geraniums for gardeners either by seed or cuttings. Seed geraniums, developed in the 1970s, are more compact, better branching, and have smaller and more numerous flowers. Some varieties are still propagated from cuttings, which tend to produce larger blooms. Within these two types, there are different flower shapes.

Cactus-flowered types boast single or double cactus dahlia-like blooms with petals twisted into

Faith Bemiss

quills. Firedragon bears fire-engine red semi-double flowers on knee-high plants.

Double and semi-double geraniums bear flowers with six or more petals per flower. The Erik Hoskins variety produces double-white to pale-salmon flowers with deeper salmon centers and green leaves splashed with brown zones.

Fancy-leaved varieties have gorgeous tricolored foliage that often steals the show from the plant's flowers. Ben Franklin brightens beds with rounded, white-edged green leaves and salmon-hued flowers.

Rosebud types generate double flowers with central petals that remain closed for a rosebud-like appearance. Apple Blossom Rosebud bears 3-inch clusters of greenish-white flowers that have pink margins on the petals.

Donna and Tom Krischan

Single-flowered varieties (below) are the simplest blossoms, bearing no more than five petals. Plants in the Black Magic series spotlight pink, rose, salmon and red blossoms with green-edged, chocolate-hued leaves.

Stellar cultivars have star-shaped blooms and pointed leaves. Bird Dancer boasts thin-petaled, pale-pink flowers that blend into salmon. These dwarf plants grow only to 8 inches in height.

The True Geranium

You might be surprised to learn that the annual geraniums you know are not true geraniums. Europeans brought *Pelargonium*, a South African native, to their gardens in the 1600s and named it "geranium" because it resembled the perennial geraniums native to Europe.

We know this perennial flower as cranesbill, though its botanical name is actually *Geranium*. By the mid-1700s, these newly named annual geraniums had made their way to the American colonies. Soon, the plant came to be synonymous with home and hospitality, and in later years, pioneers carried the popular plant to their new homes on the Western frontier.

Cultivation and Propagation

Today, geraniums are everywhere! Geraniums require full sun for optimal flowering, but will tolerate sites with partial sun. In sizzling summer climates, plants benefit from placement out of the hot afternoon sun. Geraniums should be spaced at least 12 inches apart for good air circulation, which will prevent mildew-

Richard Shiell

Plant Profile

Common Name: Geranium.
Botanical Name: *Pelargonium x hortorum*.
Bloom Time: Spring to frost.
Hardiness: Zones 9 to 11; treated as annuals elsewhere.
Height: 12 to 24 inches.
Spread: 12 inches.
Flower Colors: Red, scarlet, white, purple, lavender, pink, rose, salmon and orange.
Flower Shape: Five or more petals in clusters, depending on cultivar.
Light Needs: Part to full sun.
Soil Type: Fertile, loamy, well-drained soil.
Planting: Plant transplants in spring after last frost date. Start seeds indoors 16 weeks before last frost.
Prize Picks: Americana and Black Magic series; Apple Blossom Rosebud, Ben Franklin, Bird Dancer, Firedragon and Freckles.

R. Todd Davis Photography

FANTASTIC FOLIAGE. Don't just plant geraniums for their blooms. Look for varieties that have unique foliage, too (like those at top right and above).

R. Todd Davis Photography

Donna and Tom Krischan

Faith Bemiss

CONTAINER ALL-STARS. Geraniums are one of the most popular container plants (above). At left, these stellar blooms boast star-like flowers, and the coral-hued geraniums have double blooms.

GREEN THUMB TIP

Geraniums are long-lasting, inexpensive and easy to grow. You can even bring them indoors to use as houseplants for the winter. They are available in many colors and shapes, so there's sure to be at least one that will suit your fancy!

type diseases from attacking the plants.

Geraniums grow best in moist, loamy, well-drained soil and with regular applications of a balanced water-soluble fertilizer. You should feed container-grown geraniums throughout the season, according to the label directions. Garden-grown plants require less frequent applications, such as every 4 to 6 weeks.

Geraniums also require regular watering—be sure to check potted plants daily to ensure the soil is slightly damp. Mulching geraniums will decrease watering chores and keep the plant's roots cool.

With food and water needs addressed, geraniums are care-free plants. They require only deadheading of faded blossoms to ensure continuous bloom, and removal of damaged leaves. An occasional pinching prevents stems from becoming leggy.

As frost looms, you can bring plants inside or propagate them. Experts recommend taking cuttings or displaying the potted geraniums as houseplants instead of letting them go dormant. Cut potted geraniums back by one-third to one-half, set in a south- or west-facing window, water them regularly and allow them to grow.

To propagate geraniums, take 3- to 4-inch cuttings with three leaf nodes from the plant and remove lower leaves so just a top tuft of leaves remain. Place cuttings in pots or flats filled with a moist, well-drained potting mix or vermiculite. Set in a sunny window and keep the soil damp.

In less than 2 weeks, you can transplant the newly rooted cuttings into larger pots. By late May, you'll have a new and larger crop of geraniums for planting in outdoor containers and gardens.

Then you can start your summer out right—by enjoying the beauty of your very own geraniums.

Richard Shiell

Petunias

Marvels of nature, these energetically blooming plants deliver season-long color.

By Ann Wilson
Geneva, Illinois

My grandmother planted petunias in her gardens, while my mother potted them up in containers. In fact, every yard along our block had these cheerfully hued annuals displayed in one way or another. But, when I started gardening, I bypassed the way-too-familiar petunia in favor of more exotics (to me, at least), such as nicotiana, canna lilies and gladioli.

All good gardeners learn from their mistakes, and I learned early on that omitting petunias from my planting palette was a major blunder. One Mother's Day about 10 years back, my kids presented me with two bedding flats of hot-pink petunias.

Never one to turn down free plants—especially those from my offspring—I tucked the flowering plugs into garden holes and plopped them in pots. Amazingly, those petunias just kept trucking, spreading and flowering through July's dog days, and brightening our yard through October.

Ever since that planting season, I've been picking up flats of ruffled, hot-pink double petunias.

Plant Profile

Botanical Name: *Petunia* x *hybrida*.
Bloom Time: Spring to frost.
Hardiness: Generally treated as an annual but can be grown in Zones 8 to 11 as a perennial as long as it has winter protection.
Height: 6 to 18 inches.
Spread: 6 to 36 inches.
Flower Colors: Red, pink, purple, blue, yellow, salmon and white.
Flower Shape: Five-lobed saucer, trumpet or fluted shapes in single or double forms.
Light Needs: Sun to partial shade.
Soil Type: Tolerates poor soil, but performs best in light, nutrient-rich and well-drained soil.
Planting: Start seeds inside 10 weeks before the last frost date; plant transplants after danger of frost has passed.
Prize Picks: Blue Sky, Chiffon Morn, Frillytunia White, Merlin Blue Moon, Tidal Wave Cherry and Ultra Crimson Star. Noteworthy petunia series include Celebrity, Double Cascade, Fantasy, Razzle Dazzle, Wave and Whopper.

Alan and Linda Detrick

They've become the workhorses of my spring-to-fall gardens. Whether trailing from hanging planters or massed with sweet alyssum in a flower bed, petunias are one of the brightest lights in my landscape.

Inauspicious Beginnings

Gardeners haven't always considered petunias bright lights. In fact, it took 400 years for the plants to catch on with gardeners. Sixteenth-century Spanish explorers noticed the lanky, white-flowering South American native plant on a visit to Argentina but thought it unworthy of collecting. Local Indians called the plant "petun," which roughly translated to "worthless tobacco," summing up the explorers' viewpoint as well.

Three centuries passed before later explorers sent petunia plants back to Europe. In the early 1800s, plant breeders began crossing the white-flowering petunia (*Petunia axillaris*) with two other South American native petunias to create garden petunias—a group of lively hued, large-flowered plants that didn't always bloom true to form.

By the early 20th century, plant breeders in the U. S., Japan and Germany began to produce true petunia hybrids, which plant breeders have continually tweaked to create hundreds of modern-day petunia cultivars.

Richard Shiell

AROUND THE EDGES. This Frillytunia Tropical Red variety (above) has ruffled petals. Other petunias can have single or double petals.

GREEN THUMB TIP

Petunias can be used almost anywhere in the garden. Try planting them in perennial borders, up a slope or to outline a flower bed. They are drought and heat tolerant, but if planted in containers or window boxes, they'll require regular watering.

Four Fabulous Forms

You'll find petunias in an array of colors, flower shapes and growth habits. There are solid-hued, striped and bicolored varieties with saucer, trumpet and fluted blossoms—some are single, some are double and some have ruffled petals. Also, there are varieties that grow into upright clumps, while other varieties sprawl and cascade. Petunias generally fall into one of the following four groups.

GRANDIFLORAS boast the largest blooms of all petunias. Flowers can reach 4 or 5 inches in diameter and are available with single or double flowers. Generally, grandiflora petunias mature into 15-inch-tall mounds, but some varieties have a trailing habit. Due to their sizeable blooms, rainstorms often damage these petunias.

MULTIFLORA petunias are prolific bloomers that bear 2- to 3-inch flowers on compact plants. Single or double flower forms come in loads of crayon-box hues, sometimes with contrasting throats or striped petals. The most adaptable of all the petunias, multifloras handily weather heat, humidity and rain.

MILLIFLORAS are miniature petunias. The plants are about two-thirds the size of other petunias, and the flowers measure between 1 and 1-1/2 inches in diameter. Though their flowers are small, the plants teem with masses of colorful blooms throughout the season. A good choice for hanging baskets and containers, these petunias keep their shape and don't require a hard midsummer pruning like other petunias.

GROUND COVER (or spreading petunias) rise only to 6 inches in height, but their flowering stems quickly spread to 3 feet. Give them water and fertilizer, and they'll perform like a ground cover, winding through other plants to create a carpet of color. Abundant 2- to 3-inch flowers bloom along the trailing stems. These types (including those in the Wave series) are perfectly suited to growing in hanging baskets and window boxes.

Falcon Pink Morn and Fantasy Pink

Photos this page: Richard Shiell

From Good to Great

Although petunias will tolerate some shade and poor soil, they grow and flower best when planted in well-drained, humus-rich soil in full sun. Petunia plants tolerate drought and heat, but will require regular watering when planted in containers or window boxes.

Garden-grown petunias only require watering during long stretches of rainless days. Petunias, like other annuals, can benefit from fertilizer, but you should do a soil test to determine how much and what type of nutrients to provide.

Some petunias look messy by midsummer as they become leggy and produce fewer flowers. Prune leggy stems back to encourage new stems and more flowers. Deadheading also promotes continuous blooms, as does cutting the blossoms for floral arrangements. Petunias make fine additions to summer bouquets. Since they tend to flop, cut the stems short and display them in small vases.

Think about planting petunias in perennial borders, massing them down a bank, up a slope or lining them along a garden's perimeter. Some gardeners believe petunias are natural insect repellants and nestle them around the base of trellis-grown peas or beans. They also thrive in alpine gardens, partner well with roses and pair nicely with other annuals like portulaca, geraniums, sweet alyssum, vinca and salvia.

You can never have too many petunias. Cultivate the bounteous bloomers, and your landscape will sport lively splashes of color from spring well into fall.

Surfinia Pink Veined

Madness Red Morn

Blue Ice

Celebrity Yellow

PAINT WITH PETUNIAS, and you'll have endless options! In addition, hummingbirds and moths love these blooms.

Mark Turner

Nasturtiums

Fiery-hued flowers and distinctive leaves add zest to gardens and containers.

By Ann Wilson, Geneva, Illinois

Plant Profile

Common Name: Nasturtium.
Botanical Name: *Tropaeolum majus*.
Bloom Time: Early summer to frost.
Hardiness: Annual; some species are hardy in Zones 9 to 11.
Height: 12 inches for mounding types; vining varieties grow 3 to 8 feet in length.
Spread: 12 to 24 inches.
Flower Colors: Orange, yellow, white, red,

There are many things to love about nasturtiums. They are simple-to-grow, sun-loving annuals that flower profusely, thrive in poor soil, require little to no fertilizing and need only regular watering.

In addition to producing lightly fragrant, funnel-shaped flowers, nasturtiums also bear pretty lily pad-like leaves in hues ranging from light green to deep green shaded in purple or blue. Many gardeners also enjoy varieties with variegated leaves.

With cultivars available in mounding, trailing and climbing forms, ever-colorful nasturtiums spice up flower beds, window boxes and trellises. And, because seeds, flowers and leaves are edible, you can use nearly every plant part to add a peppery zing to your favorite recipes.

Plant Them in the Right Place

Natives of cool, mountainous regions, nasturtiums are adaptable plants that flourish where other plants may struggle. For years, I've tucked the seeds in tiny, soil-filled gaps in a set of unused flagstone steps around my house. Within weeks, flower-filled stems always spill over the rocky surfaces.

Trailing nasturtium varieties double as ground covers that handily plug up garden voids left by spring-flowering bulbs. Some gardeners insist these plants deter pests such as squash bugs, Colorado potato bugs, whiteflies and cucumber flies, so they plant them in their vegetable beds. Wildlife gardeners love the red and orange flowering

Peach Melba

David Cavagnaro

Donna and Tom Krischan

Prize Picks

Try the Jewel, Whirlybird or Alaska series (pictured here). For specific cultivars, look for Peach Melba, Empress of India and Strawberries and Cream.

pink and bicolored.
Flower Shape: Funnel-shaped with five petals; some flowers have spurs.
Light Needs: Full sun.
Soil Type: Well-drained soil.

What's in a Name?

The botanical name for nasturtiums is *Tropaeolum majus. Tropaeolum* is derived from the Latin word for trophy. A botanist thought the flowers and leaves resembled the helmets and shields that were taken from enemy forces and displayed as trophies.

Healing Powers

Early healers pickled nasturtium seeds as a scurvy preventative, and used the plant's blossoms and seed oils to ease muscle aches. Modern herbalists value the plant for its vitamin C, iron and sulfur content, as well as its antibacterial qualities. When eaten raw, nasturtiums help fight infections and keep bacterial spores from spreading. Tealike infusions are employed to relieve bronchial and sinus problems.

Climbing nasturtium mix

Empress of India

Photos at right and left, David Cavagnaro

Perk Up Your Plants

Once nasturtiums take hold and begin to flower, they need little care. But since the plants like hot days and cold nights, flower production may fall off during summer's hottest months. If a slowdown takes place, tidy up the plants by removing faded flowers and foliage. Make sure the plants have enough water, and they'll perk up again as night temperatures cool toward the end of summer.

varieties that are known to attract hummingbirds and butterflies. (The spurs on the flowers are filled with nectar.)

Get More Blooms

Nasturtiums don't transplant well, so it's best to sow seeds directly into the ground or into containers after the danger of frost has passed. Gardeners in Zones 4 to 8 should plant seeds soon after spring's last frost; in Zones 9 to 11, plant the seeds during the winter for an early-spring flower show.

Nasturtiums grow and flower best in sites that get at least 6 hours of sunlight. They're not picky about soil type, but it should be well-drained. For best results, plant seeds about a foot apart in well-tilled soil. Then keep them watered until seedlings sprout.

Happily, nasturtium leaves, seeds and flowers are not only edible, but also aid in digestion. So these plants please the eye, and also pleasure one's taste buds and sooth the tummy.

Mark Turner; VanDusen Botanical Gardens, Vancouver BC

Hydrangea

Make a statement with these big-blooming beauties.

By Margene Whitler Hucek

Keswick, Virginia

Nothing announces summer like hydrangeas. With their large, softball-sized flowers, hydrangeas are bold enough to brighten any landscape. They offer hope for gardens that can look a little tired after the initial flush of spring-blooming dogwoods, azaleas, lilacs, tulips and daffodils has faded.

Bigleaf hydrangeas (*Hydrangea macrophylla*) are easy-to-grow shrubs that start flowering in early summer. The flowers are either pink or blue, depending on whether the soil is alkaline (resulting in pink blooms) or acidic (blue). Leaves can be as big as your hand and heart-shaped.

I have two of these large specimens near our back porch about a foot from our air-conditioning unit. I planted them there to hide the unit and perk up the side yard. They did just that! Now in spring and summer, I see a sea of blue instead of an old, grey eyesore.

Plant Profile

Botanical Name: *Hydrangea.*
Bloom Time: Late spring through summer.
Hardiness: Zones 3 to 9, varies with species.
Height: 3 to 8 feet.
Spread: 3 to 8 feet.
Flower Colors: White, pink and blue.
Flower Shape: Large clusters that look like pom-poms.
Light Needs: Best in partial shade; will tolerate full sun as long as soil stays moist.
Soil Type: Light, moist and well-draining.
Planting: Plant hydrangeas in spring or fall as soon as you purchase them for best results. Dig and remove suckers from established plants in early summer or fall.
Prize Picks: Annabelle is a good smooth hydrangea, Blue Wave is a popular bigleaf variety and Alice is a fast-growing oakleaf species.

Annabelle's Charm

After I had such good luck with those hydrangeas, I knew I had to grow more. This time, I tried a smooth hydrangea (*Hydrangea arborescens*) for the opposite side of our porch.

This smooth cultivar, Annabelle, quickly became one of my favorites. By spring, it was 2 feet by 2 feet. Then in summer, it was full of apple-green flowers that matured to pure white.

By the next year, it doubled in size and had several side shoots that we dug up in fall to line the rest of the area. Now, 5 years later, we have a bed of Annabelles that's 20 feet long and 6 feet wide. They truly are a spectacular sight and have even grown large enough to peek into my kitchen window and the adjoining screened porch.

No Flowers? Here's Why

If your bigleaf hydrangeas don't bloom, it's usually because either cold weather killed the emerging buds, or the plant was pruned at the wrong time.

After flowering in summer, prune stems that bore flowers to just above an outward facing bud. Prune old branches to the base in winter. Don't cut new stems, as they will bear next year's flowers.

Many gardeners don't like the fact the bigleaf hydrangeas look unkempt after the first hard frost. Their large, black leaves hang despondently, begging for you to cut them. Resist the urge! Their appearance will improve with leaf drop.

Annabelle hydrangeas bloom on new wood, so you don't have the same problems of pruning that you do with the bigleaf ones. Their dried heads look attractive all winter and add interest to the landscape. I also find that finches like to dart about their branches, pecking at the dried flowers.

Worth the Effort

Prune these rapid bloomers in early spring to keep them under control and encourage large blooms. And, since the blooms form on new spring growth, you don't have to worry about winter kill.

In fact, we always have an abundance of cloud-like blooms on our Annabelles. But some years, our bigleaf hydrangeas produce only a few blooms due to harsh winters.

Don't let that discourage you from growing bigleaf hydrangeas, though. They are more temperamental, but their brilliant blue color makes them worth growing.

It's those captivating blooms that caught the eyes of plant collectors in the 1800s, when they were found growing wild along the rivers of Japan and China. The plants were taken to Europe, where Victorian gardeners used them as both a fresh flower and for dried bouquets.

Blooms Keep Going

When planting hydrangeas, dig a hole twice as wide and the same depth as the shrub's rootball.

Richard Shiell

Pink 'N Pretty

Set the base of the hydrangea at ground level. Fill with soil, water thoroughly and mulch to help the plant conserve moisture.

Never plant hydrangeas in the heat of summer. Instead, plant immediately in spring or wait until fall after the plants have lost their leaves. Fertilize in spring, if needed, with a balanced slow-release fertilizer.

Hydrangeas are carefree with few insect problems. Mildew can be a concern, though I haven't had much trouble with it here in Virginia, despite our hot and humid summers.

If you see white powder on the leaves, remove the infected foliage. If needed, you can also treat the plant with a fungicide.

Hydrangeas are long-lived. At my brother's home, he grows hydrangeas that were planted more than 100 years ago. They are still profusely blooming, pleased with their site on the shady side of his porch.

I can only hope mine will last that long, brightening up summer days with big, beautiful blooms of blue and white for future gardeners to enjoy.

Top 3

Try one of these favorites in your garden.

Oakleaf hydrangeas (*Hydrangea quercifolia*) are shrubs with attractive peeling bark and leaves like oak trees that turn purple in autumn. Try cultivars such as Alice, Harmony, Snowflake and Pee Wee.

Smooth hydrangeas (*Hydrangea arborescens*) are rounded shrubs with broad leaves and abundant flowers. Favorites include Annabelle, Grandiflora and Samantha.

Bigleaf hydrangeas (*Hydrangea macrophylla*) are rounded shrubs with dark-green leaves. Plants either have lacecap flower heads (flattened with small fertile blooms in the center, surrounded by larger, showy blooms) or hortesia flower heads (spherical, long sterile blooms). Try Blue Wave, All Summer Beauty and Pink Elf.

Oakleaf hydrangea

Richard Shiell

Bigleaf hydrangea

Donna and Tom Krischan

Smooth hydrangea

Mark Turner; Linden Gardens, Kaledon BC

Cannas

Bring a taste of the tropics to your backyard with this tall beauty.

By Ann Wilson, Geneva, Illinois

Plant Profile

Common Name: Canna lily.
Botanical Name: *Canna x generalis*.
Bloom Time: Summer to early fall.
Hardiness: Zones 8 to 11; dig up in fall elsewhere.
Height: 1 to 6 feet.
Spread: 18 to 24 inches.
Flower Colors: Orange, yellow, white, red, pink and bicolored.

Canna photos: Richard Shiell

Want to stop passersby in their tracks? Grab their attention by including a stand of cannas in your planting plans. These wow-powered plants contribute tropical textures and exotic forms to flower borders and oversized containers.

Why You'll Love Cannas

Bold, beautiful and care-free, cannas are the "Big Easy" of the planting world. They are one of the easiest summer rhizomes to grow, and carry season-long color on sturdy stems that stand tall without staking.

Cannas have orchidlike flowers in a rainbow's worth of shades. And it's not just the blossoms that make them a superstar. Glossy, paddle-shaped leaves that grow between 12 and 24 inches in size are equally striking. Depending on the cultivar, the foliage may be black, purple, bronze, burgundy, bluish-green, variegated or striped in multiple hues.

Cannas offer gardeners a lot of bang for their buck. Depending on where you shop and the variety you choose, canna bulbs can cost just a few dollars each. Plus, cold-weather gardeners can save the bulbs by digging them up in the fall and storing them in winter.

Growing Secrets for Cannas

Cannas usually are sold as rhizomes or container-grown plants, which you can plant outdoors after the last frost. They require little more than a sunny spot and moist, well-drained soil amended with organic material.

After the last frost, plant canna rhizomes 3 to 4 inches deep and 18 to 24 inches apart. Cannas like moisture, so give their roots a good soaking once a week. Container-grown cannas will dry out more quickly. Pay special attention to their watering needs.

As flowers fade, gently remove spent flowers to keep plants tidy. Do this carefully because there's likely to be another flower in bud on the stalk below.

When frost descends, cut stems back to a couple of inches and dig up the bulbs. Gently remove the soil and dry the bulbs, and then store them in peat moss or sawdust in a spot where temperatures stay between 45 and 50°. Gardeners in Zones 8 to 11 need only leave the stalks in place and protect the roots with a heavy layer of mulch to ensure the plants return the following summer.

If You Like Cannas, You'll Love...

Grow cannas alongside perennials and annuals that share similar light and watering needs. Fashion a tropical tableau by planting cannas with bananas, elephant ears, palms and gingers, or surround them with cottage-garden companions, such as cleome, fountain grass, cardinal flower, daylilies and salvia.

Or, plant a single canna bulb in a patio container. Just one canna supplies a showstopping display that's deserving of attention and a round of enthusiastic applause.

"I never thought I'd take the time to dig up cannas in fall...but they're worth that little effort!"
—Heather Lamb, Editor

Prize Picks

Cannas took center stage at the 1893 World's Fair Columbian Exposition in Chicago, where 76 beds, encompassing 1,000 linear feet, were planted entirely with canna lilies. One of these cannas, Florence Vaughan, endures as a tribute to early canna production.

Cannas are sorted into three size groups—dwarf (up to 3 feet), medium (up to 4 feet) and tall (up to 6 feet). Melinda Myers' favorites include Durbin, Bengal and Pretoria.

Surfinia Pink Veined

Rosemond Cole

Get to Know Their Roots

Natives of moist and open areas in Central and South America, Malaysia and Nepal, cannas made their way to Europe in the late 1500s. Three centuries later, hybridizers across the globe produced a wealth of new varieties. Some turn-of-the-century cultivars still are available through heirloom bulb companies, such as Old House Gardens in Michigan.

Flower Shape: Orchidlike panicles with three petals and showy stamens.
Light Needs: Full sun.
Soil Type: Moist, fertile and well-drained.

Plant Profile

Common Name: Bee balm.
Botanical Name: *Monarda didyma*.
Bloom Time: Midsummer to early fall.
Hardiness: Zones 4 to 8.
Height: 4 feet.
Spread: 3 feet or more.
Flower Colors: Red, pink, violet and white.

R. Todd Davis Photography

Bee Balm

Hummingbirds, butterflies and bees will love these blazing, skyrocket-style blooms.

By Ann Wilson, Geneva, Illinois

Each spring, stands of bee balm unfailingly rise to put on a pyrotechnic display come summer. These count-on-me plants amply fill their designated spaces while supplying a few extra seedlings you can use to plug up holes left by less-reliable perennials.

Bee Balm Benefits

From my personal experience, I've found bee balm to be a plant that just keeps on giving, whether planted in sunny or partly shaded sites. Their emerging burgundy-shaded leaves form an aromatic mat in early spring. Soon, the minty, citrus fragrance grows stronger as fuzzy leaves fill square stems.

Rarely a spring goes by when I'm not dividing a clump or just chopping off some roots to create new plants to give to friends or add to a flower bed. By midsummer, the plants burst into firecracker-like blooms in shades of pink, red and lilac to lure in hummingbirds, swallowtails and buzzing bees.

Get the Most From Your Blooms

As a member of the mint family, bee balm is easy to establish, spreads by rhizomes and will reseed if not deadheaded. It also has shallow roots

"When flowering wanes or plants start looking scraggly, I just chop the clumps back to about 6 inches above ground. Oftentimes, the plants plump up again to rebloom along with late-summer and early-fall perennials." —Ann Wilson

Prize Picks

When selecting new bee balm plants, opt for disease-resistant varieties. Many new hybrids are a result of crossing *Monarda didyma* with its stalwart, light-purple wildflower relative, *Monarda fistula*. Cultivars with good disease resistance include Raspberry Wine, Cambridge Scarlet, Marshall's Delight and Jacob Cline. For a good dwarf variety, try one of Melinda Myers' favorite picks, Petite Delight.

Marshall's Delight

R. Todd Davis Photography

Cambridge Scarlet

R. Todd Davis Photography

Flower Shape: Tubular petals rise in a circular form from a lower burgundy-green bract.
Light Needs: Dappled shade to full sun.
Soil Type: Humus-rich, moist well-drained soil.

Healing Powers

Valued by Native Americans for its curative powers and citrusy flavor, bee balm leaves and flowers were used to brew teas, preserve meat and treat colds and stomach distress. Earl-Grey-like teas can be brewed by steeping either fresh or dried leaves in hot water—the refreshing brew is said clear sinuses, settle stomachs and control coughing.

Photo at right, Pam Spaulding/Positive Images; below, Larry Dech

RECIPE FOR SUCCESS

Bee balm is susceptible to powdery mildew, so give each plant enough room for air to circulate around and through the plant. In spring, remove about a quarter of the stems to open up the interior of the plants.

HUMMINGBIRD FAVORITE. Not only do hummingbirds love bee balm, but the plant also is a favorite among butterflies and bees.

and has a tendency to encroach upon other areas. If that's the case in your area, hand-pull unwanted growth from the outer edges.

Bee balm prefers a sun-lit spot in gardens that boast moist, well-drained soil, but it will also tolerate some shade and will benefit from afternoon shade in hot summer climes. These plants are not drought-tolerant, and you should plant them where they will receive regular watering. They like moist feet in the summer, but are likely to fail if their winter roots become soggy.

Deadhead bee balm stems as flowers fade to encourage more blooms and to prevent plants from reseeding. As clumps begin to die out in the center, which happens every 3 years or so, divide the clumps, compost the unattractive center and replant healthy roots.

If You Like Bee Balm, You'll Love...

Grow bee balm along with other natives, such as swamp sunflower, rudbeckia, obedient plant, butterfly weed and coneflowers. Also, try partnering them with airy annuals like cosmos or cleome.

Bee balm is indeed generous in its bounty. It's long blooming, highly ornamental, wonderfully fragrant, edible and therapeutic.

Donna and Tom Krischan

Clematis

Fabulous flowering vines heighten a garden's beauty.

By Ann Wilson
Geneva, Illinois

It's no wonder the ever-popular clematis has charmed so many people. The climbing perennial vines produce plentiful blossoms for extended periods, and sometimes they will even rebloom before the growing season ends.

The plants contribute lovely silhouettes to the back of the border as they scramble up trellises and over fences. As a group, clematis bear a bounteous array of flower forms—including saucer, star, tulip, bell, double and tubular shapes—in a rainbow's worth of hues.

In fact, a whopping 2,500 clematis cultivars come from a genus that includes nearly 300 clematis species native to Europe, the Himalayas, China, Australia, North America and Central America. The sheer number of clematis varieties provides gardeners with countless options for dressing up the landscape.

Clematis make fine specimen plants, but can

Plant Profile

Botanical Name: *Clematis.*
Bloom Time: Late winter to late fall, depends on cultivar.
Hardiness: Zones 4 to 11, varies with species.
Height: 18 inches to 30 feet.
Spread: 2 to 4 feet.
Flower Colors: Blue, red, pink, yellow, white and purple.
Flower Shape: Saucer, star, tubular, tulip, bell, double and more, depending on variety.
Light Needs: Sun to partial shade.
Soil Type: Moist, well-drained alkaline soil.
Planting: Plant container-grown clematis in spring and early summer; plant dormant clematis in early spring when soil is workable.
Prize Picks: Cultivars to look for include Barbara Jackman, Betty Corning, Comtesse de Bouchard, Dutchess of Edinburgh, Etoile Violette, General Sikorski, Henryi, Lady Betty Balfour, Lincoln Star and Multi-Blue.

Alan and Linda Detrick

Alan and Linda Detrick

PERFECT FORM. Clematis have many different flower forms. Some of the shapes include the popular single flower (previous page), the four-petaled *Clematis montana* (top) and the double bloom (above).

be grown with other clematis or climbing roses to stage a season-long display of blooms. You can train them to shinny up entrance arbors, or leave them to sprawl as a distinctive ground cover.

Rules for Success

Although clematis are generally easy to grow, there are two things gardeners must remember. The first rule is to plant clematis with their "feet" in the shade and their "face" in the sun. Keep clematis roots cool with a layer of mulch or by planting perennials near the base. The perennials' foliage will shade the clematis roots and help the soil retain moisture. Meanwhile, the flowers should be facing the sun.

The second rule is to know whether the plant blooms on old or new wood. This is essential when it comes to pruning the vines properly.

One of the best things about clematis is that you can have blooms in nearly all four seasons if you plant the right varieties and live in a mild climate. Clematis species and cultivars are sorted by bloom time into the following three groups:

GREEN THUMB TIP

When planting clematis, be sure to follow one rule of thumb. Plant them with their "feet" in the shade and their "face" in the sun. If you plant the right varieties and live in a mild climate, it's possible to have clematis blooms throughout all four seasons.

Early Flowering. This group includes clematis that bloom on the previous year's growth. These plants may be evergreen or deciduous and will occasionally rebloom on the current season's new growth.

Clematis alpina and *Clematis montana* and their cultivars fall within this group. *Clematis alpina* cultivars are reported hardy in Zones 4 to 9 and bloom from late spring to early summer.

Clematis montana varieties are energetic, deciduous climbers that easily grow to cover trellises and outbuildings. Hardy in Zones 6 to 9, these varieties produce 2- to 3-inch white or pink flat or saucer-shaped blooms in late spring. Prune these varieties after they flower by clipping out damaged and dead stems and pinching back other stems. This will encourage plenty of new growth for the next season's blooms.

Early to Mid-season Flowering. This group includes clematis that bloom on new side shoots growing from the previous season's growth. These plants, generally hardy in Zones 4 to 11, may also put forth a second flush of blooms in late summer on entirely new growth.

This group produces 4- to 8-inch saucer-shaped blossoms in single, semi-double and double forms in an array of colors. Be sure to tidy these plants up in early spring before new growth appears.

Alan and Linda Detrick

John Glover/Positive Images

R. Todd Davis

judywhite/GardenPhotos.com

FROM BLOOM TO BEARD. Some people know clematis by its common name, old man's beard. You can trace the clever nickname back to the plant's silky seed heads, which develop after the flowers fade away for the season. The silvery gray seed heads are beautiful, unique and resemble a beard.

Remove dead and diseased stems and trim back living stems to visible buds. After the plants flower, remove spent blooms to encourage plants to put their energy into establishing strong roots and new growth.

Late Flowering. This group includes cultivars that grow on the current year's growth. Cold hardiness differs depending on variety. Large-flowering clematis varieties bear outward-facing, saucer-shaped blooms measuring between 3 and 6 inches in size.

These varieties produce blooms in an array of shapes from late summer through fall. Fragrant, white-blooming sweet autumn clematis, or *Clematis terniflora*, falls into this group. These varieties require a hard pruning in early spring before growth begins. You should cut plants back to strong buds, which generally appear 6 to 8 inches above the soil.

Clematis Past and Present

The genus name *Clematis* derives from the Greek word *klema*, which translates to "vine branch." Common nicknames for different species include traveler's joy, old man's beard, vase vine and virgin's bower.

Clematis x *jackmanii* is the best known clematis, and you can trace its origins back to 1860 in England. Researchers here first developed the popular bloom from a cross between *Clematis* x *hendersonii* and *Clematis lanuginosa*, a large-flowered species introduced by Robert Fortune 10 years earlier.

Since then, crosses and back-crosses with *Clematis viticella* have resulted in the wide variety of large-flowered clematis available today.

Present-day cultivars require very little in the way of care. Clematis are happiest when you plant their rootballs 2 to 3 inches below the soil in a sunny to partly shaded site at the base of a support structure. Planting them at this depth encourages plants to generate new shoots beneath the soil, which in turn results in fuller plants.

Once planted, they'll thrive as long as their roots are cooled by either a layer of mulch or shade-producing companion plants and they are pruned at the proper times.

Clematis plants also appreciate a regular watering schedule, especially during dry spells. Apply a layer of compost or well-rotted manure around the plants in the early spring to provide nourishment for the plants through the upcoming growing season.

Then all you have left to do is sit back and enjoy the show!

Lungwort

Donna and Tom Krischan

Alan and Linda Detrick

Delicate plants with a not-so-pretty name breath life into the shade.

By Ann Wilson
Geneva, Illinois

One of the first harbingers of spring, shade-loving lungworts are dual-purpose plants valued both for their flowers and foliage. The herbaceous perennials appear shortly after the snow melts to put forth cheerfully charming blooms shaded in vibrant hues that quickly banish wintertime blues.

Clusters of blue, red, pink, white or purple funnel-shaped flowers rise from clumps of narrow leaves splashed with silver or white markings. Some lungwort species produce pink buds that successively open to blue, purple or violet blooms for a plant that presents (albeit briefly) a multicolored appearance.

After the flowers fade, gardeners should remove stems and wilted leaves to encourage a second flush of leaves. These new leaves form low-growing, strikingly marked mounds that make the plant a choice ground cover for woodland and shrub borders.

A native of the mountainous and subalpine regions of Europe and Asia, lungworts have happily adapted to America's climates and most are hardy in Zones 4 to 8. The easy-care, fast-growing plants naturalize and hybridize freely in shady to partly shaded sites by spreading their creeping rhizomes or by self-seeding.

An Herbal Remedy

Lungwort bears the botanical name *Pulmonaria* because people thought the blotches on the leaves made them resemble diseased lungs. Early healers created lungwort lotions, syrups, poultices and washes to treat pulmonary problems, including wheezing and coughs, jaundice, wounds and ulcers.

Modern herbalists employ Jerusalem sage (*Pulmonaria officinalis*) as a culinary and medicinal herb. The leaves are used to craft skin balms, astringents and tonics for treating respiratory and digestive problems. People also use dried lungwort leaves like a styptic pencil to stop blood flowing from a cut.

Although you can start lungworts from seed, the resulting plants don't always stay true to type. Experts recommend buying plants and placing them in partly shaded to fully shaded spots in spring or fall. Planting beds should be humus-rich, moist, well drained and out of reach of the afternoon sun. During their first season of growth, new plants benefit from regular watering and an annual top-dressing of compost.

Lungworts are ideal companions for other

Alan and Linda Detrick

Richard Shiell

Plant Profile

Common Name: Lungwort.
Botanical Name: *Pulmonaria.*
Bloom Time: Spring.
Hardiness: Zones 4 to 8.
Height: 8 to 24 inches.
Spread: 8 to 24 inches.
Flower Colors: Blue, red, pink, white and purple.
Flower Shape: Funnel-shaped bells.
Light Needs: Partial to full shade.
Soil Type: Humus-rich, well-drained and moist.
Planting: Plant transplants in spring or fall; sow seeds in containers outside as temperatures warm in spring.
Prize Picks: Bertram Anderson, Beth's Pink, Cambridge Blue, David Ward, Mrs. Moon, Smokey Blue, Raspberry Splash and White Wings.

GREEN THUMB TIP

Lungwort is the perfect plant to spice up shady areas. Try planting Milky Way for its unique spotted leaves and delicate pink flowers that gradually fade to blue. It will add some long-lasting interest to your shade garden all summer.

shade-loving plants, such as hosta, bleeding heart and ferns. You can interplant them with spring bulbs to hide bulb plants' yellowing foliage or plant in drifts as ground covers. Larger cultivars make good specimen plants, both in borders and containers.

A Plethora of Choices

Of the 14 lungwort genera, roughly 12 are cultivated in gardens. Like coral bells (*Heuchera*), which people hybridize for leaf color, lungworts are hybridized to create an array of silvery- and snowy-patterned cultivars meant to brighten a garden's shadows. Generally, five lungwort species are available to the home gardener.

Pulmonaria angustifolia, commonly referred to as blue cowslip, boasts unspotted mid- to dark-green lance-shaped leaves and produces a profusion of bright-blue flowers on 12- by 18-inch mounded plants. Cultivars include Beth's Pink with deep coral-pink flowers.

Pulmonaria longifolia, also known as longleaf lungwort, produces narrow, white-spotted 5-inch leaves in loose 10- by 18-inch clumps. Pink buds sometimes open to blue-shaded flowers. Cultivars include Raspberry Splash with deep-red blossoms, and Bertram Anderson, a longtime favorite (above right) with bright-blue flowers.

Pulmonaria officinalis, also called spotted dog, soldiers and sailors, and Jerusalem sage, boasts hairy, mid-green leaves with white spots on loose clumps measuring 10 by 18 inches. Plants produce pink flowers with shades to reddish violet and blue. Cultivars include Cambridge Blue with heart-shaped leaves and pale-blue flowers. White Wings (above left) bears pink-eyed white flowers.

Pulmonaria rubra, or red lungwort, has velvety, elliptical leaves and produces flowers ranging from brick-red to coral on plants measuring 10 by 18 inches. Cultivars include Redstart (opposite page, right), an early bloomer with coral-red flowers. David Ward has variegated, sage-green leaves and coral-red flowers.

Pulmonaria saccharata, also called Bethlehem sage, is the most hybridized species. Saccharata refers to the plant's leaves, which look sugarcoated with splatters of silver, white or gray. They have violet or white blooms on plants 12 by 24 inches wide. Cultivars include Smokey Blue with medium to dark-blue flowers and grey-spotted foliage; Milky Way (opposite page, left) with pink flowers that fade to blue and heavily mottled leaves; and Mrs. Moon with silver-spotted foliage and blue flowers that open from pink buds.

Thanks to their reliability, beautiful blooms and interesting leaves, lungwort has become one of the brightest lights in the shade garden.

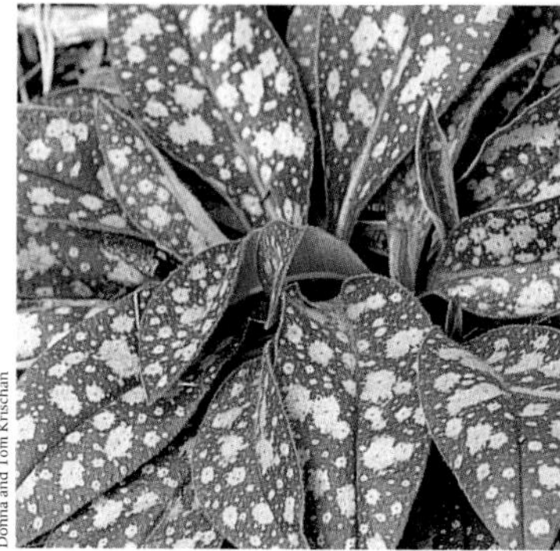

Donna and Tom Krischan

Alan and Linda Detrick

LITTLE AND LOVELY. The small flowers of lungwort are a welcome sight in spring. Many have variegated leaves (like Milky Way and Excalibur, above) for appeal all summer.

Richard Shiell

Bougainvillea

Vibrant beauties add a tropical touch to gardens and containers.

By Bernice Maddux
Weatherford, Texas

No other plants have given my husband and me more pleasure than our bougainvilleas. In the summertime when everything in our yard is dying from extreme heat, our bougainvilleas continue to bask in the sun's rays.

Our love for these plants started several years ago when our daughter brought us a small pink bougainvillea in a pot. The plant was from Florida, and I feared it wouldn't survive in our Texas climate. Happily, that original plant not only survived, but it has also produced 16 "children" and "grandchildren."

Although we grow our bougainvilleas in containers, gardeners in Zones 9 to 11 have many more options. They can plant the explosively hued flowering vines to scale arbors, frame windows or doorways, climb up trellises or spill over fences.

In these warmer regions, many people trim bougainvilleas as espaliers or erosion-controlling ground covers. You can also leave the plants

GREEN THUMB TIP

Once bougainvillea is established, it requires very little watering and regular fertilizing. Just plant it in a sunny spot with well-drained soil and give it a little care. Then be prepared to be amazed by the stunning blooms it gives you in return.

untrimmed to grow into mounded shrubs. Potted bougainvillea makes for colorful cascading hanging baskets, but you can also train it into an upright, treelike standard form (see photo at bottom right).

In colder zones, gardeners must bring their containers inside for the winter. Placed in a brightly sunlit area, where temperatures are warm day and night, the plants may continue to grow and bloom. Without enough light and warmth, the plants could go dormant. If this happens, they will require very little water—just enough to keep the soil barely damp.

Come next spring, after the danger of frost has passed, you can take your potted plants outside. There, they work to reenergize exterior landscapes with their exotic colors and contours.

Tropical Roots

A native of South America, bougainvillea was named after Admiral Louis Antoine de Bougainville, a Frenchman who found the plant in 1768 while traveling through Brazil.

The quick-growing, thorny and woody vines bear riotous bunches of blossoms made up of insignificant yellow or cream tubular flowers. The real color comes from the surrounding papery bracts (a type of leaf) in red, pink, yellow, apricot, white or orange.

Left untrimmed, the vines grow up to 40 feet in height. However, horticulturists have developed a number of dwarf or more compact varieties ideally suited to growing in containers.

Bougainvillea asks so little and gives so much. After the drought-tolerant bougainvillea becomes established, it just requires is a little water and some regular fertilization. Garden-grown vines will also need a sunny site with well-drained soil.

Since bougainvilleas flower on new growth, experts recommend removing spent flowers and cutting back the flowering shoots by a half to ensure more flowers. Pinching back growth also results in more blooms and a tidier plant.

Pruning and Propagating

Autumn is always a sad time for me because I have to prune back my still-blooming bougainvilleas. But the upside of pruning is that we will have plenty of cuttings to use to create new plants.

We trim back our bougainvilleas to between 6 and 10 inches each fall and use the pruned stem pieces to start new plants. An expert told me that severe pruning is needed to keep the plants healthy and productive—it hurts me to the put shears to their branches, but a gal's gotta do what a gal's gotta do!

When propagating the cuttings, we dip the bottom inch of each 4- to 6-inch cutting into water and a rooting compound before planting it in a small pot filled with a 1-to-1 mix of soil and peat. We add a handful of perlite and vermiculite to lighten the potting mixture. Once the cutting takes root, we move it to a larger pot.

Then we place the cutting and shorn bougainvilleas in our greenhouse to wait out the winter months. The cuttings put out new growth in just a few weeks and bloom profusely before it's time to take them outside in early spring.

When days are dreary and my spirits are sagging, I go to the greenhouse to watch the bougainvilleas blossom. It always brightens my day.

In April, we carry out the old and newly propagated bougainvilleas to perk up our landscape. Then, from spring until impending frost, they flaunt their extravagant beauty for all to see.

Plant Profile

Common Name: Bougainvillea.

Botanical Name: *Bougainvillea.*

Bloom Time: April through September.

Hardiness: Zones 9 to 11.

Height: 18 inches to 40 feet, depending on cultivars.

Spread: 6 to 40 feet.

Flower Colors: Red, pink, violet, apricot, orange, yellow and white.

Flower Shape: Three papery bracts surround a small yellow or white tubular flower.

Light Needs: Full sun.

Soil Type: Well-drained, rich loam soil.

Planting: Year-round in mild climates.

Prize Picks: Barbara Karst, California Gold, Double Pink, Jamaica White, Surprise, Ooh-La-La, Orange King, Texas Dawn.

TREE IN TRAINING. You can train bougainvilleas to grow in any number of forms, including a tree shape (like the one below). A closer look at this plant reveals its tiny, cream-colored flowers surrounded by vibrant, dark-pink bracts (below left).

Donna and Tom Krischan

Richard Shiell

Liatris

By Ann Wilson
Geneva, Illinois

Hummingbirds love these breezy, nectar-rich blooms.

Liatris is a North American native prairie plant that deserves a place in any backyard. These easy-care perennials emerge from the earth as grassy tufts. They fill in nicely around the feet of early-blooming perennials. Then, by midsummer, they seem to rise as exclamation points to punctuate flower beds.

The tall and feathery purple, rose or white spires lure in bevies of bees, butterflies and hummingbirds. Then the flowers eventually give way to fluffy seedpods, which nourish birds through fall and winter.

There's plenty to love about this flower. Also known as blazing star and gayfeather, the plant is simple to start from woody, bulb-like corms that can be ordered from a catalog, or you can start liatris from seed. Also, most gardeners can easily find plants for sale at their local garden center in spring.

One of the best things about liatris is that they're reliable. These hardy plants return year af-

GREEN THUMB TIP

Plant liatris in masses, along walkways or at the base of birdbaths and arbors to really make a statement. They will add unique texture to any garden, especially among ornamental grasses, feathery yarrows or velvety lamb's ear.

ter year, and oftentimes reseed to create colonies of colorful clumps that bring in droves of hummingbirds.

During the height of growth, the bottlebrush-like spikes of liatris grow up to 5 feet, bringing eye-catching vertical forms to the middle or back of the garden. If you look closely at one of the blooms, you'll see small, disklike flowers open from the top to bottom along the spike. This makes flowers attractive additions to bouquets, especially since they have a long vase life and keep their beauty for nearly 2 weeks.

A Notable Native

Liatris is a native of northeastern North America and naturally occurs in marshes, prairies and meadows from Ontario to Florida and New York to Michigan. One of more than 30 species in the *Liatris* genus, *Liatris spicata* is the most commonly cultivated type of this flower. *Spicata* derives from the Latin word *spica*, which means spike and aptly describes the plant's flowering forms.

Early settlers and Native Americans appreciated some varieties of liatris for their medicinal qualities. They used them to create diuretics, expectorants and analgesics. People even thought liatris balms, powders, teas and tonics would stimulate the vascular system, ease backaches and cure sore throats.

Modern herbalists add the fragrant leaves and roots to sachets, potpourris and insect repellants. They also use the plant as homeopathic remedies to relieve an array of maladies, including colic and kidney problems.

Cultivation and Companions

Liatris plants are drought-tolerant and require sunny sites and fertile, well-drained soil. The plants will tolerate a bit of shade and poor soils, but most won't tolerate wet feet. Though *Liatris spicata*, often called swamp blazing star, tolerates damp soils and is a great addition to rain gardens.

Amend soil with humus or compost to create good-draining sites, but don't plant liatris in areas where water is likely to pool. Plant corms 1 to 2 inches deep and about 8 inches apart. Space container-grown cultivars 15 to 20 inches apart. During the plants' first growing season, keep a regular watering schedule to encourage healthy roots.

Deadheading and harvesting flowering stems also promotes root growth and a second flush of flowers. For fresh bouquets, cut stems when one-third of the buds have opened. If you want to dry the stems, cut the stalks when all the flowers have opened.

Divide and Conquer

Deadhead fading blooms by cutting the stems back to the plants' basal leaves. Make new plants by allowing flowers to go to seed or by dividing overgrown clumps every 2 or 3 years.

Plants do best when you divide in spring, but you can also divide them in fall as long as transplants have enough time to develop roots before the ground freezes.

Liatris make a statement when you plant them in masses or arrange them as drifts trailing through prairie-style plantings. Place shorter varieties along walkways and at the base of birdbaths and arbors. Showcase liatris' airy, upright silhouettes by interplanting them with perennials and dwarf shrubs that boast rounded forms, such as stonecrop, perennial geraniums or spirea.

Create textural garden groupings by combining liatris with strappy-leafed daylilies, ornamental grasses, feathery yarrows and velvety lamb's ear. Pair the prairie natives with other natives that bloom around the same time, such as coneflowers, black-eyed Susans and goldenrod. The adaptable plants also partner well with cottage-garden favorites coreopsis, phlox, catmint and mallow.

It doesn't matter what planting companions you use. This easygoing plant is always a standout—truly a blazing star in any midsummer garden.

Plant Profile

Common Names: Gayfeather, blazing star.
Botanical Name: *Liatris spicata.*
Bloom Time: Midsummer to fall.
Hardiness: Zones 3 to 9.
Height: Up to 5 feet.
Spread: 18 inches.
Flower Colors: Purple, rose and white.
Flower Shape: Fluffy, disklike blossoms open on stiff spikes.
Light Needs: Sun, tolerates part shade.
Soil Type: Most prefer well-drained soil, but various varieties will tolerate both dry and damp.
Planting: Plant corms in spring or fall; plant container-grown plants any time during the growing season.
Prize Picks: Alba, Blue Bird, Kobold, Floristan Violet, Floristan Weiss and Snow Queen.

Richard Day/Daybreak Imagery

Dragon Wing begonia, wax begonia

Begonias

Prolific bloomers bring nonstop color to gardens great and small.

By Ann Wilson, Geneva, Illinois

Plant Profile

Common Name: Wax begonia.
Botanical Name: *Begonia* x *semperflorens-cultorum.*
Bloom Time: Summer to frost.
Hardiness: Tender perennial in Zones 10 and up; used as annual elsewhere.
Height: 6 to 12 inches.
Spread: 6 to 12 inches.
Flower Colors: Pink, red, white and bicolored.
Flower Shape: Multi-petal, rounded blossoms.
Light Needs: Partial shade to full sun.
Soil Type: Moist, humus-rich, well-drained soil.

Alan and Linda Detrick

It's easy to see why wax begonias are one of America's favorite bedding plants. These frost-tender perennials, generally grown as annuals, enliven shady and sun-bright borders from late spring to frost.

Key Benefits of Begonias

When you plant wax begonias, not only do you get bounteous blooms, but you also get great waxy foliage. Flowering in shades of pink, red and white, wax begonias sport glossy green, copper, bronze or white-variegated leaves that showcase the perky blossoms and spark interest in planting beds and containers.

Wax begonias are heat-tolerant plants with sturdy, compact forms that bear masses of small single or double flowers, oftentimes centered with bright-yellow stamens. Because of their uniform and mounded forms, wax begonias work well when planted together in sweeping masses or as edgings for perennial borders. The tough bloomers need minimal deadheading, and you can bring them inside to overwinter or easily propagate them from late-season stem cuttings.

Growing Secrets for Your Garden

Wax begonia seeds are tiny and take nearly 4 months to grow from seeds to transplants, so a gardener's best bet is to purchase transplants in containers or flats and set them in the garden after the danger of frost has passed. When buying transplants, double-check their light requirements. Most do well in partial shade, but some require more sunlight.

Begonias thrive in moist, well-drained soil. Space plants 8 to 12 inches apart to avoid moisture-related diseases such as powdery mildew and stem rot.

Before frost, cut back plants by one third, dig them up, put them in a pot and take them inside to enjoy the blooms through winter. During winter, hone your green thumb by propagating stem cuttings to produce new wax begonias that you can add to next year's garden.

If You Like Begonias, Then You'll Love...

Tuberous begonias (*Begonia* x *tuberhybrida*) are larger and have softer green foliage. They grow 18 inches tall and bear large rose, camellia and carnation-shaped blossoms in a variety of colors.

"Begonias are great additions to the landscape or container garden," says Melinda Myers. "My favorite is the Dragon Wing begonia. I love its glossy leaves, bold texture and flowers."

Get to Know Their Roots

Natives of Brazil, wax begonias are one of more than 1,300 species in the begonia genus. Their common name alludes to the waxy texture of their leaves. And their scientific moniker—*semperflorens*—translates to "ever blooming." French botanist Michael Begon took begonias back to France in the late 1600s. The plants eventually made their way to America in 1880, and the American Begonia Society formed in 1934.

Prize Picks

Wax begonias have been continually hybridized, so there are numerous cultivars available to the home gardener. One bright-green leafed variety is Senator Pink (bottom). The Ambassador series has large green leaves and big flowers. For bronze leaves, try cultivars in the Cocktail series, like Gin (below). The Victory series also features bronze leaves with showy blooms.

Gin

Flower photos this page: Donna and Tom Krischan

Senator Pink

Shasta Daisy

David Cavagnaro

This classic flower still shines brightly in gardens.

By Ann Wilson
Geneva, Illinois

As Shasta daisies burst into bloom in early summer, gardens brighten and gardeners' spirits soar. The tried-and-true charmers illuminate sunlit borders while evoking memories of lazy childhood days crafting daisy chains and plucking petals as "loves me, loves me not" predictions.

Shasta daisies have long been a "gotta have it" inclusion in gardens. Shasta daisies are valued for their large, yellow centers and white blooms.

Hybrid cultivars are available with petals in single, semi-double and double forms and in sizes ranging from dwarf to towering. Some Shasta varieties boast fringed petals, and others have mounded mum-like flower heads. Blooming from early summer through frost, daisies' perky profiles and striking hues beautifully partner with any number of perennials and annuals.

Unfortunately, gardeners can't always count on Shastas to return indefinitely. The short-lived perennial will only bloom profusely for a few seasons, and then eventually fail to show up one spring.

Luckily, those voids are easy to fill. You can start Shasta daisies from seed, and potted plants are readily available at garden centers and through mail-order gardening catalogs.

GREEN THUMB TIP

Shasta daisies will eventually stop returning each spring. While you can't prevent their demise, you can ensure they get a good start when initially planted. To give them a greater chance of success, plant them in a sunny area with moist, well-drained soil.

Plant Profile

Common Name: Shasta daisy.
Botanical Name: *Crysanthemum.*
Bloom Time: Early to late summer.
Hardiness: Zones 4 to 9.
Height: 1 to 3 feet.
Spread: 1 to 2 feet.
Flower Colors: White petals with yellow centers.
Flower Shape: Daisy shaped in single, semi-double, double and fringed forms.
Light Needs: Sun to partial shade.
Soil Type: Moist, well-drained soil.
Planting: Start seeds indoors in spring; transplant bare-root plants and seedlings after danger of frost has passed; plant container-grown plants in spring and early summer.
Prize Picks: Aglaia, Alaska, Becky, Crazy Daisy, Esther Read, Little Miss Muffet, Snow Lady and Little Silver Princess.

Make 'Em Last

Garden expert Melinda Myers offers the following tips for prolonging the life and bloom time of this beloved perennial. First, give Shasta daisies a good start by planting them in a sunny site with moist, well-drained soil—good-draining soil is essential to the plant's winter survival. In southern regions, Shasta daisies will tolerate part shade and do best out of afternoon sun.

Shasta daisies are easy to grow. Simply space plants 18 to 24 inches apart, lightly fertilize in spring, keep the soil moist through the growing season and mulch to cool roots and prevent weeds.

Keep the plants vigorous and long lived by dividing clumps in the early spring every 2 or 3 years. Control taller varieties by pinching the stems back to 6 inches in late May or early June. Melinda notes that pinched plants will bloom a few weeks later than usual, but most won't require staking.

Prolong flowering by cutting blooms back to side buds once the plants have finished their initial flowering. This pruning gives the plants a neat appearance, encourages root growth and promotes another round or two of flowers later in the season.

Here, There and Everywhere

Shasta daisies are well suited for planting in a range of garden designs. Magnets for winged creatures, Shastas are a must for butterfly and wildlife gardens. Compact varieties step up interest when arranged along paths and at the edges of formal borders.

Frank Moegling/The Image Finders

Try making an eye-catching statement with clumps of taller varieties, assembled to frame an entry walkway or sprinkled as white splashes through wildflower plantings. You can also grow Shastas in large containers, and they're great in cut bouquets.

A few good garden companions for Shasta daisies include balloon flower, gaillardia, catmint, purple coneflower, perennial salvia, black-eyed Susan, Siberian iris, daylilies, bee balm and ornamental grasses.

A member of the *Asteraceae* family, the Shasta daisy first appeared on the gardening scene in the early 1900s. Renowned American horticulturist Luther Burbank created it from several other popular daisy flowers, including wild ox-eye daisies, English daisies, Portuguese field daisies and Japanese field daisies. Working near Santa Rosa, California at the time, he named the large, white flower for the nearby snowcapped Mt. Shasta.

Daisies and their many attributes have been noted in story, song and poetry since the time of Geoffrey Chaucer. Today, descendents of those once-revered wild daisies bring joy to gardeners—gardeners who may even wax poetic as their Shasta daisies unfurl into a dazzling sea of ever-cheerful blooms.

170

166

174

168

All About Hummingbirds

Chapter 6

176

Photos: black-chinned hummingbird, Sid and Shirley Rucker; hummingbird in flight (opposite page), Mark Bettis; Anna's hummingbird, Charles W. Melton.

182

178

Hummingbird photos by Sam Alfano

If I had known my photo would be E-mailed to millions of people around the world, then I probably would have put on a little makeup.

Amazing photos have baffled people all over the world.

As told by Abigail Alfano
Covington, Louisiana

Story by Stacy Tornio
Managing Editor

Hi. I'm Abigail. Many people know me as "The Hummingbird Lady." I'm the woman pictured hand-feeding hummingbirds in my pajamas (above).

Photos of me were part of a massive E-mail chain. I've heard from people all over the world who've asked about the photos and questioned their validity. Well, I'm here to tell you that they are 100% real. My husband, Sam, is a great photographer, and he did not do anything to alter the photos.

But I'm getting ahead of myself a little bit. First, let me tell you how this whole thing started.

Two years ago, when we were living in Pine, Louisiana, I was drinking my coffee and watching the hummingbirds feed from our sugar-water feeder. I did this every morning and loved watching the traffic at the feeders increase around migration time.

On this particular morning, I looked over to my husband and said, "Oh, I wish I could hold one of those hummingbirds."

He replied, "Why don't you go out and try?"

WORLD-WIDE LEGEND. These photos (left and above) have traveled all over the world, thanks to the Internet. Many people know Abigail as a local singer (below), but now even more people know her as "The Hummingbird Lady."

So I went outside, held the hummingbird feeder and stood as still as possible. The birds swarmed around me, feeding at the sugar-water feeder but not daring to land on me. I did this for a few days so they could get used to having me around.

Next, I removed the feeder and mounted a red cap filled with sugar water on an old milk jug. It didn't take the hummingbirds long to find the new food source, and soon they were buzzing around it, too.

Then came the day when Sam took these legendary photos. It was a typical morning with hummingbirds swooping around our backyard. I saw the buzz of activity, so I grabbed my cowboy boots and headed outside. I took the red cap the birds had been feeding from and put it in my palm.

The next few minutes took my breath away. Hummingbirds were flying around me at every angle and even landing on my hand to feed! They were light as a feather and amazing to watch at such a close distance. Sam snapped away with his camera, getting 50 or more photos of the moment.

Afterward, Sam picked his favorite four or five photos and E-mailed them to about six people. Within a month, I started hearing from friends, saying that they had received an E-mail with my pictures in it!

From then on, the photos traveled like wildfire. One woman in Lexington, Kentucky even passed one of the photos off as her own for a local photo contest. We learned our lesson from that, and Sam has since branded the photos with our name.

It has been 2 years since we took those photos, but we know the E-mail chain is still circulating all over the world. I get E-mails from people nearly every day!

I am by no means a hummingbird expert, but I do offer a few tips for people who ask me about how to hand-feed. I tell them that it just takes a lot of patience and a little luck.

When I'm not watching birds, you'll likely find me singing. I'm in a musical group with two other guys, and we play a lot of acoustic soft rock and country at local places on the weekend.

Sam still does a lot of photography, and I love seeing what he comes up with. It's amazing to think that my love of hummingbirds and his love of photography started this whole thing. I suppose people will always know me as "The Hummingbird Lady," and that's okay with me!

5 Steps to Feeding Hummingbirds in Your Hand

It's one thing for a hummingbird to eat from a container that you're holding. But it's another thing to actually feel one of these jeweled fliers in your hand. Abigail Alfano was determined to touch a hummingbird. And with a little practice and patience, she finally did. Here's how she did it.

1 Get hummingbirds used to your yard by offering multiple sugar-water feeders.

2 As the traffic around your feeding area increases, start spending time out there so the hummingbirds get used to you. Even if you scare them off at first, be patient. They will come back.

3 Once they get used to your presence, hold the sugar-water feeder in your hand. If you are patient, they should eventually start feeding from the one you're holding.

4 When you have good hummingbird traffic one day, remove your other feeders. Next, place a small feeder filled with sugar water in the palm of your hand (Abigail used an old milk jug lid).

5 Now you just have to sit outside and wait. If you choose a day with good hummingbird traffic and remove the other food sources, you'll have better chances. Be patient and stick with it. You just might feel the flutter of a hummingbird in your hand.

Rolf Nussbaumer

Black-Chinned Hummingbird

This subtle beauty is the best-kept secret in the West.

By Sheri Williamson
Bisbee, Arizona

It's human nature for us to gravitate toward the rare, the exotic and the spectacular. When we think of hummingbirds, it's usually the superstars that come to mind—the fiery rufous, the musical broad-tailed, the elfin calliope and the tall, dark magnificent hummingbird.

Yet of all the hummingbirds that inhabit the American West, the black-chinned is the one that most embodies Western values. What this down-to-earth, blue-collar hummer lacks in feathered finery, it makes up in toughness and adaptability. It gets the pollination job done from the Southwestern deserts to the foothills of the Rocky Mountains and from wilderness to suburban gardens.

The black-chinned's charms are subtle by almost any standard. It takes patience and luck to see a flash of violet at the base of the male's gorget, but his velvety-black head and crisp, white collar set him apart from males of most other species. Tiny notches on his inner primary feathers produce a dull whine in flight, a sound much less dramatic but no less distinctive than the wing trills of a male broad-tailed, rufous or Allen's.

The female is a picture of understated elegance, with a slim, graceful neck and long, slightly decurved bill to distinguish her from female ruby-throated, Anna's and Costa's.

My husband and I are conservationists and researchers working in hummingbird-rich southeastern Arizona. We've banded more than 3,000

BIRD-WATCHER'S SECRET

Male black-chinned hummingbirds, which are only common in the western region of the United States, have a distinguishing feature—a signature black chin with a violet band just below it.

black-chinned hummingbirds over the last 20 years, which has deepened our admiration of these mild-mannered gems.

Our main study site is on the San Pedro River, a major migration corridor as well as excellent breeding habitat for black-chinned species. Some birds return to the river year after year, allowing us to gather valuable information on how they cope with the hardships of desert life.

The oldest wild black-chinned on record is one that we banded—a female at least 10 years old when we last encountered her. Though we try to maintain the proper scientific objectivity, it's hard not to feel a personal connection as we follow "our" birds through good times and bad.

One female, "Checkers," earned her nickname from the pattern of dark markings on her throat. She was one of our regulars on the San Pedro, with 17 captures over 5 years.

One summer, Checkers entered our trap at the beginning of a 2-hour banding session. We verified her band number, took the usual measurements, let her drink from a feeder on the banding table and sent her on her way.

At the end of the session, as I was packing my tools, I heard the thrum of wings and looked up into a familiar face. It was Checkers, and her eyes were darting from me to the feeder on the table, then back to me. I leaned back and folded my arms to look less threatening. "Go for it, lady," I murmured.

She took a tentative sip, sneaking a peek around the feeder to make sure I was staying put. Once satisfied, she settled on the perch and drank her fill before making a beeline to a green ribbon of cottonwood trees.

Like all hummingbirds, the female black-chinned is a single parent, raising up to three overlapping broods per season with no help from the male. Under totally natural conditions, broadleaf trees and large shrubs provide preferred nest sites.

Females nesting in urban areas may take advantage of wires, light fixtures, wind chimes, or hanging plants under the shelter of porches and roof overhangs. Once her young have feathers and no longer need constant attention, the mother may use her free time to build another nest and incubate a new clutch of eggs.

Fellow hummingbird banders Steve and Debbie Bouricius of Palisade, Colorado have an apple orchard that hosts a healthy population of black-chinneds. Over the years, they've observed more than 250 nests.

One thing they've noticed is that females tend to build their second nests within sight of the first to better watch over both broods at once. They've also noted that quiet corners of the orchard make the best nurseries.

"Females regularly visit our large feeding stations," says Steve, "but they'll never nest anywhere near all those aggressive males that chase and harass them every time the girls come to drink."

Luckily, it doesn't take a river or an orchard to make the black-chinned feel at home. All these undemanding birds need are flowers or feeders for energy, a few trees and shrubs for shelter, water for bathing and lots of pesticide-free insects to feed their ever-hungry youngsters. If only every hummingbird was so easy to please!

Photos this page: Sid and Shirley Rucker

UNDERWRAPS. Look closely at the base of the male's black chin to see a flash of violet. Above, a female black-chinned feeds a nestling.

At a Glance

Size: Black-chinneds are 3-3/4 inches long with a wingspan of 4-3/4 inches.

ID Tips: Male has a black chin with a violet band below it.

Voice: A high, weak warble.

Nesting: Nest is a round cup made of plant down, about 1-1/2 inches across and coated with spiders' silk. Usually attached to a drooping branch or a tree fork 4 to 30 feet from the ground. Females lay two pure-white eggs that hatch after 16 days. Young leave the nest about 20 days after hatching.

Diet: Flower nectar, tree sap and insects.

Fun Facts: As summer progresses, black-chinneds may move higher in the mountains, as the flowers bloom later there.

How to Attract: Sugar water.

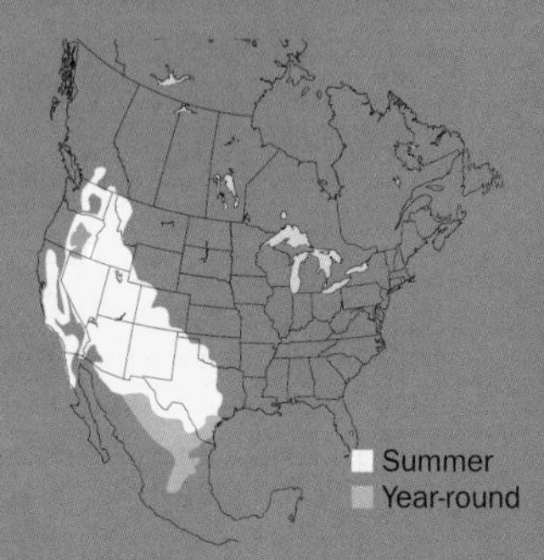

Practice Makes Perfect

By Mark Bettis
Villa Ridge, Missouri

This amateur photographer has mastered a technique for taking hummingbird photos.

Photographing hummingbirds is like going fishing with a cane pole. Both require the "sit, watch and wait" technique.

With fishing, you're eagerly waiting for something to take your bait, giving the slightest bit of action to your bobber. This is similar for hummingbirds, too, though your bait becomes a flower, and your fishing pole translates to a camera.

When I photograph these amazing birds, I cast my focus on a single flower and then wait for one to take the bait. It can take a while, but once one shows up, I snap as fast as I can until it's gone. Sometimes, hummingbirds only stay for seconds at a time, so you always have to be ready.

I first became interested in photographing hummingbirds while preparing for a trip to Alaska. I was planning to photograph whales there, and I knew I needed to practice taking speed shots if I wanted to get any good photos.

You only have only a few seconds to capture a whale photo, and since hummingbirds are quick and flighty, I thought they'd be perfect for practice. It worked great. I got plenty of great whale shots and lots of good pictures of hummers.

THE RIGHT FOCUS. Mark Bettis has spent hours perfecting his technique for taking hummingbird photos. His best tip: First focus on a flower (like the petunias at left), and then wait for a bird to arrive.

The following spring, I decided to try to improve my technique. Soon, I was spending all my spare time outside on my patio and deck, shooting photos of the hummingbirds visiting our backyard.

My wife had filled the area with colorful flowers, so I got a couple of good shots right away. But then the traffic tapered off, and my patience grew pretty thin.

Then it suddenly occurred to me why the numbers were low. We had a hummingbird feeder up, so, of course, they preferred its convenience to the flowers! I removed the feeder, hoping it would

7 Hummingbird Photo Tips

It takes a little practice to get great hummingbirds photos, but it's always worth it in the end. Here are a few technical tips and tricks that I've learned.

1 I was photographing hummingbirds with a shutter speed of 1/2000th of a second, but I found I can get even more detail with a 1/4000th of a second.

2 If you do use a faster shutter speed, then you'll need a wider aperture setting.

3 To get a wider aperture setting, set the shutter speed and let the camera figure out the aperture. Or you can go to a manual setting where you set both the shutter speed and aperture. The manual mode takes a little practice, but it's worth it.

4 I use a manual setting on my camera because I like hummingbird pictures a little overexposed verses what the camera would calculate on its own.

5 Don't forget to set a high ISO value. I usually have an ISO setting of 1600 and no less than 800. In other words, a higher shutter speed requires a higher ISO.

6 Use a single focus point when taking a picture.

7 Use your camera to its fullest potential. You'll never be sorry.

send the birds back to the blooms.

It worked like a charm! For about the first 15 minutes or so after removing the feeder, the deck flowers were abuzz with hummers. Sitting in a lawn chair with the camera remote in my hand, I was shooting these speedy birds like nobody's business.

Thanks to my digital camera and its delete feature, my success rate was about 40 to 50%. My so-called bad shots contained birds out of focus, exposure problems, or sometimes the bird was absent from the picture altogether.

This was mostly my fault, though. I sometime had a slow reaction on the snap. So if I had even the slightest pause, I often missed my picture.

I've taken more than 2,000 hummingbird pictures that I consider keepers. But in all fairness, I deleted an equal number of photos as well.

I like to name some of my best photos, much like an artist would name their painting. I've dubbed one "Reflections" (top left) because of the way the red bloom is reflecting directly onto the bird's belly.

Photographing hummingbirds is not only fun, but also addicting. I can't wait to see what I "catch" this summer.

Fact or Myth?

We're setting the record straight about hummingbirds.

It's not easy to tell the difference between facts and myths, especially when it comes to hummingbirds. After all, it seems like these amazing little birds can do anything!

But the truth is, there are lots of myths floating around about hummingbirds. In fact, we get dozens of questions each year from readers who have heard various rumors.

Don't be fooled any longer. We're debunking myths and setting the record straight once and for all. How many of these have you heard?

Myth: Hummingbirds sip nectar through their bills like a straw.
Fact: Hummingbirds use their tongues to lap up flower nectar and sugar water at a rate of 13 licks per second.

Myth: Hummingbirds hitch rides on the backs of geese as they migrate south.
Fact: This legend is entertaining but untrue. Hummingbirds and Canada geese migrate at different times and to different destinations.

Myth: Hummingbirds' only natural predators are other, larger birds.
Fact: Besides other birds like hawks, hummers have to watch out for cats, spiders, snakes and even frogs.

Myth: Leaving hummingbird feeders up late into fall delays migration.
Fact: You won't interfere with hummingbirds' migration; they know to fly south as the days get shorter.

Myth: Hummingbirds eat only nectar and sugar water.
Fact: Insects and small spiders also are an important part of a hummingbird's diet.

Myth: All hummingbirds migrate.
Fact: Most, but not all, hummingbirds migrate south for winter. The Anna's hummingbird stays along the West Coast year-round.

Myth: Adding red dye to sugar water will attract more hummingbirds.
Fact: It isn't necessary to dye sugar water. In fact, *Birds & Blooms* birding expert George Harrison recommends leaving it clear. Feeders with red parts do the trick.

Myth: Hummingbirds feed only from red flowers.
Fact: While red blooms draw them in, these sweet-toothed fliers will gladly feed from any color flower that produces nectar.

Myth: Hummingbirds and other small birds are carried long distances by powerful storms.
Fact: High winds don't blow hummingbirds around. Small fliers will take shelter in bad weather.

Myth: Hummingbirds have as many taste buds as humans.
Fact: Hummingbirds have between 40 and 60 taste buds, while humans possess about 10,000.

Myth: Hummingbirds don't have a traditional call or song like other birds.
Fact: People know hummingbirds for the buzz of their wings, but they also have a twitter or chatter they emit while resting or chasing other hummers.

Myth: Hummingbirds have no feet or legs.
Fact: While they possess feet and legs, hummingbirds can't walk. They use their feet to perch on branches and feeders.

Illustrations by Kevin Rechin

Bring more jeweled fliers to your feeders with these reader tips.

Hummingbirds

Head-Feeding Hummingbirds

Our friend Rick loves to watch hummingbirds. So, to get up close and personal, he built this device (left) by taking a hardhat and mounting a sugar-water feeder to the front.

It works great, and Rick definitely gets the up close view he was after. In fact, he said he learned the hard way that safety glasses are required when you're wearing the hat.

It only has one feeding port, but Rick has had as many as 10 hummingbirds buzzing around his head at one time!

—Don and Gayle Martens, Duluth, Minnesota

Stepping Gingerly

I read in an old issue of *Birds & Blooms* how you can keep ants away from the bottom of your hummingbird feeder pole by putting old grass clippings around it. We don't have a lawn, so we found another solution.

Just sprinkle a little ground ginger around your feeder pole. Once you do, the ants won't go near the area. And, as an added benefit, it smells good. Good luck to everyone who tries this!

—Carson Tyree, La Grange, California

Speedy Sugar Water

I developed a quick and easy way to make sugar water on busy days. First, put 1 cup of water into a glass pitcher and bring it to a boil in the microwave. Carefully add and mix 1 cup of sugar to the hot water until it's dissolved. Then add 3 more cups of cold water and mix again.

The cooler water evens out the boiling water, and then it's immediately ready to serve to the hummingbirds.

—Ann Novacek, Greenbush, Minnesota

Hummingbird Hangout

For years, we used shepherd's hooks to hang our sugar-water feeders. Then we recently decided to exchange all our old hooks with a single folding clothesline (left).

We hung 15 hummingbird feeders from it, and the traffic really took off! The clothesline is the perfect size for the birds to perch.

The contraption revolves, making it easy to refill the feeders. And it folds up at the end of the season. It's a great way to bring in more hummingbirds at one time. I think there are close to 100 hummingbirds perched or feeding in this photo.

—Darlene Potts, Grandview, Indiana

Hanging Basket for Hummingbirds

You don't need a big garden to attract hummingbirds with flowers. A container or simple hanging basket (like the one at right) will work just fine.

Gardening expert Melinda Myers says the most important thing to remember when planting a container is to group plants by lighting needs. For example, this trio of annuals will do well in the shade.

Fuchsia
two plants

Begonia
three plants

Sweet potato vine
one plant

Galore

No Crossing Zone

Ants kept getting into my hummingbird feeder, so I set out to find a fix. I noticed that other feeders had built-in ant guards and water barriers. I looked around my house and found a cap from aerosol can and a paperclip that I thought could work similarly.

The cap had a center section, so I heated my paperclip with a candle flame and easily slid it through the middle. Then I filled the outside of the cap with water. This didn't work so great. The weight of the water made the lid tilt and wiggle the paperclip, and ants were still able to get around the edges. So I tried a second, smaller container to help hold the paper clip in the original cap (right).

This stopped the shifting, and the ants finally disappeared.

—*Arlene Siegwarth, Matawan, New Jersey*

Protection from Above

My hummingbird feeder hangs in full sun. This causes the sugar-water solution to spoil quickly in hot weather. To keep the solution fresh longer, I attached a red plastic plate as a shade above the feeder (above).

I poked a hole in the center of it then put it on the wire from which my feeder hangs.

This creates a wide area of shade directly over the feeder. And, as an added bonus, it adds a large, bright spot of red to help attract flying jewels!

—*Linda Bussell, Imperial, Nebraska*

Pulley Makes It Easy

We love to hang our sugar-water feeder in front of our high kitchen window, but we did not like having to climb a ladder just to fill it.

I created a way to raise and lower it so there's no climbing required! I bought a small pulley at the hardware store and rigged it with about 20 feet of fishing line (above).

Now, we can watch hummingbirds outside the window and easily fill the feeder when it's empty.

—*Paul J. Trulson, Monteagle, Tennessee*

Cool Down

We have 16 sugar-water feeders for hummingbirds, which means we can have 30 to 40 hummingbirds at a time!

We noticed that the sugar water in the feeders was getting very hot and spoiling quickly. We wanted to keep the mixture cool longer, so we cut the bottom out of plastic bottles (left) and placed them over the feeders as insulation. Now the feeders stay cooler, keeping the sugar water fresh longer.

—*Helen and Jerry Johnson*
Fillmore, Missouri

Hanging from a Thread

To prevent ants and other insects from drinking all the sugar water in my hummingbird feeder, I hang it from clear nylon sewing thread.

The thread is too fine and slippery for insects to climb. It's sturdy, too. The weight of the feeder has never broken the thread, but it definitely keeps insects away!

—*Bernice Binginot, Stowe, Vermont*

Soak It Up

I've heard of many different ways to clean hummingbird feeders, but I think my method is easiest of all. I just soak my feeder in warm water and dish soap, then rinse it thoroughly.

Sure, it sounds simple—because it is! With some good, quality soaking time, my feeders always come out sparkling clean.

—*Marie Longtin, Bennington, Vermont*

Editor's Pick
HUMMER HOT SPOT
2008

Legend of the Southwest

You won't find a better—or friendlier—place to watch hummingbirds.

All photos by Charles W. Melton

By Stacy Tornio
Managing Editor

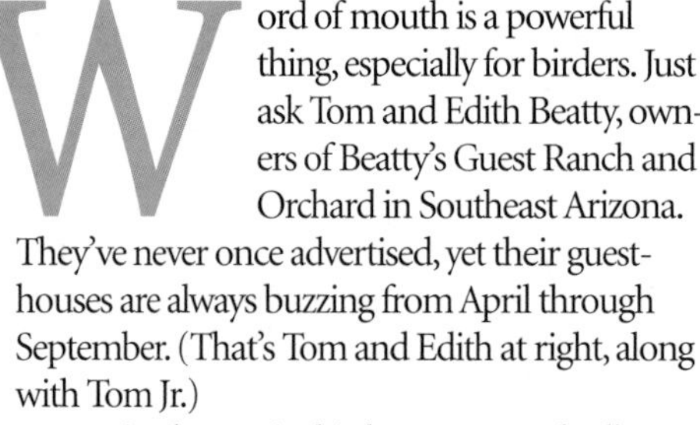

Word of mouth is a powerful thing, especially for birders. Just ask Tom and Edith Beatty, owners of Beatty's Guest Ranch and Orchard in Southeast Arizona. They've never once advertised, yet their guesthouses are always buzzing from April through September. (That's Tom and Edith at right, along with Tom Jr.)

Rufous

During hummingbird season, people all over the world gear up for a trip to Beatty's Guest Ranch near Miller Canyon. The Beattys host more than 5,000 visitors in any given season and have welcomed people from Norway, France, Australia and Holland.

The ranch has a reputation among birders that other birding hot spots can only dream about. If you're in the Southwest and searching for hummingbirds, it's impossible not to have Beatty's on your list.

It's easy to see why the ranch is so popular. After all, it holds the U.S. record for the most hummingbird species spotted in 1 day with 14. And bird enthusiasts insist it's the best place to consistently find rare hummers.

"You can see 15 different species of hummingbirds at Beatty's. That's impressive!" says nature photographer Charles Melton, who lives nearby. "And this is the only place in the U.S. to reliably see the white-eared."

Charles has been going to Beatty's to see hummingbirds for more than 10 years. He has taken several thousands of photos and many hours of video on their ranch. In fact, he took all the photos for this story there.

"The location is spectacular," he says. "It's a 10-acre apple orchard in the middle of a national forest, surrounded by mountain peaks and cliffs. The hummingbird viewing areas are amazing."

When Tom and Edith bought the property in

1967, they knew they had something special, but had no idea it would evolve into the popular spot it is today.

Right away, they noticed a large number of hummingbirds around their land. And pretty soon, others started noticing, too.

"At one point, we had 15 birders leaning over our fence to get a closer look at a white-eared hummingbird at our feeder," Tom says. "That's when we knew it was time to create a public viewing area."

Today, they have four public areas. The most popular is a controlled access site in their orchard, open only to their guests or those who pay a small access fee.

"One of my favorite memories is the time I helped my grandson carry his 89-year-old grandmother uphill to the controlled access site," Tom says. "She had heard about the area and wouldn't take no for an answer."

Tom and Edith have four children. Their oldest, Tom Jr., lives on-site and helps manage the ranch. The others help out and visit when they can.

The family's hospitality amazes visitors. Sam Wilson lives in Scottsdale, Arizona, and he'll never forget his first trip to the ranch. He was driving around the canyon, looking for the right place, when he came to the Beattys' private drive. Tom came walking up, and Sam immediately started apologizing.

"The next thing I knew, Tom was telling me to park on the side of the road," Sam remembers. "Once we stepped out of our car, we looked up and saw what seemed like a million hummingbirds. They were zipping all around and dive-bombing us. I had never seen so many hummingbirds."

Tom and Sam hit it off right away and started talking like they had known each other their entire lives. Today, Sam still goes back to the ranch to see hummingbirds and visit Tom and Edith.

"Tom is one of the most down-to-earth and honest men you'll ever meet," Sam says. "Yet, he's stern in a good way because he wants to protect those little birds."

Tom and Edith Beatty are happy to share their little piece of paradise with others, and they don't plan on stopping anytime soon.

Beatty's Guest Ranch may not use advertisements or have a fancy Web site, but it doesn't matter. Word gets around, and the visitors keep coming.

White-eared

Broad-billed

Calliope

Anna's

Hummer Happenings

Readers recall rare hummingbird encounters.

Hand-Feeding Success

While vacationing in Maine at my friend's home, my daughter Aimee and I were sitting on the deck watching the many hummingbirds that were feeding on the flowers. I picked a petunia bloom, and much to my surprise, a hummingbird came and drank from the flower! Luckily, Aimee was able to capture this wonderful experience on film.

—Kathy Peterson, Lisbon, North Dakota

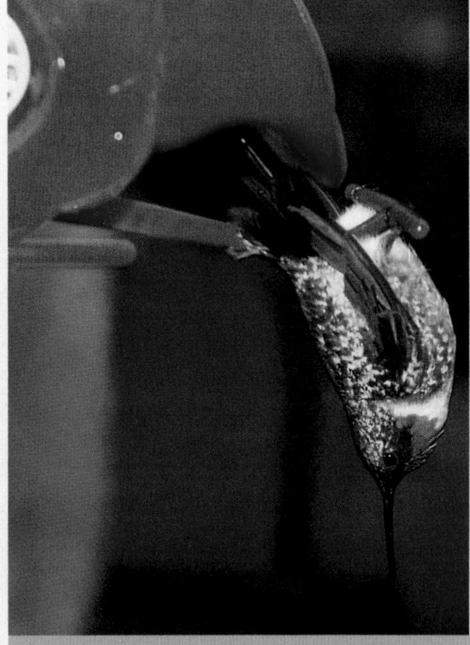

Lifeguard on Duty

Our 6-year-old granddaughter, Delaney, was down on the beach playing. Suddenly, she came running into the house and said, "Grandma, get the bug net. There's something in the water, and I've got to get it out!"

By the time Grandma got there, Delaney had pulled a hummingbird out of the water and was holding it in her hands. We think it fell out of a nest about 15 feet over the water.

Delaney carried the bird to the house and fed it sugar water. It took a test flight, which only lasted about 8 feet. Soon, the hummingbird took off on its own. Delaney swears she sees her hummingbird, "Wiggles," at one of our feeders every time she visits.

—John Evers, Kendallville, Indiana

Unusual Behavior

One chilly September morning, my husband Bill noticed an unusual sight at our hummingbird feeder. A hummingbird was perched backward and upside down. We had never seen anything quite like this.

I went outside to get a better look, but as I got closer, the bird chirped and flew away. A few minutes later, it came back and perched on the feeder right side up, before falling backward again. We mentioned its behavior to friends and they told us it might have been in a state of torpor, or rest, to stay warm.

We were so excited we had the opportunity to see this sight.

—Pam Wyatt, Rives Junction, Michigan

Getting to Know "Oskar"

A few years ago, when we were living in Washington, I had the most amazing hummingbird encounter. While looking out my kitchen window at our sugar-water feeder, I saw a juvenile calliope hummingbird. My husband, John, later dubbed the bird "Oskar" as he began to acquire his distinctive red-streaked throat.

On that morning, Oskar seemed confused and exhausted as he perched on the feeder. He stayed there for a long time, intermittently drinking and dozing, so I was able to stand very close.

Oskar eventually recovered, and from then on, never showed any sign of fear when I approached. He even let me pet his head and neck feathers once—what a thrill!

It was probably my imagination, but I could swear Oskar recognized me whenever I came outside. Or maybe he just recognized the wide-brimmed summer hat I usually wear.

As the summer wore on, we got more and more familiar with each other. I even began to recognize his peeping noises, which usually indicated something was wrong at the feeder, like invading ants or yellow jackets.

The little guy would fly right up to me as soon as I came outside, then hover about an inch from my left eye. This was rather unnerving at first, given the length of his sharp little bill. He would fly back to the feeder, then back to me again. So I'd go check out the feeder and take care of whatever was amiss. Here is one of my favorite photos of Oskar (right).

One morning after a hard rain, I heard his loud and insistent peeps and found him trapped under a tarp that covered our grill. I put my finger under him as he hovered, and he eventually settled on it, completely worn out. I brought him into the sunlight, where he rested for a few moments before flying away.

When the hummingbirds left for the season, I wondered if I'd ever see Oskar again. Sure enough, the following summer, while out on the back deck one bright, sunny day, a hummingbird flew up and hovered about an inch from my left eye.

I know some people might wonder if it really was the same hummingbird; I believe it was. Oskar perched on the brim of my hat. I was glad he was back!

—Collene Karcher, Cullowhee, North Carolina

Overseas Exposure

One spring, I filled the sugar-water feeder my daughter had given me as a Christmas stocking stuffer. Then I waited for the hummers to arrive.

At the time, I was hosting a foreign exchange student from Japan. She was amazed when she saw the hummers come to feed, and asked what kind of birds they were. She'd never seen hummingbirds before, and told me there aren't any in Japan.

I could hardly believe this after visiting many Japanese hanging gardens filled with flowers. But she was so adamant that I finally looked it up in an encyclopedia—and she was absolutely right! Hummingbirds are only found in the Western Hemisphere.

I was glad we had the opportunity to expose her to something truly unique during her stay.

—Christie Eddlemon, Malvern, Arkansas

Friendly Welcome

My friend had just dropped me off from a girls' weekend at the beach. I realized I had left my keys inside the house, so I lugged my bags to the backyard to wait for my husband and son to return home from church.

It was a beautiful September morning, and I sat down under the umbrella to look at my photos from the weekend. I must have dozed off for a bit because I woke up to a boisterous buzzing. It was coming from a charming little hummer, innocently eating from my hibiscus, flitting from blossom to blossom. It was a great way to welcome me home from my vacation.

—Fran Klassen, Annapolis, Maryland

Landing Gear Down!

My husband, Charlie, and I love to catch photos of our hummingbirds throughout the year in a variety of different poses. This is one of our favorites. It looks as if this particular hummingbird is gearing up for the perfect landing.

—Jann Kiesel
Fort Branch, Indiana

Treat for Cold Feet

Last April was one of the coldest on record here in South Texas. One weekend, the temperatures dipped down to a chilly 33°.

I noticed our hummingbirds were desperately trying to cope with the frigid weather, so I put warm sugar water in the feeders so they could eat. Then I turned on my outdoor twinkle lights (above) to see if they'd sit on the lit bulbs to warm their little feet. I was so excited when they actually took me up on my offer!

—Judy Bratten, Lago Vista, Texas

Smile for the Camera

When I first saw a hummingbird in our yard, I went right to a store and bought a feeder, hoping to encourage it to stick around. Not only did the female stay, but she also made a nest in some ivy branches entwined in an elm tree.

I checked on the nest every few days by holding a hand mirror up above it. After the eggs hatched, it was even more fascinating to watch the babies. I eventually got bold enough to set up a ladder on the tree, which allowed me to see even better.

The picture I'm sharing (below) is my favorite out of all the images I took over the course of several weeks.

—Shirlee Wilson
Mojave, California

A Little Help from a Friend

My cousin Joyce and her husband, Tom, were visiting with us during breakfast one day, when I looked outside and saw what appeared to be a bat hanging from our hummingbird feeder. It was a frosty October morning, and most of the hummingbirds already had migrated south.

When we went to investigate, we discovered it was a hummingbird. Joyce, who has been in the medical profession for more than 35 years, immediately told me to warm up a cloth and fix some sugar water. She wrapped the hummer in the warm cloth and put its bill in sugar water.

It slowly began to sip, and she could feel it coming back to life. After it finally took some long sips, she sat it on the feeder.

It immediately flew away, and we never saw it again. We later learned the bird was in a torpid state to save energy.

—Marcy Embry, Greenwood, Missouri

Hummingbirds by the Gallon

I can't wait until April 15—and it's not because I enjoy paying taxes to Uncle Sam. No, I get excited because it's the day that hummingbirds usually return to our area of Washington.

We're on the migratory path of several species of hummingbirds, including the calliope, black-chinned and rufous. We've been putting up feeders since 1978, and plant nectar-producing flowers, too.

As we add more and more trees, shrubs and flowers to our yard for food and cover for birds, the number of hummingbirds increases each year. It has reached the point where I now use a gallon of sugar water a day to fill our five large feeders.

At times, we might see almost 2 dozen hummers swarming around a single feeder. There is nothing like the sound of their squeaky "talk" as they constantly zip to and from the feeders.

One morning in May, I decided to try to feed the hummers by holding a small container of nectar in my hand. I didn't know what to expect, but I asked my husband to grab the digital camera, just in case.

Within minutes, hummers were hovering all around me (above)—as well as my husband, who was wearing a red hat. I wore a red shirt, which prompted the birds to probe the buttons with their bills in search of more food. At times, they even perched on my collar.

It's sad when our little friends begin to migrate back to their winter homes in Mexico. I gradually pare down the number of feeders as the hummer population declines. The only good thing is that April 15 always seems to be right around the corner. And by then, I think I will have earned enough money to pay Uncle Sam—and support my hummingbirds' sugar-water habit!

—Debara Lawrence, Inchelium, Washington

Randy to the Rescue

Our friend Randy Timm lives in a log cabin in a remote area of West Virginia. Because he often leaves the doors and windows open during the summer, birds sometimes fly into the cabin. Once inside, the birds often get confused and can't find their way back outside.

One morning, Randy found a hummingbird passed out on the floor. He not only revived the bird with drops of sugar water, but he managed to take this great picture (above) before it flew away.

—Carol Raschka, Pasadena, Maryland

Coming in for a Landing

My husband, John, and I were visiting his parents in Sun City, Arizona one Christmas when we took this beautiful picture of a Costa's hummingbird (above). We were all gathered around the table with the feeder in the middle, and the bird came right up to us. It was a very nice Christmas moment!

—Kathy Fribley, Auburn, Indiana

Bird's-Eye View

The newest addition to my many hummingbird feeders is a twin feeder, which gives me eight feeding stations to watch right outside my kitchen window.

One day, while filling the new feeders, the hummingbirds were trying to eat while the feeder was still in my hand! My daughter ran to get my camera, and I put my head right in between the two feeders, so the birds were right in front of my face. It was the closest I've ever been, and probably will ever be, to their tiny wings.

—Lester Doss, Ringgold, Virginia

Rufous Invasion

My husband, Joe, took advantage of a sunny November day to wash and wax his Jeep. All of a sudden, a bright-copper bird charged at him several times.

I watched and laughed in amazement as he ran all over the yard with the bird following close behind. It took me a moment to recognize it, but it was actually a male rufous hummingbird!

We decided that the hummingbird liked the sweet-smelling car wax that Joe used as well as the bright-red color of the Jeep.

We still laugh to this day about how he ran all over the yard trying to escape that tiny, charging hummingbird!

—Sherri Fallin, Katy, Texas

Best Hummingbird Photos

Amazing reader photos from the past year.

Putting on a Show

"At our vacation home in California, we noticed this male Anna's hummingbird aggressively protecting his territory by zipping between three perches and chasing other hummers away," write Randy and Barbara Steufert of Mason Neck, Virginia. "He would sometimes fly up over 50 feet in the air and do loops, as if he was showing off."

Beginner's Luck

My wife and I purchased our first home together in Kansas. Right away, we were anxious to set up some sugar-water feeders in hopes of attracting hummingbirds. I was also looking forward to trying to photograph them once they arrived.

It didn't take long for our new guests to find our feeders, and I was more than ready with my camera. With the help of a tripod, a good flash and an extra-long shutter release cable, I got this great shot (left) from inside the house.

—Glenn Davis, Leavenworth, Kansas

Finally Picture-Perfect

"I noticed a few hummingbirds checking out my bee balm," says Jonathan Jenkins of Utica, New York. "So I camped out on my picnic table in hopes of getting some great photos. I took about 100 shots in 2 days. This one is my favorite."

Warning: No-Fly Zone

My husband, Phil, and I spend a lot of time photographing hummingbirds. We captured this image of a male ruby-throated hummingbird by placing a stick between two perches. He loved watching for any rivals that dared encroach on its territory from this lookout post.

—Diane Allen, Fishing Creek Valley, Pennsylvania

Camp Hummer

"The first summer in our new home started with a single hummingbird feeder and a couple of ruby-throated hummers," writes Julie Hodder from Canton, Georgia. "Three summers later, our bird family has grown into a hummingbird camp. My husband, Dennis, and I have come to love the time of year that they spend with us. We can't wait to get home from a long day and spend the evening on the deck, relaxing and watching these amazing, tiny birds."

Caught in Midair

"I am so proud of this picture (below)," says Donna Richardson of Creaola, Alabama. "The buds of the fuchsia were just about to open when this hummingbird flew in for a drink."

A Rare Bird

We have tried to attract hummingbirds for several years. Last year, we were thrilled to have a few; this year, we had several at our feeders!

One afternoon, I looked out the window to see this little white hummingbird sitting on the feeder. I quickly grabbed my children to show them. I took a few photos, thinking this rare beauty would be gone in a flash. Much to our surprise and delight, it stayed around for 3 weeks!

—Mary Dobbs, Decatur, Alabama

186

198

192

196

190

Chapter 7
Backyard on a Budget

190

Photos: flowers (top left), Faith Bemiss; yellow-rumped warbler, Richard Day/Daybreak Imagery; spiderweb, Bryan E. Reynolds.

194

188

Faith Bemiss

Garden Bargains

Find great deals on plants at the end of the season, and learn how to care for them.

By Melinda Myers
Contributing Editor

The lazy days of summer are a great time of year for planting. No, this is not a marketing ploy to help nurseries clear out their surplus inventory toward the end of the season. The end of summer is the perfect time to increase your planting success and get a jump start on the next season.

Ideal Conditions

As summer slowly starts to wind down, planting conditions are ideal. The warm soil speeds up establishment, and the cooler air temperatures reduce transplant shock.

Keep in mind that you still need to provide sufficient water and care for your plants. But this will be easier since the soil won't dry out as fast and need as frequent attention as it does during the heat of the summer.

In addition, the milder weather is easier on you as a gardener. Therefore, you'll be better able to keep up the care.

Many garden centers receive a fresh supply of plants in the fall. Professionals have been properly caring for these plants all summer. Some plants may have spent the summer on the garden center lot. As long as they were properly tended, they make good (and often inexpensive) candidates for late-summer and early-fall planting.

RDA/GID

Look for signs of healthy, quality plants whenever you shop. They should have proper color, minimal browning (a sign of drought stress), and be free from insects and diseases. After all, there's no need to bring more work and problems into your landscape.

Better with Time

You can get some great bargains during the late-summer months, and the deals only get better as fall and winter get closer.

This is when the risk takers and green thumb gardeners look for the really big deals and steals. They often discover that the reduced prices are worth the challenge of establishing plants before winter.

If you're one of these people, you'll find that you can increase your success by selecting plants that are reliably hardy to your area. Don't plant borderline hardy plants if you're not willing to take a gamble. Of course, proper post-transplant care will increase your chances of success.

Beat the Odds

Mulch the soil around your new plantings. This will help keep the soil warm for extended rooting. As the weather cools, the mulch will help moderate temperature extremes and also will conserve moisture.

Water new plantings thoroughly whenever the top few inches of soil are crumbly and moist. Continue watering until the ground freezes or plants go dormant.

Surround tender shrubs and broadleaf evergreens with hardware cloth sunk several inches into the soil. Once the ground freezes, fill the enclosed area with straw, marsh hay or evergreen boughs. You can remove this when temperatures start hovering near freezing in the spring.

Now that you know how to care for your garden bargains this season, it's time to go out and find some at your local nursery or garden store. It won't be long before your new plants are poking through the ground next spring. Good luck with your bargain hunting!

DIG IN! You can get some great deals in late summer and early fall. So grab your shovel, dig in and start planting! Whether you're planting new plants or dividing some of your old ones (see the box below), be sure to water them well. Early on, this is one of the most important steps to establishing new plants.

Divide and Save with Perennials

You can easily find a bargain in your own backyard. Scope out your perennials and see what can be divided. It's like creating a whole new plant! Follow these simple steps to divide your perennials...

Photos: RDA/GID

1. **Dig** around the outside edge of the perennial and gently lift it out of the ground.

2. **Divide** the plant, depending on its original size and how many divisions you want. Amend the planting sites with organic matter.

3. **Replant** divisions at the same depth they were growing. You may want to put one of the divisions in its original location. Or, share them with friends.

Secrets to Grow on

The "best of the best" home-tested gardening secrets.

All-Natural Containers

When I discovered a dead tree, I knew I had to do something with it. My husband cut it down with his chain saw and then divided it into several pieces. After that, we hollowed out the centers.

Now these old logs make great containers for my impatiens. I placed them in my flower bed. They look wonderful in the natural setting. They're some of my favorite plant containers, and they all came from nature!

—Alma Deutsch, Raymore, Saskatchewan

Easy with a Spout

I was tired of the mess involved with mixing water-soluble plant food every time I wanted to feed my plants. It made a mess of the table, and I always got green hands from the fertilizer.

Then I discovered a great alternative. I use a recycled 300-ounce detergent container (below). It has a pouring spout, and it is easy to mix up a big batch all at once.

You have to clean out the container thoroughly, but it's worth it. It's been a simple way for me to feed my plants a little at a time.

—Al Hanson, Eau Claire, Wisconsin

Zip It Up

For the past few years, I've started my own seeds in spring. I don't have a lot of space, so I use my windowsills. They're too narrow for the store-bought seed-starter kids, so I just use zip-top sandwich bags instead.

I start by filling the bags halfway with potting soil. Then I soak my seeds for a few days and plant them in the bags. I water them and zip up the bags. Then, after a few weeks, I vent them slightly.

The growth seems to speed up with the mini greenhouses. As the plants continue to grow, unzip the bags to accommodate growth. I've had great luck with this method, and I plan on doing it again this year.

—Marcia Ciak, Blackstone, Massachusetts

Cardboard Magic

My garden used to be filled with weeds. Then, a couple of years ago, when I had a surplus left over from moving, I got the idea to bury cardboard around my garden plants. I covered it with woodchips from a local tree company.

Now my garden is a lot easier to weed and it doesn't require as much water. Cardboard is easy to obtain. Go to your local appliance dealer and ask for some. Just watch out for staples and don't use any wax-covered cardboard.

—Alex Thurlow, Brooklyn, Connecticut

Staking Solution

After years of trying everything from wooden stakes to bamboo poles, I wanted to find a new way to support "dinner plate" dahlias.

I bought some 20-foot lengths of rebar at the local lumberyard, which are typically used to reinforce concrete. I asked the workers to cut them into 4-foot sections. Then I simply stuck them into the dirt and tied the stalks to them. It worked great, and it's inexpensive!

In the fall, I simply pull them up, hose off the dirt and store them in a dry spot until next year.

—Peggy Fick, Yreka, California

Aphid Aversion

Having been plagued by aphids on my roses over the years, I have stumbled upon an organic and nontoxic remedy—I simply let dandelions grow next to my rosebushes.

The aphids seem to prefer the dandelions to the rosebush. They cover the dandelions, but leave the roses alone. I don't know if this method will work for everyone, but it has done wonders for me!

—Betty Yuill, Bloomington, California

Canning Flowers

I love using large flowerpots, but I don't like filling them with soil. It can get expensive, and the plants usually don't need that much soil.

To avoid this, I put empty aluminum cans in the bottom of the pot. This keeps my pots much lighter, and I still have gorgeous flowers.

—Vi Concannon, Fair Oaks, California

Tomato Head Start

The first year I started seeds in my basement, it was too cold for the tomatoes to sprout. So the next year, I put the seeds in 4-inch pots, and then I put those in larger pots. I covered the big pots with clear plastic lids and set them under a lamp. The seeds sprouted quickly.

Try this if you want to get an early start on your tomatoes. It saves money, plus you'll get plump tomatoes earlier than ever!

—Irene Jones, Chardon, Ohio

A Sweet Idea for Starting Seeds

I've tried many different ways to germinate flower and vegetable seeds over the years. I often had trouble keeping the soil moist, but not too moist, which leads to root rot. Then I finally found a good solution.

A couple years ago, my wife, Laura, returned from the grocery store with some strawberries. As much as I love those red berries, I was more excited to see the packaging the strawberries came in.

The first thing I noticed is that the top of the container had a hinge, which allows for easy opening. I immediately saw a new way to propagate seeds in these containers (right).

Here's how it works. First, place your strawberry containers in shallow, plastic seed-starting trays that don't have holes in the bottom. Next, plant your seeds in small pots as you normally would. Then place those pots into the plastic strawberry containers.

Fill the shallow seed-starting trays with water, adding some water-soluble fertilizer to a level just above the bottoms of the small pots. This allows the soil to get wet while allowing proper ventilation at the same time. The clear plastic also lets sunlight or artificial light reach the small pots.

After the seeds germinate, you can open the containers to allow more room for the plants to grow. Once the seedlings become large enough and it's warm enough outside, transplant the seedlings to their permanent location in your garden.

I've used this method for 2 years now, and I've been very successful.

—John Hoepfner, Appleton, Wisconsin

Climbing the Ladder

Plant stands don't have to be fancy or expensive. Last year, I used a stepladder (right) as a stand for some of my flower containers.

It's been a great way to display my marigolds and other annuals. This is an old wooden ladder, so it is very sturdy. This year, I'd like to plant a vine to cover the ladder as well.

—Frances Moore, Burgessville, Ontario

Take a Stand

I have an idea to complement existing containers. For many years, I've had fun creating beauty out of discarded objects.

When I found an old lamp at a garage sale, I immediately pictured it as a plant stand. I brought it home, took out the old lightbulb and removed the wiring.

While washing it, I discovered just how beautiful it really was. The lamp had intricate carving and a touch of gold.

I glued a wooden dowel in the center of the stand, and once it dried, I put my bougainvillea pot on top (right). Now it welcomes visitors at the front entrance of my home.

—Lottie Bradshaw, McCarney, Texas

Eye-to-Eye with Flowers

Get close to nature and save money by spending the day outside with your camera.

By Tammy Anderson
Keyser, West Virginia

I never knew what I was missing until a year ago. I've always enjoyed nature and being outside, but I hadn't really noticed the small things in my own backyard.

I live on the outskirts of the small town of Fort Ashby, West Virginia, and I'm thankful to have access to land where I can enjoy the wildlife and changing seasons. But it wasn't until I became interested in photography that I realized I was missing out on the beauty of some of nature's best hidden treasures.

It was my husband, Dale, who first got me interested in photography. He used to be the only one snapping pictures, but after borrowing his camera a few times, I was hooked! We purchased another camera just for me. Now when I go for a walk, I never leave the house without it!

Spring and early summer are great times to head outdoors. Some of my favorite things to photograph on my walks are flowers. By getting down on the level with blooms—and sometimes even lower—you get a whole different view. I never realized how many beautiful stages a flower can go through before it's actually in full bloom.

Flowers are everywhere, whether they're wild or planted in a neighbor's garden. I've learned that you can get some great photos by just being patient.

A lot of times, I'll be sitting there waiting, and a bee or butterfly will come by to enjoy the flower I'm photographing. For me, this is like an extra reward for my patience.

Don't forget to look up, too, whenever you go for a walk. The birds, leaves and seeds on the trees all have different shapes, colors and textures. You never know when an American robin, mourning dove, blue jay or other bird might want to join you.

I encourage you to take the time to go for a walk and enjoy the scene around you. Slow down, get close and really look at the details of nature.

Sometimes you need to see the small things before you can see the true beauty of the big picture. It's amazing how you can get lost in the quiet and scenery of your own neighborhood.

Go ahead and get out there. Who knows? Getting close to nature might even turn into a passion you can't get enough of.

SNAPPY SHOTS. Tammy's subjects include, clockwise from top right: mimosa, clouded sulphurs, an emerging coneflower, bird's-foot violets, a bee, blooming purple coneflowers and Jerusalem artichoke (above inset).

EDITOR'S PICK
LOW-COST
GARDEN HOBBY
2008

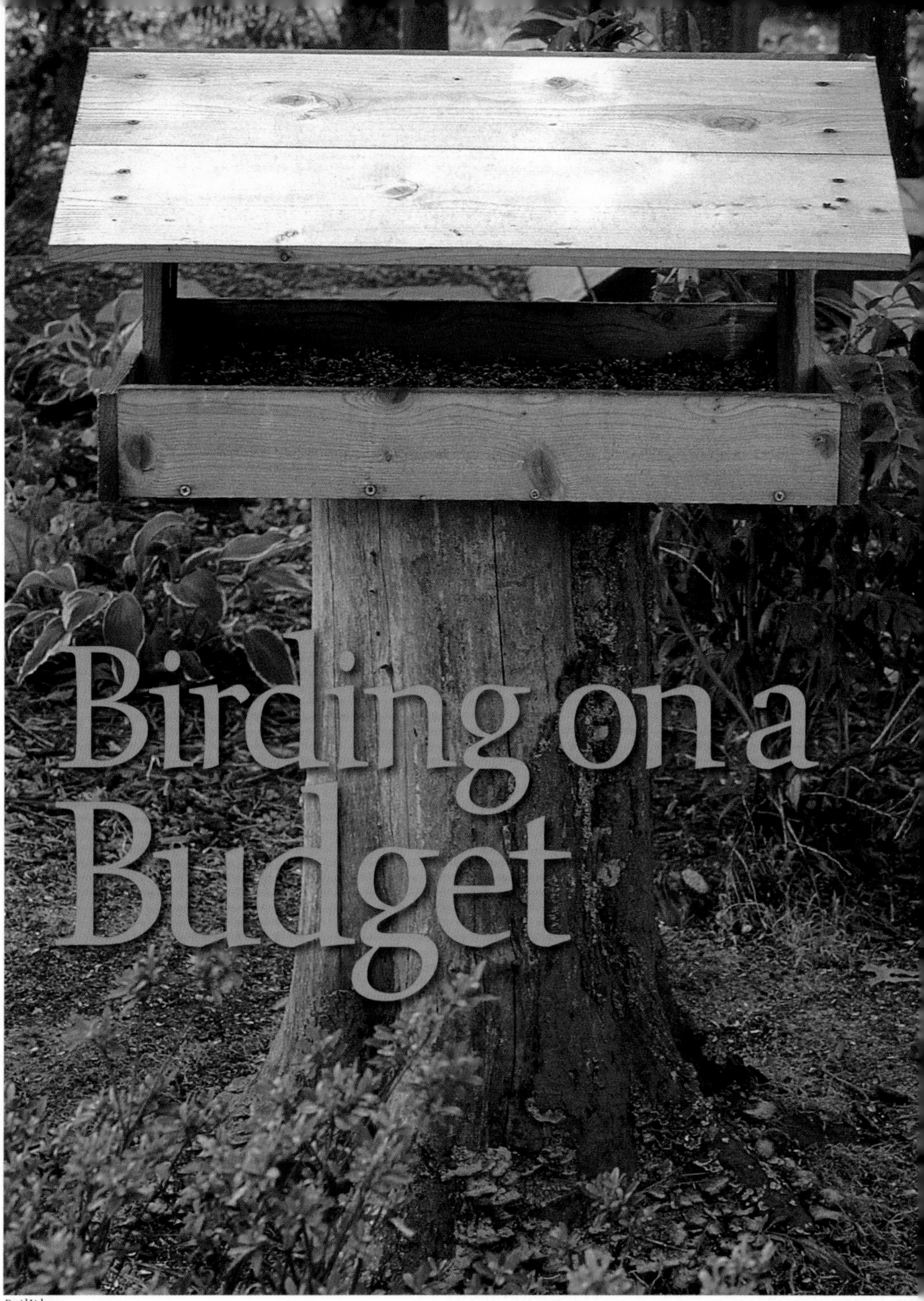

Birding on a Budget

Attract more feathered friends to your backyard with these eight easy, money-saving ideas.

By George Harrison
Contributing Editor

David Liebman

Roland Jordahl

Here's a secret I'd like to share: You don't need to spend a lot of money to attract birds to your backyard. There are many inexpensive ways to host birds. I have a few simple ideas that will keep costs down while still bringing in plenty of winged traffic.

1 Make Your Own Food. You can prepare food in your kitchen for birds like hummingbirds and orioles. For instance, make hummingbird nectar by mixing 1 part sugar to 4 parts water. You don't need to add food coloring; just boil the water, cool and serve. Orioles also like sugar water, oranges and grape jelly (left).

2 Bargain Suet. Another inexpensive food source is suet (fat from around the beef kidney). If you can't get it free from your local butcher, then you can usually purchase it at a low cost. This pure suet is better than the premade suet cakes from the store.

3 Venison Alternative. If you are a deer hunter or know one, ask for the deer suet that comes with butchering. I've used venison suet for many years, and I think birds actually prefer it over beef fat.

Richard Day/Daybreak Imagery

Richard Day/Daybreak Imagery

CLEVER WATERING. You can easily create your own birdbath with a garbage can lid (above) or old pan (right, with this yellow-rumped warbler). Don't fill your container with more than a couple inches of water so the birds can stand in it.

4 Buy in Bulk. Instead of buying small bags of seed mix, you can get more with your money by purchasing large bags of black-oil sunflower, cracked sunflower, safflower seed or nyjer. Most of the popular backyard birds actually prefer the pure seeds instead of mixes.

5 Plants They Can Eat. One of the easiest ways to feed birds is with plants. Birds relish berries from mountain ash, crabapple, highbush cranberries and more throughout fall and winter. In addition, be sure to leave out some of your perennials like sunflowers, coneflowers and black-eyed Susans. Birds will feed on the seed heads throughout the year.

6 Build It Yourself. It doesn't take an architect to build a birdhouse or feeder. Free patterns are readily available from a variety of sources.

As far as materials go, you can often find scraps for free. You might even have some around your home. With a little time and a few supplies, you can make a durable birdhouse (like those at right) or feeder (left) to attract birds to you yard.

7 Birdbaths in an Instant. Another easy item you can make yourself is a birdbath. It doesn't have to be expensive or elaborate with waterfalls and pools. A garbage can lid, discarded saucer, bowl or pan will do the job. Just keep it filled with fresh water at a depth of no more than a couple of inches so that the birds can stand in the water.

8 Cover Creations. All yards should have cover for birds, but this doesn't mean you have to invest a lot of money in an expensive landscaping project.

You can transplant greenery from friends or order it for free from many state Departments of Natural Resources. Or use discarded brush and old Christmas trees to create cover. Then grow your own vines, annuals and other plants by starting seeds indoors. It'll take longer, but you'll save a lot of money in the long run.

With a little ingenuity, anyone can devise ways to attract and care for birds without breaking the bank.

Easy-to-make, bargain birdhouses

Building your own birdhouses is a great way to save money. Plus, it is a fun activity you can do with your family. Visit our Web site, *www.birdsandblooms.com*, for the step-by-step directions on how to create these two birdhouses, as well as other tested and approved favorites.

To make the coffee can birdhouse (above right), you'll only need a few materials. And you probably already have one of them in your kitchen—a coffee can! You can even get creative and paint it however you want.

This one-board birdhouse (right) is perfect for a beginner builder or even kids. And you truly only need one board!

Dollar $avvy Gardens

You don't need a lot of money to create a garden haven in your backyard. Over the years, we've learned hundreds of money-saving secrets from gardeners like you. Here's a collection of our favorites...

An old bathtub makes a great raised bed.

Steve Terrill

Forget landscape fabric. Save money by laying down newspaper or cardboard under your mulch.

Protect your seedlings from frost with a 2-liter plastic bottle with the bottom cut out.

Keep soil moist on your indoor seedlings by covering them with a clear shower cap.

Use cardboard egg cartons for seed starting...and plant them right in the garden.

The holes in the center of cement blocks are perfect for planting flowers and creating a pretty display.

Don't toss out old bird feeders. Fill them with soil and flowers.

Hanging shoe caddies are great places to store garden items in a shed or garage.

A wooden chair without a seat makes a great holder for a flowerpot. Look for an old chair at garage sales.

Borrow a child's plastic sled or wagon (above) to transport garden items.

Turn your old birdbath into a container for a colorful display of flowers in your yard.

Create a "saucer" of soil around your plants to conserve water.

Place crushed milk containers or soft drink cans in the bottom of a large planter to conserve soil and make it lighter overall.

Start flowers from seed in a plastic cake container. The lid that comes with the container will help the soil moist.

Turn rotted-out old logs into rustic planters.

Cut up spare mini blinds to make garden markers.

Save this year's annual trays to start seeds next season.

Yogurt cups with clear lids are great for starting seeds.

Forks and spoons are great for digging weeds in the garden.

Cotton balls placed on top of seed trays help retain moisture.

Save money on annuals by taking cuttings in fall, overwintering them and then moving them outside in spring.

Place foam packing peanuts in the bottom of containers to provide drainage and to help keep pots lighter.

Recycle old pots and pans for flower containers.

Saxon Holt

Use an old tire (or even a truck) for a creative container.

Steve Terrill

Get a better grip from your best garden tools by wrapping them with some baseball bat tape.

Place old burlap or paper birdseed bags over plants as winter protection.

Old wheelbarrows are great for plants.

Gently cover newly planted seeds with soil using an old crank flour sifter.

Drag a chopstick through soil to create a perfect trench for planting seeds.

Recycle a mailbox and use it in your garden for storage.

Use pipe cleaners from the craft store to tie back tomatoes and other plants you need to stake.

Slip plastic grocery bags over your shoes and tie them before going into a wet, muddy garden. They'll stay clean and you won't bring mud into the house.

Old plastic film canisters are perfect for storing dried flower seeds.

Old musical instruments make unique and interesting flowerpots.

Use landscape cloth as a windbreak to protect evergreens from winter winds.

Keep soil from falling out of a flowerpot by lining the bottom with a dryer sheet.

Large coffee cans will protect plants when mowing.

Use twist-ties from bread bags to mark your favorite flowers. You'll know which seeds you want to harvest at the end of the season.

Save on birdseed in the winter by drying your sunflower heads.

Old wagon wheels make good trellises for climbing plants and vines.

Use a ski pole to form holes for spring seeds.

Set out tin barrels in your yard to collect rainwater for your plants.

Latex gloves are thin enough that you can feel what you're doing in the garden. Plus, they are inexpensive.

Butter knives are great for weeding.

Rinse and relabel household spray bottles for weed killer or fertilizer mixes.

Organize a seed swap with your friends.

Use tree prunings as plant stakes.

Make an inexpensive stepping-stone by filling a springform cake pan with cement.

Plastic drink bottles make perfect mini greenhouses.

Start seeds in plastic ice cube trays.

Rake and dig leaves into the garden in fall to improve soil for spring.

Cowboy and work boots make unique planters.

Terry Wild Stock

Thrifty Backyard Projects

The best homemade garden projects of the year.

Fountain From Scratch

My wife has always wanted a fountain in our yard, so instead of buying one, I decided to make my own. It's made of old galvanized parts and a heavy steel base.

The pump feeds water through a bent piece of pipe that connects to both the watering can and the bucket at the top. The water then falls into an old washtub. It looks great on our deck, and my wife is really happy with how it turned out.

—Mark Daily, Cardinton, Ohio

Relaxation Station

Last spring, my husband, David, and I decided to build a pond. I wanted to make it a backyard refuge for the birds and anything else that would come along.

We built the pond where an old mimosa tree was barely living. No matter what we did or how far down we dug, the tree kept sprouting.

By fall, we'd completed the project. The joy this pond has given us and our neighbors have been phenomenal. Anyone is welcome to come sit and relax by the pond.

It's only 7 by 13 feet, which is not the biggest, but when you're digging the hole yourself, it is not the smallest either. I certainly recommend a pond to anyone who loves nature. It has brought us so much pleasure.

—Carol Sawicki, Fairhaven, Massachusetts

No House Here

My husband, Ron, created this fence to hide the propane tank in our yard. The wood is recycled from an old barn that collapsed on our road.

We love the view, but we're sure the birds are disappointed none of the holes have houses behind them.

—Sue McCreery, Milan, Ohio

Seat Made of Feet

After unsuccessful shopping trips to find a bench for the front of our house, my husband, Kevin, decided to make one himself. We saw a children's bench crafted from boots that we loved, so Kevin decided to make a similar one for our yard.

He bought cheap rubber boots and lined them with chicken wire, so they'd retain their shape when he filled them with concrete.

Kevin waited a few months to let the concrete cure before adding the top, which is actually a large garden stepping-stone. He attached the stone with epoxy.

This unique bench gets a lot of attention—and a lot of use—from our family and friends!

—Elaine Stoltzfus, Lancaster, Pennsylvania

Stylish Seat

When I brought this chair home, my husband said that it would take a lot of work to get it fixed up. But I told him that it was perfect the way it is.

All it needed was a circular hole cut into the seat. I placed a pot of million bells petunias in the hole. It's a great way to reuse something that another person was throwing out!

—Shirley Leath, Bowling Green, Kentucky

Garden Gator

My husband is a truck driver and one day while traveling the interstate, he saw a bunch of "road alligators." (This is trucker slang for tire retreads.)

He picked one up and decided it would make a great addition to our garden. With a little bit of paint and a few screws, he soon turned that road gator into a garden gator. It's a great addition to our yard.

—Darlene Reinoehl, Klingerstown, Pennsylvania

Creative Yard Birds

Using an old shovel and random scraps of metal I found behind my muffler shop, I came up with a perfect project: yard birds.

Not only do these birds look great, but since putting them on display, we no longer have crows hanging around. It's amazing what you can make with just a few scraps.

—Joan Hardan, Pahrump, Nevada

Insect Allies

Save money by letting these good insects do the work of expensive insect and pest-control products.

Story and photos by Bryan E. Reynolds, Lexington, Oklahoma

To thousands of insects, your garden is a buffet. The leaves, flowers, stems and roots in it serve as food for a myriad of these hungry creatures.

There is good news, however. You have allies that can help you protect your plants, which means you'll save money by not buying insecticides. Many insects and spiders will hunt the pests in your garden. In fact, the majority of backyard bugs *are* beneficial in some way—whether they pollinate flowers, help convert plant debris to compost or eat harmful bugs.

Having a basic knowledge of these beneficial bugs and what they can do to help you is the first step to keeping them as allies. The second step is to stay away from insecticides—they don't distinguish the good bugs from the bad.

Have a look at some of the friends you have in your garden. Take flies, for instance. Although most people think of flies as nuisances that land on the potato salad at a picnic, there are predatory flies that help control garden pests. These flies include robber flies and hoverflies.

ROBBER FLIES (1) grab insects in midair and stab them with their modified mouthparts. Many perch on a leaf or twig to await their next victim. Some are convincing mimics of bumblebees.

The HOVERFLY (2) is another mimic. Some look like wasps. You may have seen them hovering in one spot before quickly darting away. As larvae, some hoverflies will devour aphids.

Other insect larvae that eat aphids include LACEWINGS (3). As adults, they are lime-green insects with clear wings. They gather around outdoor lights at night, and you can also find them in your garden during the day.

DRAGONFLIES (4) and damselflies are renowned for their mosquito-hunting abilities. Both have excellent eyesight and scoop up their prey as they fly by forming a basket with their specially modified legs. Their larvae live in water, and they are also known for eating larvae of mosquitoes.

Two other effective predators are ASSASSIN BUGS (5), which have poisonous saliva that subdues their prey, and ICHNEUMON WASPS (6), which lay eggs into other insects.

Another interesting group of garden allies are spiders. There are several types of spiders, and they can be roughly divided into those that use a web and those that don't.

The common web builders are orb weaving spiders, cobweb spiders, sheet-web spiders and funnel-web spiders. Some of their creations, like this orb web (right), are among nature's most artistic.

Most ORB WEAVING SPIDERS (7) construct their webs at dusk and take them down at dawn. Orb webs capture flying insects such as beetles, moths and other garden-munching pests.

Sheet webs and funnel webs are similar in appearance—both are flat, silken sheets. Sheet-web spiders await prey underneath the sheet, while funnel-web spiders tunnel into one of the web's corners.

Cobweb spiders build messy looking snares that capture a wide range of crawling pests.

Hunting spiders don't use webs. This group includes jumping spiders, wolf spiders and crab spiders.

JUMPING SPIDERS (8) have the best vision of spiders. These large-eyed predators actively hunt during the day. Most are less than 1/2 an inch across and are ferocious hunters.

Wolf spiders typically hunt at night. Female wolf spiders are sometimes found carrying their egg sack. When the baby wolf spiders hatch, they ride around on their mother's back for a while. Wolf spiders chase and pounce on their prey.

CRAB SPIDERS (9), on the other hand, wait patiently for prey to come to them. Some wait on the surface of leaves; others lurk in flowers.

Together, these good bugs are "at work" night and day, helping control the insects that might otherwise ravage your garden.

1

2

3

4
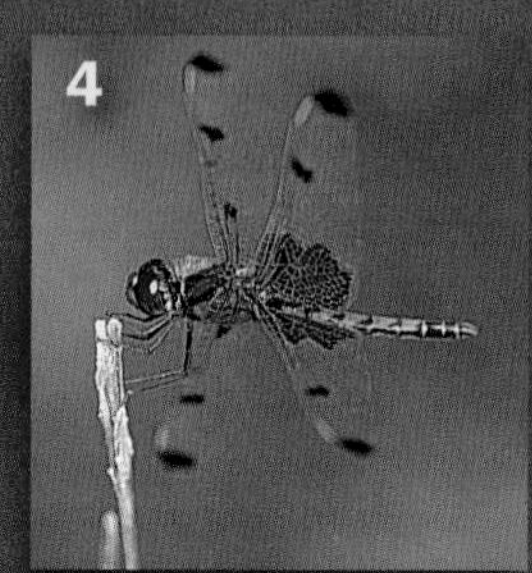

5

6
7
8
9

208

202

218

216

210

212

Chapter 8
Glad You Asked!

Photos: cats, Gerard Fritz/Unicorn Stock Photos; checkered white, Kathy Adams Clark/KAC Productions; sharp-shinned hawk, Roland Jordahl; black checkerspot, Rick and Nora Bowers/KAC Productions.

Gerard Fritz/Unicorn Stock Photos

The Cat Factor

Keep your felines entertained and backyard birds safe.

By George Harrison
Contributing Editor

Cats are one of the most loved (and hated) pets in the country. Anyone who owns a cat probably isn't surprised to learn that 90 million U.S. homes include cat residents, making them the country's top house pet.

But what does surprise many cat owners is that their pets are one of the biggest threats to birds.

Studies in the United States and Great Britain dramatically confirm that house cats, including those well fed at home, are responsible for the deaths of millions of small birds every year. This contributes to the decline in some species of birds, which doesn't sit very well with birders.

Dr. Stanley Temple, a professor of wildlife ecology and conservation at the University of Wisconsin-Madison, completed a 4-year study on this topic with his colleague, John Coleman. They looked at the impact free-ranging domestic cats have on rural wildlife.

By radio collaring many farm cats, the researchers found that in Wisconsin alone, cats kill at least 19 million songbirds and 140,000 game birds annually. Surveys from Cornell Laboratory of Ornithology confirm similar results.

Keeping "Tweety" Safe

Studies like these recommend cat owners keep their felines indoors at all times, but this isn't always convincing. Cat owners argue that their pets aren't content to stay inside.

As a cat owner myself, I understand where this concern is coming from. If you have a cat that is used to being outdoors, then of course it will show signs of wanting out.

Perseverance pays off, though. It could take days or even weeks, but eventually your cat will adapt beautifully to its pampered life indoors. I know people who have retrained their cats to stay indoors, and without exception, they are delighted they made the change. If you're starting with a kitten, it makes it easier.

The various cats that have shared my life and home over the years have all been kept indoors from the start, and they've never shown the desire to go outside.

Purr-fect Entertainment

If there is any negative aspect to keeping a cat indoors, it's that they can get bored. You can easily cure the boredom by providing them with entertainment that is safe and natural. Bird-watching is the perfect solution.

Cats can still satisfy their stalking instincts by watching birds from indoors without going out to kill or injure them.

It's a winning situation for everyone. You'll cater to the birds' needs and provide endless entertainment for your cat. At the same time, you'll pick up a new hobby for yourself.

It's a hard decision to bring your outdoor cat inside, but start now. Then set up bird feeders, birdbaths and natural cover for birds outside your cat's favorite window. Now your cat will be happy, and the birds will stay safe!

NO, KITTY! Keeping pet cats indoors keeps them from endangering backyard birds. From inside, they can watch birds from the window.

Faith Bemiss

Keep Squirrels Away

While cats are a common backyard problem, squirrels' antics constantly trouble backyard bird-watchers. Readers are always sharing new ways to keep squirrels from snatching bird food and taking over birdhouses. Here are some of their best tips.

Private Dining
Squirrels used to empty and ruin my bird feeders until I started putting a couple scoops of sunflower seeds under the pine tree for them. Now the squirrels eat those seeds and leave my feeders alone.

—Deloris Bowen, Columbia, Connecticut

Soda Bottle Solution
After years of feeding birds, this is the only squirrel-proof solution we've found. We cut the neck off of a 2-liter soda bottle and slipped it on the pole below the feeder. It really works for us!

—Lenore Mather, Waverly, New York

Squirrel Deterrent
I have built many birdhouses over the years, and I've learned how to keep squirrels from destroying the entrances. I attach a flat steel washer around the entrance hole, either 1-1/4 inches or 1-1/2 inches, depending on what type of bird will inhabit the house.

—Roy M. Seppala, Pembroke, Massachusetts

Easy Fix
To keep squirrels from climbing feeder poles, we've used motor grease as a deterrent. It's messy, but effective.

—Gordon Price, Dayton, Ohio

Tricilla Berlin

Above, Rick and Nora Bowers/KAC Productions; left, Kathy Adams Clark/KAC Productions

Butterfly look-alikes take a little practice to identify.

By Tom Allen
Contributing Editor

Double Take

Butterfly identification is both easy and...not so easy. There are several butterflies out there that are simple to recognize immediately, like monarchs and swallowtails. But it also can be difficult because so many look alike!

In the past, I've often talked about mimics—butterflies that mimic the look and behavior of others as a form of protection. There are several flying flowers, however, that are simply hard to tell apart.

Luck Be a Lady

Two butterflies that often confuse us include the American lady and painted lady. They are closely related but feed on different host plants.

To separate these two species, you need to take a look at the undersides of their hind wings. The painted lady has five small eyespots along the outer margin, while the American lady has two large eyespots.

Fritillaries are another group that closely resemble one another. They fly at the same time of year, and all use violets or close relatives as host plants.

The great spangled, Aphrodite and Atlantis fritillaries all fly in similar areas. The best way to tell the differences among them is to look at the undersides of their hind wings. Atlantis fritillaries have a greenish cast, Aphrodites have a reddish cast, and great spangleds have a broad band near the outer crescents.

Other factors make it even harder to distinguish these species, but a good field guide with range maps will help you. They will include valuable information about your area fliers.

Confusing Cousins

Other groups of butterflies that we mistake for one another are the whites (above) and sulphurs. The cabbage white, an introduced species that is a pest to vegetable crops, is easy to confuse with its close cousin, the checkered white.

These two species usually feed on different

Kathy Adams Clark/KAC Productions

Rick and Nora Bowers/KAC Productions

Atlantis fritillary, Tom Allen; great spangled fritillaries, Bill Leaman/The Image Finders

Question mark — Rick and Nora Bowers/KAC Productions

Comma — David Liebman

host plants, and you can also separate them by the black markings on their wings. Cabbage white males have a single black spot in the center of their upper forewings, while the female has two black spots. In addition, they also often have a black patch at the tips of their forewings and a yellowish hue on their undersides.

Checkered whites, on the other hand, have several black or charcoal patches on the forewings. Also, they appear gray in color when flying.

Cabbage whites also closely resemble a couple of their woodland relatives, the mustard white and West Virginia white. And in the West, checkered whites are often confused with their cousins, the western white and Becker's white.

Uncovering Sulphurs

As for sulphurs, many species look alike, especially those found in the West. Three sulphurs found over much of the northern U.S. that are confusing include the clouded, orange and pink-edged sulphur.

Look for pink-edged sulphurs near blueberry patches, since this is their host plant. Clouded sulphurs feed on legumes and have a rapid flight.

Orange and clouded sulphurs are difficult to tell apart and often interbreed. But true individuals are yellow as clouded sulphurs, orange as orange sulphurs, and hybrids are somewhere in between. To further confuse matters, both species have a virtually identical white female form.

There are many more look-alike butterflies out there. Anglewings, such as the question mark and comma (pictured above), are often very difficult to tell apart. Some of the lesser fritillaries, like the meadow fritillary and silver-bordered fritillary, resemble one another as well.

Then there's the pearl crescent, northern crescent and silvery checkerspot that all look alike. Lastly, many hairstreak species and blues are similar in appearance. Only a trained eye can separate the banded and hickory hairstreaks!

For most of us, a little practice is all that's needed to identify the mysterious flying flowers that visit our gardens. But the best way to help you separate look-alikes in the field is a reliable field guide. Most good field guides use small arrows to clearly point out key characteristics between hard-to-identify butterflies.

So, get out there, and have fun discovering the beauties in your yard!

TAKE A CLOSE LOOK. Some butterflies are harder to tell apart than others, like the whites (opposite page), American and painted ladies (left), fritillaries (top right) and those in the anglewing family (above).

Water-Wise Gardening

Make conservation a priority in your garden.

By Melinda Myers
Contributing Editor

We all want to do the right thing for the environment, but this doesn't mean you have to sacrifice beauty in your garden. You can be a good steward of the Earth and still have a beautiful yard.

A few adjustments in your gardening habits can yield major results. For some, you only need to make minor adjustments to your current method, while others may need a bit more work. Either way, the effort will be worth it when you see the beautiful results in your garden.

Water is foremost on many gardeners' minds. Droughts, watering bans and the high cost of water have many concerned about our natural and cultivated landscape.

You can find solutions, though. No matter where you live, you might want to consider incorporating some of these water-wise gardening strategies.

Start by making the most of the rainfall you receive. Amend fast-draining soils with organic matter to help soils hold onto the water longer. Add about 2 to 4 inches of compost, peat moss, aged manure or coir (coconut husks) to the top 6 to 12 inches of soil. This will give you good-looking plants with less water.

Another easy way to conserve water is to capture rainfall and runoff from your roof in rain barrels and cisterns. This allows you to store water for later use. If you do a quick search on the Inter-

Mark Turner

Mark Turner

SAVE A RAINY DAY. Make water go further with tools like a rain barrel (top) and soaker hose (above). Then reduce your need for a watering can by mulching around plants.

5 Drought Busters

You can increase your yard's winged population and decrease your water bill with these five water-wise plants. Once established in the garden, they will easily adapt to dry conditions, requiring little to no supplemental water during the dry season.

1 Agastache (*Agastache* species)
Known as hummingbird plant, licorice mint, Mexican hyssop or anise hyssop, depending on the species. Trumpet-shaped flowers attract hummingbirds, sphinx moths and butterflies. Seed heads provide food for birds. Zones 5 to 11; blooms from summer to fall.

2 Butterfly weed (*Asclepias tuberosa*)
Flat-topped flower clusters are a nectar source for butterflies and hummingbirds. Includes milkweed, the caterpillar host plant for monarchs. Zones 3 to 9; flowers in summer.

3 Coreopsis (*Coreopsis* species)
Nectar-rich blooms appeal to butterflies, such as skippers, buckeyes and painted ladies. Seeds provide food for sparrows, chickadees, finches and other seed-eating birds. Zones 3 to 11; summer to fall blooms.

4 Salvia (*Salvia* species)
These annuals, biennials and perennials attract hummingbirds, butterflies and moths. Perennials are hardy in Zones 4 to 11, though it differs by variety; summer blooms.

5 Sedum (*Sedum* species)
Diverse group of succulents provide nectar for butterflies and, occasionally, hummingbirds. Late autumn to winter seed heads attract birds, including finches and chickadees. Zones 4 to 11; spring to autumn flowers, depending on species.

All photos to right RDA/GID

net or sift through garden catalogs, you'll see that there are lots of attractive possibilities. And many professional landscapers are now offering water-wise solutions that incorporate several water-saving strategies for home landscapes.

Select drought-tolerate plants best suited to your climate. Once you get them established, these plants will thrive with much less water. Yarrow, sedum and yuccas are just a few drought-tolerant plants commonly used in gardens. Also, consider incorporating plants that are native to your region.

Here's another great water-conservation idea—add a rain garden to your landscape. Strategically placed and specially designed, these gardens capture storm water as it runs off roofs, walks, drives and other hard surfaces.

The water in a rain garden filters through the soil and plant roots before recharging our ground water. Rain garden plants like marsh milkweed, Joe Pye weed and liatris are able to tolerate temporary flooding and drought. This is a good solution for those gardening in areas with periods of heavy rain and drought.

Overall, you should group plants together according to watering needs. You will waste less water and save time as you provide the right amount of water for each grouping of plants.

Mulching is another great basic rule. This conserves moisture, reduces weeds and improves the soil. A layer of woodchips, shredded bark, evergreen needles or shredded leaves can be attractive and functional around trees, shrubs, flowers and vegetables.

When you do need to water, do it in the morning so you lose less water to evaporation during the hot part of the day. Also use drip irrigation and soaker hoses to put water on the soil surface where you need it.

Try making a few adjustments this season to conserve water. After all, you'll yield beautiful results for yourself and the environment.

Northern harrier

All hawks have hooked beaks, short and strong round heads, strong feet, and curved talons.

Kathy Adams Clark/KAC Productions

Not all birds of prey have the word "hawk" in their name. Kites, eagles, osprey, falcons and the northern harrier (above) are all examples.

Common Birds of Prey Calls

Sharp-shinned hawk
—kik-kik-kik-kik

Cooper's hawk
—cack-cack-cack-cack

Great horned owl
—hoo, hoo-hoo, hoo, hoo

Screech-owl
—a tremulous, descending wail

Birds of Prey

Discover why so many people are fascinated with raptors.

By George Harrison
Contributing Editor

Roland Jordahl

Bill Leaman/Dembinsky Photo Associates

Owls' ears are located behind their facial disks, which work to gather and funnel sound. Some owls, like the great horned and screech, look like they have large ears on the top of their heads, but those are actually tufts. Snowy owls (left) don't have these tufts.

Birds of prey are amazing creatures. Many people, including me, are fascinated with these carnivores of the bird world.

All of these raptors—hawks, falcons, kites, eagles, owls and even shrikes—eat unlike any other birds. They use their beaks (not bills) to tear meat. Birds of prey tend to get a bad rap because they attack the songbirds at feeders, but I don't think that's any reason to write them off. They are really amazing birds and unique in their own way.

I remember the day I was watching my feeder when all the birds suddenly panicked and desperately searched for safe cover. At least two birds hit the big picture window closest to the feeders. One of those birds, a dark-eyed junco, knocked itself unconscious and fell into the snow.

The ambush worked. A sharp-shinned hawk glided down from above the patio, pounced on the junco and carried it back to its perch to enjoy its meal.

Cruel? Perhaps in human terms, but in nature's terms, it was just another meal for this raptor.

Watch You Like a Hawk

Two of the most common backyard raptors across the country are the sharp-shinned hawk and its slightly larger look-alike, the Cooper's hawk. Hawks, though mainly diurnal, can see objects three times farther away than humans can, thus the term "hawk-eye."

Owls have equally exceptional eyesight. At night, great horned and screech-owls take over the feeder watch in search of sleeping birds and active small mammals.

Their eyes have full binocular capability and are oversized in relation to the bird's body. The eyeballs of a 2-foot owl, for example, are as large as the eyeballs of a 6-foot man. In addition, they can rotate their heads an extraordinary 270 degrees, which covers a wide field of vision.

Go Where the Food Is

Most birds of prey move seasonally in search of food. Snowy and great grey owls are good examples. If their main source of food—lemmings, mice, rabbits and squirrels—is scarce during a particular winter, these big birds will move south into golf courses, farm fields and anywhere else to find food.

One well-known wintering site for snowy owls is Boston's Logan Airport.

"The owls go about their lives at the airport much as they would in the barren expanses of their home in Greenland and northern Canada," says Norman Smith of the Massachusetts Audubon Society, who banded 36 of the owls at Logan a few years ago.

Though many people who have feeders in their yards do not like birds of prey, they are spectacular creatures with exceptional survival tools. They are an important part of the ecosystem that we ought to admire. I know I certainly do.

Rob & Nora Bowers/The Image Finders

Eagles are actually large hawks. Their name comes from their large size. While old folktales claim eagles have carried away children, this would be physically impossible.

Richard Day/Daybreak Imagery

The Circle of Butterfly Life

Not all flying flowers follow the same path from egg to butterfly.

By Tom Allen
Contributing Editor

Most people are probably familiar with the basic life cycle of a butterfly. The female lays an egg. The egg hatches into a caterpillar. The caterpillar forms a chrysalis. Then the adult butterfly emerges.

So, do all butterflies follow this same sequence? Simply put, yes. Not all butterflies follow the same pattern in a timely fashion, however. This is the reason we see different species of butterflies at different times of the year.

Of course, there are exceptions to every rule, but in general, the average time period for a butterfly to develop from an egg to adult is about 4 to 5 weeks. Variables that could influence this include climate changes and host plant availability. Rain, unusual temperatures or lack of plants can all make a butterfly dormant, slowing down the process along the way.

The Right Moment

Butterflies living in areas where the climate is warm year-round often feed on a variety of host plants. Therefore, they generally develop straight through from egg to adult.

In these areas, species often produce several broods each year. But, in arid regions, where rainfall is sporadic or almost nonexistent, the life cycle of some butterflies may be interrupted for several years. Then, once the rainfall does come, a species can have several broods in a single season.

These species generally remain in the chrysalis stage until rains bring new plant life to the region. Then they emerge, mate and lay their eggs for the next generation. Black checkerspots are good examples of this behavior.

Butterflies that depend upon specific host plants in a certain stage of growth typically produce one brood per year. Hairstreaks, for example, feed on the buds or flowers of their host plant and time their development to coincide with the flowering of plants.

These butterflies remain in the chrysalis stage for several months each year until the next blooming cycle of the host. Henry's elfin is a good example of this behavior because they feed on the flowers of redbud trees.

Checkerspots, a group of Nymphalids, often split caterpillar development between years. Their cycle begins with females laying eggs on a specific host. When the caterpillars are partially grown, they diapause (or hibernate) for the remaining summer and through fall and winter.

The following spring, they complete their feeding as caterpillars, often on different hosts. Then they pupate and emerge as butterflies in time to lay their eggs on the primary host.

Unfavorable Conditions

Most butterflies have to go through some sort of dormant period in order to take advantage of varying conditions. For some, such as the mourning cloak, this means hibernating as adults. Other butterflies, like the monarch, migrate to more favorable climates.

These aren't options for most butterflies, though, so they must find other means to avoid unfavorable conditions. I already mentioned some of those, but there is yet another group that finds hibernating in the egg stage or newly hatched caterpillar stage the best option.

European skippers hibernate as eggs over winter until early spring when the caterpillars can feed on the young sprouts of their favorite grasses.

Fritillaries hibernate as unfed, newly hatched caterpillars in order to take advantage of the new violet leaves pushing up in the first warm days of spring. This process is vital for them. Otherwise, the old leaves of violet plants would poison young caterpillars if they tried to eat them in fall.

Over the years, butterflies have adapted their development cycles to coincide with the growth stages of their host plants. This isn't always easy, especially in extreme climates or years with unusual weather. But butterflies' survival depends on it.

So the next time you see a caterpillar, butterfly or chrysalis, remember that there's a lot that goes into their life cycle. It could take weeks, months or even more to complete!

WINTER COVER. European skippers (below) hibernate as eggs. Henry's elfins (top right) spend winter in the chrysalis. Fritillaries (top left) hibernate as young, unfed caterpillars.

Rick and Nora Bowers/KAC Productions

Rick and Nora Bowers/KAC Productions

Weathering the Weather

RAIN BRINGS LIFE. Species living in dry regions, like this black checkerspot (right), must wait for rain to bring new vegetation to the area before they can complete development. During times of drought, these butterflies remain in the chrysalis stage (1) before emerging as adults (2), laying their eggs (3) and hatching into caterpillars (4).

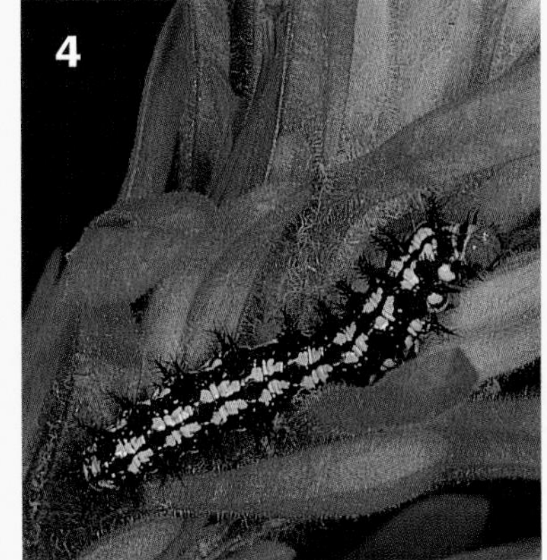

Four black checkerspot photos by Rick and Nora Bowers/KAC Productions

Donna and Tom Krischan

Raised Gardening

Take your plants to new heights with one simple secret.

By Melinda Myers
Contributing Editor

With the fresh start of spring, you might want to consider starting a new trend in your garden. Raising your garden beds even a few inches will help improve soil drainage and speed soil warming. Plus, you don't have to worry about keeping feet—large or small—from tromping your plants' roots.

Keep It Small

Before you start building a raised bed, take the time to develop a plan.

First, make sure it's easy to reach all parts of your raised garden. Most freestanding beds are no more than two arm reaches wide and as long as you like. This allows you to reach into the middle of the garden from either side.

Make sure you can maintain the area around the beds, too. Though straight edges and flat bed sides aren't as interesting as stone and curves, they are a lot easier to mow around. It helps to keep curved edges gentle.

Many vegetable gardeners make raised beds within their garden. To do this, simply rake the soil into 4- to 6-inch-high beds surrounded by lower pathways. I find this helps when growing onions, carrots and other root crops in heavy clay or poorly drained soil. Other vegetables and flowers will also benefit from improved drainage.

If you're looking to create a decorative as well as functional raised bed, then you might want to consider long-lasting timbers, plastic lumber, fieldstone or interlocking blocks. Select the material that complements your landscape and meets your needs.

First Aid for Sore Backs

An added benefit of using these types of long-lasting materials is that they allow you to raise

Alice M. Prescott/Unicorn Stock Photos

Richard Day/Daybreak Imagery

LOFTY EXPECTATIONS. Raised beds have many advantages, from providing better soil drainage to easing sore backs. Just pick the size and materials that make sense for you, from timber (left) to stone and concrete (above photos).

Take It Up a Notch

Frederick Ryan of Schenectady, New York has a small yard, only 50 by 75 feet. That doesn't give him a lot of room to garden. But he found a great solution—raised beds. He has built 18 wooden planters himself throughout the years he's been gardening.

Most notable are his V-shaped planters (above left). He designed them himself. They're one of his most eye-catching creations.

"I wanted them to look like they were balancing on each end," he says.

Frederick prefers planting hostas, but almost all of your favorite flowers and vegetables will easily grow in raised beds.

your garden several feet high or more. This is especially helpful for people with bad knees or backs.

Design the raised bed so the plants' roots have plenty of room to grow. You can add to the existing root zone by building your raised bed on good gardening soil. This allows water and plant roots to move through the raised bed into the soil below.

You can also create a free-standing raised bed that is contained by providing drain tiles or gravel at the base, a layer of landscape fabric and then at least 12 inches of soil to top it all off.

Once you build your raised bed, you need to fill it with a good soil. Mix quality topsoil with compost, peat moss or coir (coconut waste by-product).

Another option is to purchase a planting mix that drains well, yet holds moisture for better root development.

However, avoid adding sand that either creates concrete or excessive drainage when improper amounts are used. Reserve vermiculite, perlite and similar drainage materials for containers and square-foot gardens. Otherwise, they break down and lose their benefits when you walk on or work the soil.

With all raised beds, you want to crown it so the center is higher than the edges. Then wait a week for the soil to settle before you start planting anything.

Planting Time

Once the raised bed is ready, fill your garden with your favorite flowers, herbs and vegetables. You can also plant trees and shrubs in larger beds if there's sufficient soil for root development and enough insulation from extreme temperatures.

Don't forget to adjust watering and care to accommodate your raised garden bed. As the growing season progresses, you'll see that all your hard work, planning and planting will pay off with beautiful and healthy plants. Plus, you'll get the satisfaction of knowing you created it yourself!

Glad You Asked!

Best Butterfly Questions 2009

Tom Allen shares his butterfly know-how.

Lauri Mazigian

Many Happy Returns

Is Pacific Grove, California the only place that hosts overwintering butterflies? Where else can you find butterflies in winter, aside from butterfly houses? And when do monarchs (like the one at left) return from their wintering grounds?

—*Sue Strysick, Farmington, Minnesota*

Tom: Actually, there are about 25 sites along the California coastline where monarchs from the regions west of the Rocky Mountains gather for the winter months. Those populations east of the Rockies fly south, many crossing the Gulf of Mexico into the Sierra-Madres of central Mexico. With this migration, some fly more than 3,000 miles.

In Mexico, the monarchs winter in roughly 12 small, 7-1/2-acre locations. They gather by the millions where the near-constant temperatures protect them during the winter.

In early March, monarchs begin their migration north. Once they cross back into the United States, they will mate and begin to lay their eggs. It is the offspring of these butterflies that will repopulate northern habitats.

Most butterflies that migrate move north in spring as the weather warms. These species build their populations in the south and then move north with the advancing spring temperatures. In southern, warmer regions of the country, butterflies are active throughout the year.

Endangered Mystery

We live in northeastern New York and have heard that there's a butterfly in the area that is an endangered species. All we know is that it's blue. Can you give us more information?

—*Ed and Mary Benson, Ballston Spa, New York*

Tom: You are referring to the Karner Blue (*Lycaeides melissa samuelis*). This butterfly originally earned the name for its type locality at Karner, New York, near Albany.

You can find this butterfly in sandy oak and pine habitats where its host plant, lupine, grows. The species' range in the state extends in small populations throughout the sand belt in the Hudson Valley. You can also find them from the Albany Pine Bush north to the Glens Falls area. In New York, the most intact population probably occurs in Saratoga County.

Northwestern Indiana, Wisconsin, Michigan, Minnesota and New Hampshire have similar habitats. Fire is a very important tool in keeping those sandy habitats in an open condition so that the lupines can grow. Human activities have been responsible for the decline of the Karner Blue. Urbanization and reduction of fires has led to a loss of habitat.

Mystery Moth

I can't find anyone who can tell me what this moth (below right) is. Can you help?

—*Linda Francis, Providence, Texas*

Tom: This is one of the members of the hawk moth family, and people also know it as the banded sphinx. This tropical species flies across the southern U.S. from Florida to Arkansas and Texas.

The caterpillars, which often reach sizes of 4 inches or more, feed on such plants as primrose-willow and other evening primroses. This moth has a northern cousin called the pandorus sphinx. They resemble each other quite a bit, except the pandorus lacks the cross bars on its wings. The pandorus sphinx feeds on grapes and Virginia creeper instead of primroses.

Marcia Flanagan

Orange Accessories

I found this flier (above) in my garden on my Orchid Frost lamium. I love its fuzzy orange legs. Can you tell me what it is?

—Helen Grumbein, Annville, Pennsylvania

Tom: Very nice photo! This is the eight-spotted forester moth, found over most of the eastern United States. You can often spot them along woodland edges, or in yards where Virginia creeper or grapes grow.

The caterpillar of this species is quite attractive. They're white with many black cross bands and spots, and they also have an orange cross band at each segment. Their heads and tails are also orange.

Rub-a-Dub-Dub

My daughter and I were out taking photos of wildflowers and butterflies when we came upon this unusual flier (above). It would rub its wings together, so that at first glance it looked like two butterflies. Can you tell me more about it?

—Donna Richardson, Creola, Alabama

Tom: This is the great purple hairstreak. There must have been mistletoe growing on a tree nearby, as it is the host plant for this butterfly.

Hairstreaks are unique butterflies. If you take a close look, you'll see that these beauties rub the rear portion of their wings together a lot more than the front.

By rubbing their rear wings together, they attract attention to the rear of their bodies. They have two, and sometimes four, small, feather-like tails on their rear wings, which look like antennae to a predator. Hairstreaks often also have bright-red, orange or blue spots at the rear as well. These resemble eyes.

A bird trying to catch this butterfly will attack the moving rear, mistaking it for the head. Even if the bird takes a snip out of the wings, the butterfly is able to escape, virtually unharmed.

Searching for Sugar Water

I had a butterfly come to my hummingbird feeder for several days. I think it was drinking the sugar water. Is there a way I can offer nectar for butterflies?

—Carol Landaal, Waupun, Wisconsin

Tom: Some butterflies will visit hummingbird feeders for sugar water, especially red-spotted purples.

There are butterfly feeders available for purchase. Most of the butterfly feeders found in stores are made to be hung in a tree or placed on a post in your butterfly garden. Some of the feeders even have a platform where you can put a banana or other fruit for the butterflies as well.

You can find specific nectar for butterflies in some stores as well. You can also make your own sugar water by mixing 1 part sugar to 10 parts water. If you do this, add a little pinch of vitamins, too.

Glad You Asked! Best Gardening Questions 2009

Melinda Myers offers remedies for common garden problems.

Sprouting Ferns

In late spring, these tall plants (left) come up in our patio bed. At first there were three or four, and now there are 10.

The branches almost look like ferns. Can you tell me more about them?

—Jeannie Moore, Germantown, Tennessee

Melinda: People will often grow this fine-textured plant for its foliage, which turns brilliant red in fall.

Farmers in dry regions also use this as a drought-tolerant forage crop. Kochia (*Bassia scoparia*) is a fast-growing annual that easily reseeds itself. Because of this, some people consider it a weed.

This plant tolerates full sun and dry conditions. It matures into a 1- to 5-foot cone-shaped plant. Variegated and more compact varieties are also available for ornamental plantings.

Looking for the Same Results

My neighbor has the most beautiful deep-purple lilacs I've seen. How can I get a cutting of it to root?

—Judith Cicierega, Bridgewater, Massachusetts

Melinda: Timing is critical when starting woody plants from cuttings. This is especially true with lilacs. Take 4- to 6-inch cuttings just before the end leaves reach full size. Dip the cut end in a rooting hormone, which you can purchase at most garden centers. These products contain hormones that encourage rooting, as well as fungicides to discourage rot.

Stick the cuttings in a container filled with sand or a well-drained potting mix. Mist frequently or loosely cover with plastic. Be patient and don't be discouraged as lilacs are one of the more difficult shrubs to root.

Persistant Yuccas

I want to get rid of the yuccas in my yard. We've been here 10 years and no matter what we do to get rid of them, they always come back more lush. Any ideas on how we can tame them?

—Judith Browne, Plymouth, Massachusetts

Melinda: I seldom hear Northern gardeners complain about yuccas becoming a weed. Most people enjoy yuccas (like the one at right) because they are easy to grow and a drought-tolerant plant. You must have the perfect growing conditions and green thumb.

Cut existing plants back to the ground and cover the area with cardboard or newspaper and leaves or woodchips to kill the plants and prevent the yucca seeds from germinating. If the problem is more scattered, you may want to kill the existing plants and mulch the soil around your other garden plants to reduce seed sprouting.

Environmentally friendly plant killers contain fatty acids, vinegar or citric acid that burns the leaves of plants. You will need to repeat applications if you want to kill established plants, roots and all. Or you could try painting Roundup, Finale or other total vegetation killers on the leaves of the yucca plants. These chemicals kill the tops and roots of plants they touch. Be sure to read and follow all label directions carefully.

Tree Trouble

My maple has small, white and fuzzy-looking insects all over the leaves and on the branches. They are about the size of mosquitoes. There also are small black spots on the leaves. What's happening, and what can I do to save my tree?

—Donald Phelps, Barryton, Michigan

Melinda: No need to worry about these pests as long as your tree is otherwise healthy. The white fuzzy things are woolly aphids. These insects suck the plant juices from the leaves of your trees and secrete a clear, sticky substance called honeydew.

Lady beetles, lace wings and other natural predators will usually keep these aphids under control. A heavy rain or strong blast of water from the garden hose will knock many of the aphids off the tree.

The black spots could be sooty mold, a fungus that feeds on the honeydew. If the black bumps look like someone spilled tar on the leaves, the problem is tar spot. Neither fungal disease threatens the tree's health. Rake and destroy fallen leaves to reduce the source of tar spot next season.

String It Together

I received this cascading plant (below) from a friend. To me, it resembles a string of peas, but I can't find its name. Can you help?

—Inge Marks, Peabody, Massachusetts

Melinda: Often called string of pearls (*Senecio rowleyanus*), you'll find this old-fashioned plant growing on windowsills or cascading over the edges of shelves.

As a native of southwestern Africa, this plant has adapted to survive droughty conditions, though it prefers full sun and well-drained soil.

To care for this plant properly, water it thoroughly when the top few inches of soil are dry. In winter, you only need to water it enough to keep the leaves from shriveling. When the plant matures, there's a chance it will reward you with small, white flowers.

Aggressive Plants

I have garden phlox (right) and gooseneck loostrife growing in my perennial garden, and they're starting to take over the beds. I keep digging them up to no avail. What should I do to keep them under control?

—Madeleine Hadrian
Amherstburg, Ontario

Melinda: The best thing you can do is to regularly deadhead these plants to prevent reseeding and new seedlings from growing in the garden. This usually is enough to keep garden phlox contained.

The loosestrife, which also spreads by rhizomes, will probably need a bit more control. Divide these plants yearly to keep them in bounds. Or grow them in a location where they have plenty of room to grow or are contained by sidewalks, walls or other barriers.

In the meantime, invite a few gardening friends to share in the bounty. Be sure to let them know the secrets to controlling these vigorous garden beauties.

Double the Beauty

It was a real treat to see my gerbera daisies produce this Siamese bloom (right) in my flower bed. How common is this, and does it happen more in certain types of flowers?

—Brandi Wotring, Bay City, Michigan

Melinda: Your two-headed gerbera daisy is the result of fasciation. This physiological disorder (which simply is a change in plant growth) causes flattening of stems, proliferation of buds and blooms, and two-headed flowers like you found on your daisies.

This result is just the plant's response to the environment. It certainly grabs your eye in the garden.

In fact, so many people appreciate this type of growth that plant breeders have deliberately propagated fascinated plants to sell. Some of the propagated varieties that have come from fasciations in plants include fan tail willow and crested celosia.

Enjoy the show. While it's not necessarily rare, it is a unique treat in the garden.

Glad You Asked!

Best Birding Questions 2009

George Harrison answers some of your toughest birding questions.

Messy House

We've lived here for more than 20 years, and we've put up a lot of birdhouses. This one (left) truly baffles us. What kind of bird builds a nest like this?

—Marlene Cardenas, Vermontville, Michigan

George: Indeed, there is no room for a bird to enter this house. This leads me to think that this was the intention—the animal responsible for this likely stuffed the entrance to keep others away.

Wrens will often build "dummy" nests to keep other wrens from building nests in their territories, but this does not look like the work of a wren. It's more likely the work of house sparrow that intends to create a globe of trash for nesting. It could also be a European starling that wants to keep other birds from nesting inside.

If none of those birds are the perpetrator, then it's probably another animal altogether. For example, a mouse could have filled the birdhouse with nesting material, and this is the overflow.

Sit-in Without a Cause

This American robin (left) was sitting on this nest, but there were no eggs in it. Can you tell me why was it doing this?

—Debra Dunlop, Stittsville, Ontario

George: American robins can often be strange when it comes to nesting. My guess is that the bird in your photograph was shaping the nest and getting used to sitting on it before she laid the eggs.

Some robins are very indecisive about where to build a nest. I've heard of one robin that built 13 nests before finally deciding on one to lay her eggs.

Cruising Buddies

While on a cruise off the coast of Florida in October, we were treated to a pair of birds landing outside the ship. I think they were some kind of raptor. I snapped this picture (above) of one of the birds. Can you tell me what it is?

—Joan Jernegan, Bothell, Washington

George: The birds you watched on your cruise are juvenile peregrine falcons, natives to many countries. The fact that your cruise was during October suggests that the birds were migrating, which often takes them well out to sea. These long-distance migrants were using your ship as a resting station.

Peregrines were threatened from the 1940s to 1970s by concentrations of pesticides, which caused them to have reproduction failures. Peregrines are considered the fastest birds in the world, diving on prey birds at speeds approaching 200 mph. How fortunate you were to view these very special birds at such close range!

Missing Color

This bird (right) flew into our window. I noticed it has unusual coloring. Can you explain?

—Karen Whightsil, Topeka, Kansas

George: The bird is an adult American robin, probably a male. The unusual white markings on its face and body are due to a lack of pigment in those feathers, which people also refer to as partial albinism.

If the robin were a total albino, it would be all white with pink eyes, bill, legs and feet. Partial albinos are much more common than albinos, and occur frequently in American robins.

Too Hot for Comfort

Summers heat up quickly here, and sometimes the water in my birdbaths gets really hot by the afternoon. I change the water twice a day. Does the hot water hurt the birds if they bathe or drink it?

—Maria Bostwick, Sparks, Nevada

George: I would not worry about the temperature of the birdbath water. Birds are not harmed by drinking or bathing in warm water, and they know enough not to drink or bathe in water that will burn them.

It is good to replace the water on really hot days. Also, placing the birdbath in the shade will help keep the water cool.

Unwelcome Song

We have a northern mockingbird that comes to our yard and sings day and night. We love its song, but not at 2 a.m. What can we do?

—Ronda Patterson, Warrenton, Virginia

George: I had the exact same problem with a male northern mockingbird singing at 2 a.m. one bright, moonlit night in Richmond, Virginia. After throwing a shoe in its direction to flush it, I decided that ear plugs were a better solution. Of course, closing the door and windows and cranking up the air-conditioning or fan would help, too.

Dining Preference

We tried to attract hummingbirds for several years, but never succeeded. Finally, we switched from a glass and metal feeder to a plastic one. That did it! Can you explain this?

—Nan Cavalier, Vernon, Pennsylvania

George: It just sounds like the hummingbirds preferred to feed from the plastic feeders. Perhaps it's because the plastic feeders were red-colored, and the metal and glass one was not. It's difficult to say for sure, but stick with what works. If the plastic feeder works, then keep using it.

Banish the Blackbirds

I have a large number of cardinals that visit my bird feeders in winter. Problem is, I also have a large number of blackbirds. How do I keep them away?

—Sharon Conley, Joppa, Illinois

George: If you are selective about what you feed the cardinals, you can eliminate the blackbirds. For example, cardinals love safflower seeds, but blackbirds do not.

Also, blackbirds are less likely to eat sunflower seeds in the shell, which requires cracking to get to the meats. Finally, blackbirds are more seasonal than cardinals. From my experience, my cardinals stay in my backyard year-round, but the blackbirds come and go.

Overall, use a different seed, and don't give up. Hopefully, the blackbirds will soon let the cardinals eat in peace.

Bizarre Bill

The first time we saw this chickadee (right), we thought it had a seed stuck to its bill. Then we realized that it wasn't a seed. Can you explain this?

—David and Donna Langley
Orange, Texas

George: The chickadee in the picture has a deformed bill. It may have injured it while the bill was growing when the bird was a nestling. Or it may have just grown that way due to a genetic problem.

Apparently, the bird is able to eat, crack seeds and drink. Otherwise, it would not have survived long enough to become an adult. It is one of those amazing adaptations in nature

234

228

240

Chapter 9

The Best of Birds & Blooms Bonus

Photos: cabin bird feeder, Krivit Photography; patio garden, George Harrison; hand pruner, RDA INC./GID; ladybug bowling balls, Jim Wieland/RP Photo; rudbeckia, Jim Wieland/RP Photo; caterpillar, Nancy Rotenberg; cleome, RDA/GID.

Dinner's served at this cozy cabin

Birds flock to this easy-to-build woodsy feeder!

By Eric Smith, St. Paul, Minnesota

Pretend you're a chickadee or a white-breasted nuthatch (or even a humble house sparrow), tiredly flapping your little wings through the trees in search of food. Which is more appealing: a hurried bite at one of those bland industrial plastic tubes, or a relaxed meal with friends at an inviting thatch-roofed cabin?

Here's my idea of that cozy place for our feathered friends to stop and munch.

SHOPPING LIST

- One 2x4 x 4' cedar (or pine)
- One 1x6 x 4' cedar (or pine)
- 1/16" acrylic (cut to size at home center or hardware store)
- 1 lb. 2-1/2" rust-resistant screws
- 1 lb. 4d galv. casing nails
- 12 #6 x 1/2" pan-head screws
- Cut roof thatch from two brooms (old ones are fine), or try hay, twigs, reeds or similar material.

CUTTING LIST

Item	Quantity
1-1/2" x 3-1/2" x 16" sides	2
3/4" x 5-1/2" x 8-1/2" roof (A)	1
3/4" x 4-3/4" x 8-1/2" roof (B)	1
3/4" x 3-1/2" x 9-1/2" feeder tray	1
3/4" x 1-1/2" x 3-1/2" top brace	1
5" x 10" x 1/16" acrylic	2
1-1/2"- to 2-1/2"-dia. x 8-3/4" branches cut lengthwise and mitered for roof edge	4
1-1/2"- to 2"-dia. x 3" branches cut lengthwise for sides of feeder tray	4
1-1/2"- to 2"-dia. x 5" branches cut lengthwise for front of feeder tray	2
1/4"- to 1/2"-dia. x 8-1/2" twigs to hold thatch on roof	4

1 Cut the sides of the feeder from a 2x4 and the roof, top brace and feeder tray from a 1x6. Attach with 2-1/2-inch rust-resistant screws and exterior glue. Don't attach the roof to the sides—it slides up hanger wire so seeds can be poured into the bin from the top.

2 Rip a 1-1/2- to 2-1/2-inch branch in half with a jig- saw, miter the ends, then attach to the roof edges with 2-1/2-inch screws. Predrill all screw holes, and don't worry if the cuts are rough and uneven—they're supposed to be. The branches should be more or less flush with the bottom edge of the roof boards.

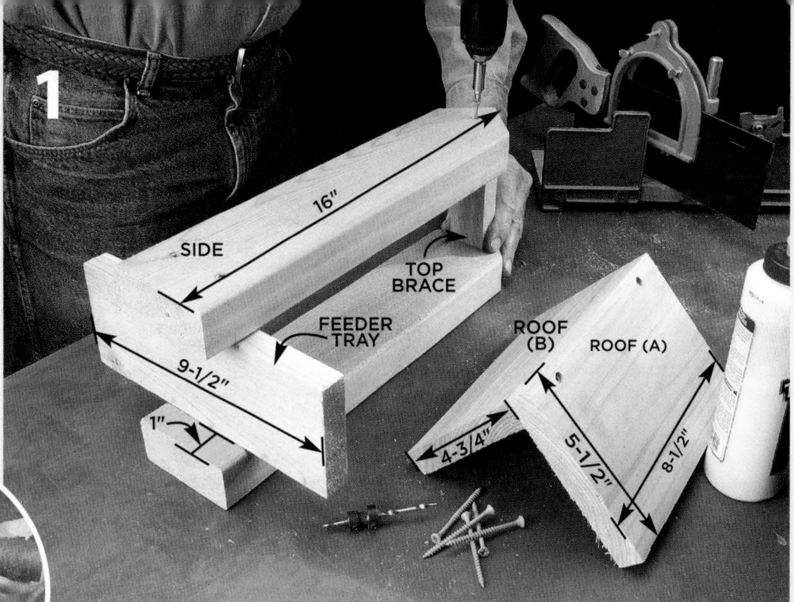

3 Tape the thatch from brooms to hold it together, then cut it 7-1/2 inches long with a sharp knife. Arrange the thatch on the roof and nail two green twigs to each side to hold it in place. The feeder makes a convenient brace (right inset). Trim ragged edges with scissors after the thatch is nailed down.

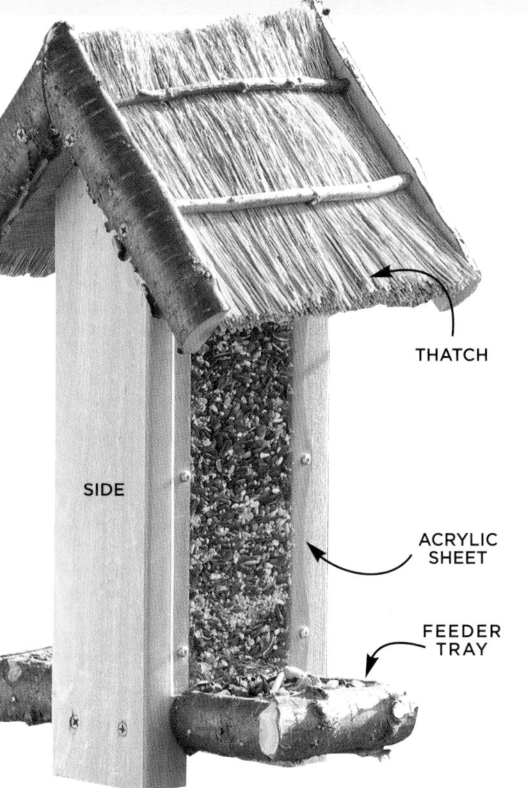

4 Drill three screw holes slightly bigger (5/32 inch or more) than the screw size through each side of the acrylic. Attach each piece of acrylic with six pan-head screws, but don't overtighten, or it might crack. Leave a 1/2-inch gap at the bottom for the bird feed to flow out. Screw or nail on half branches around the perimeter of the feeder tray to keep the feed in place. Finally, drill a hole at the center of the roof and the top brace, and slip wire or rope through for the hanger.

Container Recipes

Readers share their most successful combinations for container planting.

Shopping list:

- A Yellow marigolds (3)
- B Dusty miller (3)
- C Pink portulaca (3)
- D Dahlias (4, mixed colors)
- E Spike (1)
- F Vinca vine (2)

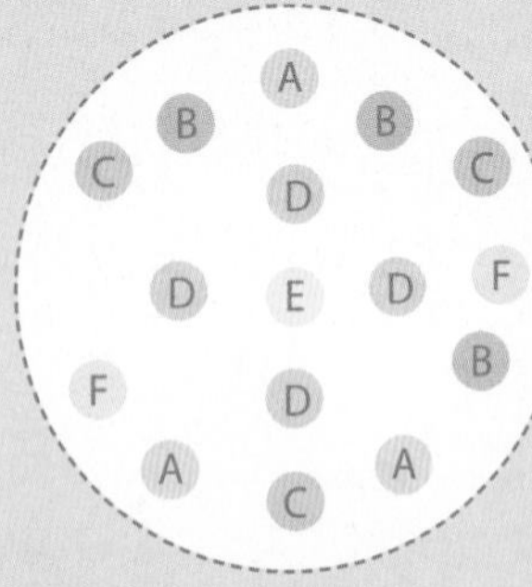

Pot with Pizzazz

This container is sure to be the talk of your patio or deck this season. The plants are easy to find, and you can mix and match the dahlias to suit your color palette.

Diane Augustus of Ellington, Connecticut created this beautiful combination in early May, and it bloomed throughout the season. "I like this combination because it's low-maintenance. Just use a regular potting soil mix and add fertilizer. I use slow-release granules," says Diane.

Why it works: The spike in the center of the arrangement creates a focal point. The rest of the plants fill in fast, so you get brilliant color without the wait. Cheery spring colors like pink and yellow complement each other, while dusty miller and vinca vine fill in the gaps.

Planter size: 18-in.-diameter pot
Growing conditions: Full sun

Simple Summer Pleasures

There are a lot of different textures in this combination by Patricia Sutherland of Apple Valley, Minnesota. The fountain grass and sedge are perfect accents to the flowers.

"This pot really dressed up my backyard this season," says Patricia. "The purple-hued Persian shield, surrounded by shades of pink and lime green, takes center stage."

Why it works: These colorful plants are perfect container partners because they are both tough and low-maintenance.

Planter size: 16-in.-diameter pot
Growing conditions: Full sun

Shopping list:

- A Purple fountain grass (1)
- B 'Life Lime' coleus (1)
- C Persian shield (1)
- D Purple geranium (2)
- E Pink petunia (1)
- F 'Evergold' sedge (1)
- G Alyssum (1)
- H Cosmos (1)

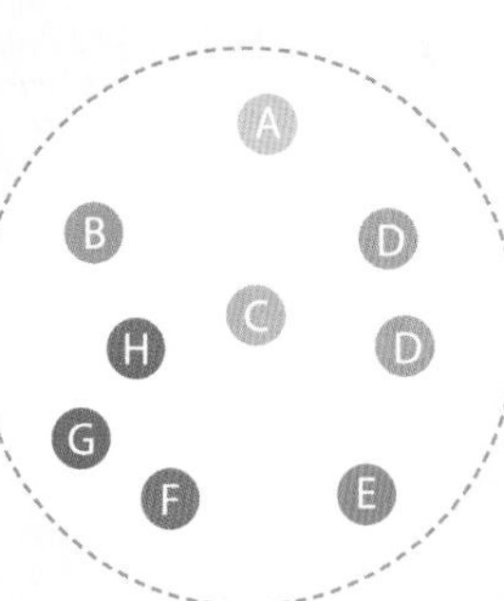

Tropical Twist

"This is my favorite container combination," says Michelle Van Heuvelen of Ocheyedan, Iowa. "I love its tropical feel and how all of the plants blend so beautifully together.

"To give it an impressive presence in my garden, I chose a 36-inch-tall container. It really shows off the plants' vibrant colors and different types of leaves," adds Michelle. "Plus, since it's mostly foliage plants, there is little need for deadheading or for maintenance other than watering."

Why it works: Containers featuring foliage are gaining popularity. These types of plants are perfect for low-maintenance options for colorful containers. This one works because it features a variety of colors and textures. The tall canna provides height and a tropical touch, while the other plants are perfect for filling in and trailing over the side of the planter.

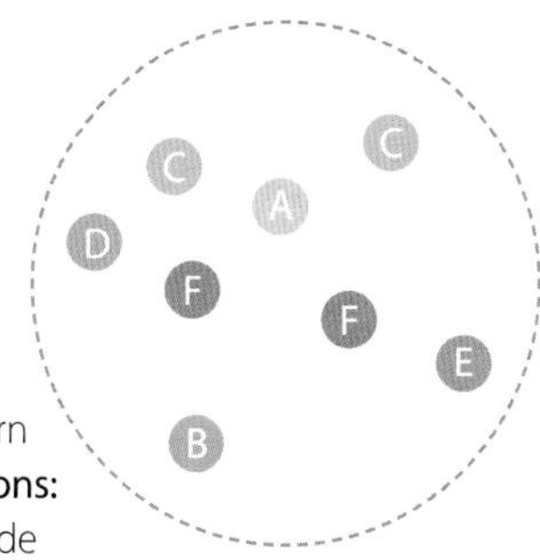

Planter size: 18-in.-diameter urn
Growing conditions: Sun to partial shade

Shopping list:
- A Canna 'Pretoria' (1)
- B Lysimachia 'Goldilocks' (1)
- C Coleus 'Gay's Delight' (2)
- D Ipomoea 'Blackie' (1)
- E Ipomoea 'Sweet Caroline Bronze' (1)
- F Variegated pelargonium (2)

Autumnal Bliss

The warm colors of this container line Gladys Fell's driveway in West Chester, Pennsylvania. Its orange and crimson hues make for a perfect fall display.

"People always remark on the unusual plant combination and different textures in this container," says Gladys.

Why it works: Gladys combined a variety of container-friendly plants. The vertical element of the hibiscus adds height, while the coleus, sweet potato vine and flowering maple fill out the center of this pretty container.

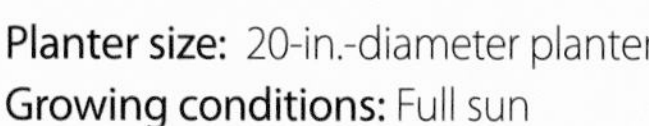

Planter size: 20-in.-diameter planter
Growing conditions: Full sun

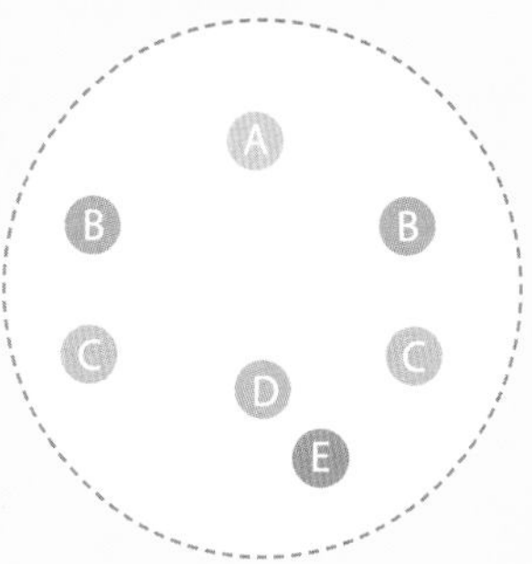

Shopping list:
- A 'Maple Sugar' hibiscus (1)
- B 'Blackie' sweet potato vine (2)
- C 'Copper Queen' coleus (2)
- D Orange flowering maple (1)
- E English ivy (1)

Butterflies Welcome

Living in the suburbs has many advantages, but one major disadvantage for Damien Anne Siegle of Indianapolis, Indiana, is that she rarely sees wildlife in her backyard.

"I love butterflies," says Damien. "But I've had to work to attract them. Creating a container like this invites butterflies to my yard, while the shelter that my other plants and shrubs provide keeps them here. They must like the colors in this container, as I have several fluttering about. I've even noticed a praying mantis lingering among the marigolds."

Why it works: Marigolds typically don't create vertical interest in a container, but they tower above the other plants in this colorful combination. Penta, lantana and snapdragon fill out the rest of the pot. A piece of whimsical garden art, like the decorative wire-bound glass ball shown, effortlessly helps to dress up any container.

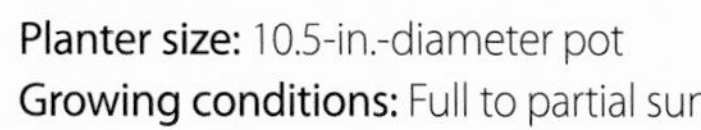

Planter size: 10.5-in.-diameter pot
Growing conditions: Full to partial sun

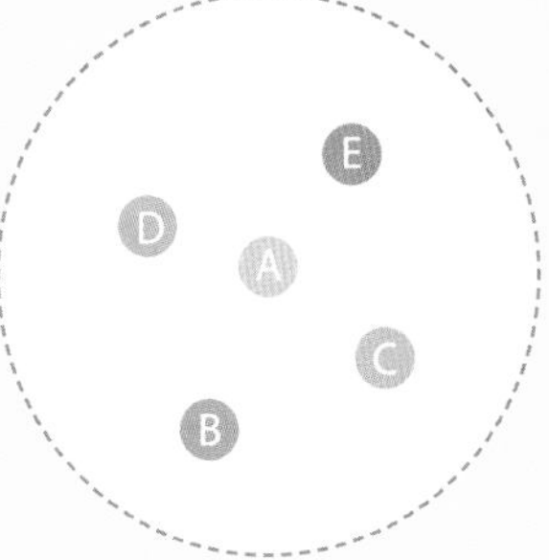

Shopping list:
- A White marigold (1)
- B Yellow lantana (1)
- C Pink penta (1)
- D White penta (1)
- E Burgundy snapdragon (1)

Serene Scene

Shopping list:

- A Apricot Iceland poppy (3)
- B Peach trumpet daffodil (4)
- C Dusty miller (3)
- D White daisy (3)
- E Trailing ivy (1)

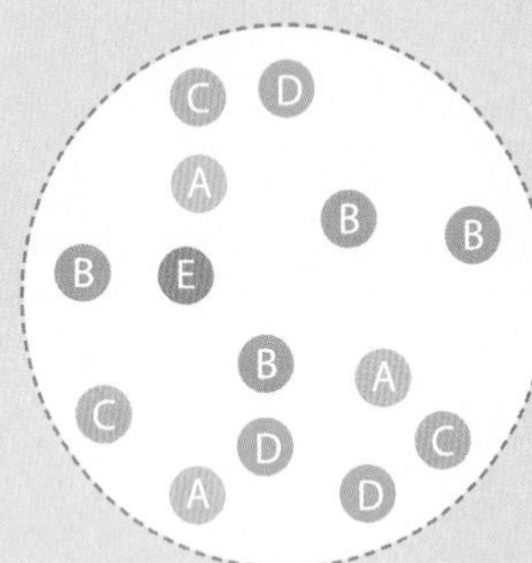

The pale, subtle beauty of this spring container came as a surprise to Eileen Gieser of Lakeport, California. That's because the white daffodils with peach-colored trumpets, pictured here, were sent to her by mistake. But the faux pas worked to her advantage as they became the focus of this enchanting combination.

"The flowers look especially elegant with the iron trellis in the background," Eileen says. "The pale, apricot-hued Iceland poppies complement the peach trumpet daffodils perfectly."

Why it works: Not only is this container combination fresh and calming, it's easy to care for, too! All the plants have sparse water demands. And when the daffodils, daisies and poppies have finished blooming for the season, the display is still gorgeous as the silver foliage steals the show in summer.

Planter size: 22-in.-wide planter
Growing conditions: Full sun

Out of the Shadows

Patty Sutherland of Apple Valley, Minnesota wanted a soothing color combination for her woodland garden. "The soft coral colors of this container really stand out against the coleus," she says.

Why it works: Bright color that survives in the shade is hard to find. Patty used impatiens, which grow well in containers and is a sure thing for spicing up an otherwise dark area.

Planter size: 18-in.-diameter pot
Growing conditions: Shade to partial sun

Shopping list:

- A Life Line coleus (1)
- B Dragonwing begonia (2)
- C Double impatiens (2)
- D New Guinea impatiens (1)
- E Golden moneywort (2)
- F Freckles coleus (1)

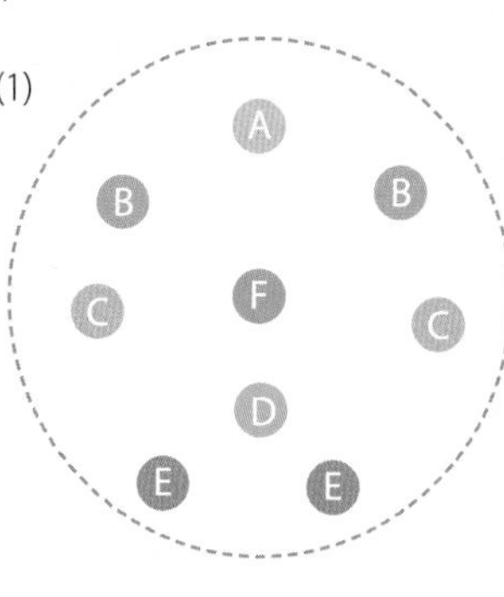

Classic Coleus

Josette Grimske of St. Clair Shores, Michigan loves this container combination because, she says, it's difficult to find plants that bring color, texture and richness to her yard. And there's no arguing that this combo does just that!

Why it works: Coleus is a classic container plant because it looks great and is easy to grow. Josette likes the bold, striking colors of the coleus and shamrock plants, but relies on the pink impatiens to soften the look.

Planter size: 12-in.-diameter pot
Growing conditions: Shade to partial sun

Shopping list:

- A Pink impatiens (1)
- B Purple leaf shamrock (1)
- C Picture Perfect coleus (1)
- D Atlas coleus (1)

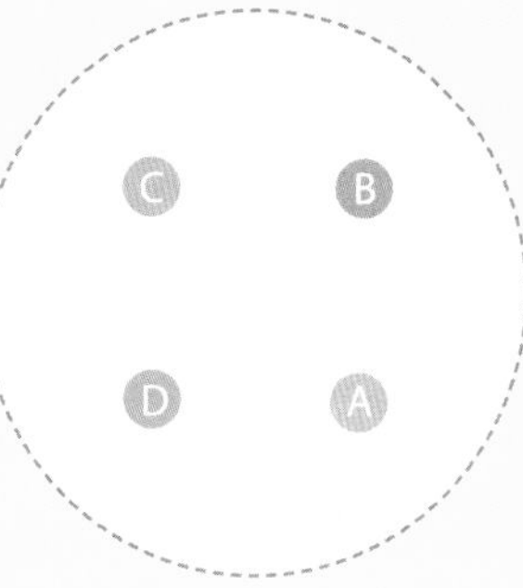

Pretty Hang-Up

Judith Schwerdt of Beaverton, Oregon found a great way to dress up her condo, which offers limited space for gardening.

"This hanging planter does very well, even though it faces the grueling sun almost all day," she says.

Why it works: Not only will this mixture of easy-to-grow plants hold up against the heat, it looks great all season long, too. The geraniums add height, and the sweet potato vines soften the container's edges and add visual impact.

Planter size: 34-in.-long planter
Growing conditions: Full sun

Shopping list:

- A Midnight Blue lobelia (2)
- B Pink geranium (3)
- C Dark lavender trailing ivy geranium (1)
- D Comedy '07 ivy geranium (1)
- E Marguerite sweet potato vine (1)
- F Blackie sweet potato vine (1)
- G Genta Pink View diascia (1)

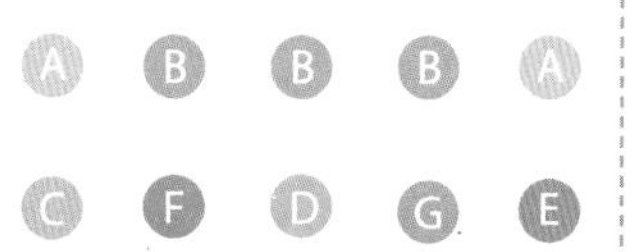

A Warm Welcome

"I love the color combination of this container and how it grabs your attention the minute you see it," says Mary Jo O'Connor of Arlington Heights, Illinois. "Located at the front of the house, it's a showstopper."

Why it works: Blue, purple, pink and yellow...there's so much color packed into this little urn. It's a good idea to plant taller plants like the fountain grass and salvia in the back and leave the smaller Million Bells and vinca vine to fill out the front of the container.

Planter size: 16-in.-diameter urn
Growing conditions: Full sun

Shopping list:

- A Blue salvia (1)
- B Purple fountain grass (1)
- C Pink 'Knock Out' begonia (1)
- D Purple Million Bells (2)
- E Yellow Million Bells (1)
- F Vinca vine (1)
- G Dahlia (mixed) (2)

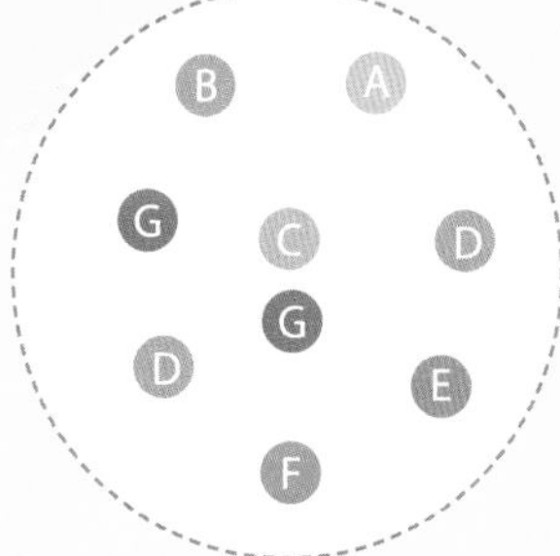

Welcome blue jays with seed mix.
Flora Marlatt

Splish splash... this robin's taking a bath!
Karen Bilka

A western tanager peeks around a bottlebrush bloom.
www.garykramer.net

All Decked Out for Birds

Simply supply the basics if you seek the company of feathered friends.

By George Harrison, Contributing Editor

Goldfinches on a tube feeder.
Richard Day/Daybreak Imagery

If you spend any time on your deck or patio and also enjoy watching birds, there's an easy way to combine both interests. Invite the birds to join you! Doing so makes outdoor living more enjoyable. Just imagine...beautiful wild birds singing and flitting from railing to post, up close and personal.

This can happen if you deck your deck (or patio) with a few simple items—specifically, three ingredients most all life needs: shelter, food and water. Supply those, and the birds will most definitely come!

Give 'Em Shelter

If trees, shrubs and ground cover don't already surround your deck or patio, it's easy to create natural shelter that birds can retreat into if threatened by predators or foul weather. Potted evergreens placed in the corners of your outdoor living space create the kind of instant cover that make birds feel safe when visiting...plus, they're pretty to boot!

Another trick is to plant vines beneath deck railings, allowing them to grow up. This provides more natural cover, as well as food (depending on the type of vine you plant), for the birds.

Potted flowers placed on the railing and around the deck or patio give birds another place to hide—and, for some birds, nectar to eat.

It's Nutty

I place a handful of peanuts on my deck whenever I see blue jays in the backyard. As a result, they associate me with food and come to visit me often. —*Connie Coloutes, Portland, Oregon*

Set the Table

Putting out potted plants that sport red blooms, such as geranium, fuchsia and petunia, will attract hummingbirds if they reside in your area. Just imagine being rewarded with the sight of these flying jewels sipping nectar from blossoms a few feet away from you.

Once you woo them with flowers, keep them coming back by setting out sugar-water feeders. By mixing one part sugar to four parts warm water, you will have the perfect nectar food for both hummingbirds and orioles. Both of these species will eat sugar water from May through August, and sometimes into September. Just be sure to hang the feeders on rods or hooks out from the railing so that the sugar water doesn't

This patio is set up for birds with its colorful container gardens and hanging bird feeders.

George Harrison

drip onto the deck.

For seed-eating birds, like northern cardinals, rose-breasted grosbeaks, finches, chickadees and titmice, tube feeders, filled with sunflower or safflower seeds, keep the birds coming every few minutes. A couple of tray feeders filled with wild birdseed mix and mounted on the railing attract other birds, such as sparrows, doves and finches. And suet cakes, placed inside a laminated cage-like feeder and hung from a railing or post, will bring in as many as four different kinds of woodpeckers, nuthatches and, perhaps, a brown creeper.

Offer a Drink

Water features add beauty to any deck or patio, even if it doesn't attract birds. But the good news is that most will. The best water feature is one that moves the water to several levels with a pump, making a splashing noise that birds can hear at some distance.

Be sure that the pools have shallow areas, only an inch or two in depth, so that birds can stand in the water to bathe. If it's any deeper than that, provide a rock or two that they can rest on. If it's hummingbirds you're after, include a spray in the water feature. These winged beauties are apt to fly through it to bathe.

More Feeding Tips

Keep It Clean

When birds eat, they're not concerned with where seed shells fall. But deck owners may want to take some measures to keep the area clean.

By mounting feeders on arms that extend out from the railing, the empty seed casings will fall on the ground, not on the deck or patio. Feeders mounted on the deck can be equipped with a seed catcher, such as a tray or screen, that's larger than the feeder and placed beneath it to catch debris as it falls.

Nighttime Nature Viewing

Many animals help themselves to a meal on a deck or patio after dark. By mounting a spotlight on the house, above the feeding area, and turning it on after dark, wildlife, both birds (owls) and mammals (flying squirrels), can be watched and even photographed!

SEEDS KEEP BIRDS COMING! Sunflower (left) and safflower (below) seeds will keep birds at your feeders.

Pruning Q&A

By Melinda Myers, Contributing Editor

Late winter is often the time to head outside to do some seasonal pruning, so you confidently leave the house with pruning tools in hand. But as you reach to make your first cut, pruning paranoia sets in. You know. . .the fear that you'll make a mistake, maim your plant or, worse yet, kill it.

Don't worry. This paranoia strikes everyone as they make their first attempt at pruning. To help reduce your anxiety—and improve your pruning results in record time—I've answered some common pruning questions for deciduous shrubs.

Q: When is the proper time of year to prune?

A: In general, most plants respond best to late-winter or early-spring pruning. Save major rejuvenation pruning for then—plants will quickly recover and put on new growth.

Time routine pruning based on flowering. Spring-flowering shrubs like lilacs, bridal wreath spirea, forsythia and the summer-blooming blue and pink hydrangeas bloom on old wood. They set their flower buds the summer before spring or summer bloom. Prune spring-bloomers right after flowering to accomplish pruning goals and have a spring floral display.

Summer- and fall-blooming shrubs flower on new growth. So prune anytime during the dormant season—I prefer late winter. That way, I can clean up any winter or animal damage at the same time I'm pruning. Besides, I'm eager to get into the garden by then.

Q: What shrubs require pruning?

A: Most plants need some pruning to establish a strong and attractive framework and to remove dead, diseased, insect-infested, crossing, rubbing or damaged branches. But always prune with a purpose in mind. Too often, gardeners feel they must prune because it's spring or because their neighbors are doing it.

A properly selected and sited shrub will need minimal pruning. One that is too big for the location will need regular pruning to control its growth. Sheared plants pruned into neat, geometric shapes will need regular pruning to maintain their tidy forms in the landscape.

Q: What are the benefits of pruning?

A: Besides creating a strong framework, proper pruning keeps plants healthy and improves their overall appearance. Plants subject to scale or borer-type insects, such as viburnum and lilac, benefit from regular pruning. Renewal pruning removes older stems and encourages fresh growth less susceptible to these pests.

Younger stems of red- and yellow-twig dogwoods are much more colorful than the old growth. Removing older brown shoots to the ground maximizes the color and beauty of these shrubs.

Proper pruning also opens up the plants, allowing more sunlight to reach all the stems, reducing disease problems and increasing flowering and fruiting.

Q: What are some proper pruning techniques?

A: Let the plant guide you. Suckering shrubs, like American cranberry bush viburnum, spireas, lilac, forsythia and red-twig dogwood continually produce new stems. Gradual pruning removes a few older, thicker stems to ground level. Repeat yearly for 3 or 4 years on overgrown plants. By the end of this time, you'll have a smaller plant with leaves from top to bottom.

Rejuvenation pruning, as its name suggests, is used to rejuvenate an old, overgrown shrub. It involves cutting the whole plant to the ground. Anyone growing privet, potentilla or Japanese spirea may have used this technique. All the stems are cut back 4 to 10 inches above the ground. This type of pruning is stressful on the plant as well as the gardener.

Before you begin, make sure the shrub you are pruning can tolerate rejuvenation pruning. Even if the shrub tolerates severe pruning, that may not be the best solution. The plant's energy is directed into forming new growth, so it may grow taller than preferred. And some shrubs, like potentilla and Japanese spirea, get a bit floppy when pruned this way.

Maintain the health and natural form of the plant by making all cuts at a slight angle 1/4 inch above a healthy bud (where a branch meets an-

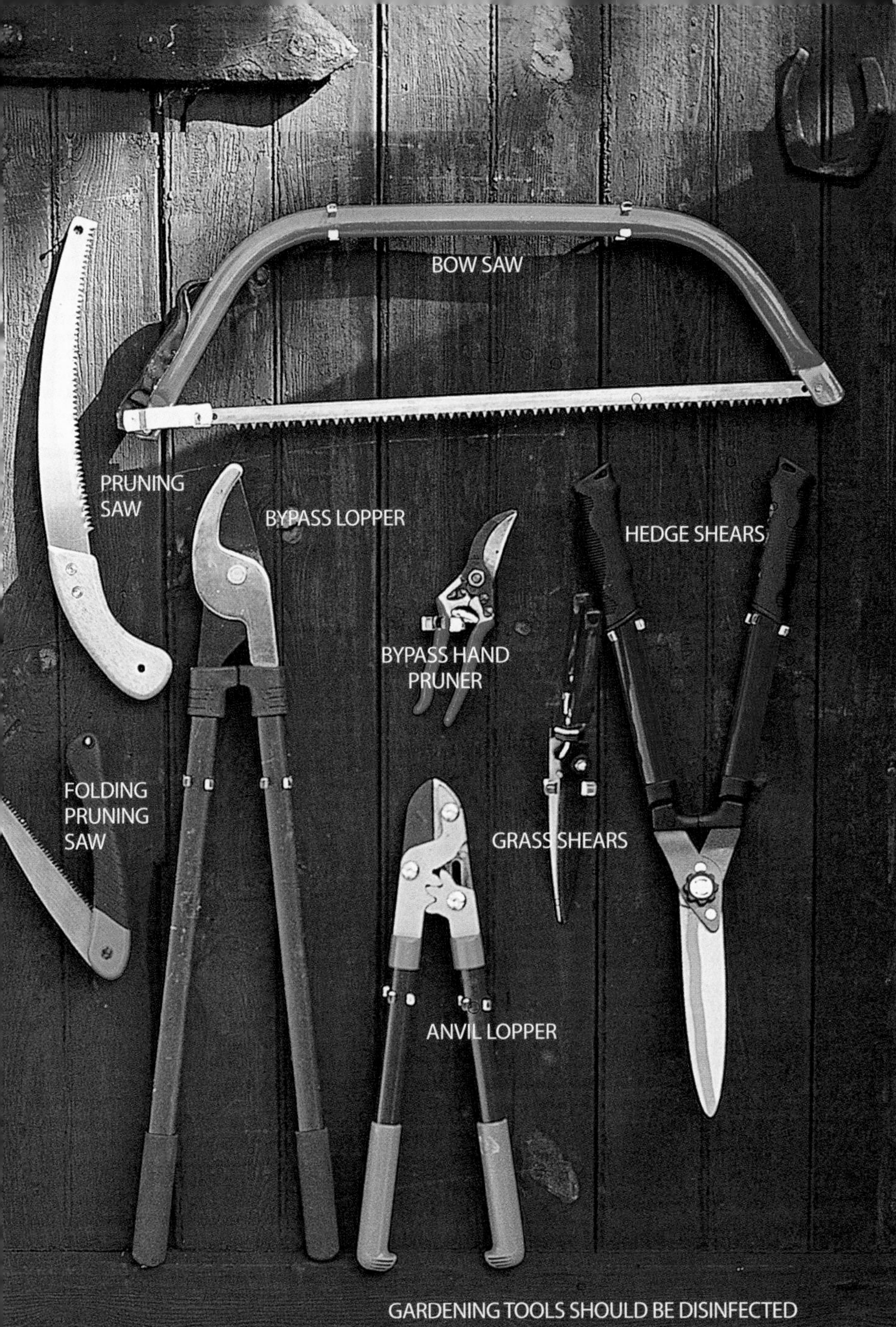

GARDENING TOOLS SHOULD BE DISINFECTED BETWEEN CUTS TO REDUCE THE SPREAD OF DISEASE.

Photos: RDA INC./GID

Q: How often do I need to prune?

A: Unfortunately, there is no set schedule. Climate, growing conditions, maintenance practices and the plant variety determine rate of growth and need for pruning.

However, there are a few guidelines. You should remove diseased, insect-infested or damaged branches as soon as you find them. Wait 1 or 2 years until the plant is established to start training and shaping it. Once established, prune as needed to maintain size, encourage new pest-resistant growth and improve bark color, flowering and fruiting. Sheared shrubs need pruning once or twice each season to maintain a formal appearance.

other branch) or back to ground level. Cutting too close or too far from the bud results in stubs. These dead tips are great entryways for insects and disease, which is why I am not a fan of shearing. However, if you do shear, make sure the top of the shrub is narrower than the bottom. This allows sunlight to reach all parts of the plants and encourages leaf growth from the tip of the branches to the ground.

Be sure to cut above a bud or stem facing away from the center of the plant, as the buds determine the direction of the new growth. You can also reduce future pruning by training the plants to grow away from (not toward the center of) the plant.

Q: What equipment do I need? Does it need to be sanitized?

A: Hand pruners work best on small-diameter branches of 1/2 inch or less. A bypass hand pruner is a must-have for gardeners. They have two sharp blades and make a clean cut like scissors. Anvil pruners have one flat and one sharp blade that crush stems. These should be used only for removing deadwood.

Loppers are long-handled pruners that extend your reach into the shrubs, increasing leverage for cutting larger-diameter branches. Check the manufacturer's guidelines for the branch sizes that can be cut with your loppers. In general, don't ever cut branches thicker than the diameter of the closed blades.

A short-bladed pruning saw is good for larger branches. The short blade allows you to negotiate the dense thicket of stems. Some gardeners use a reciprocating saw. The power and narrow blade allows it to remove hard-to-reach stems in the center of the plant.

Hand or powered hedge shears should be used only when shearing plants into hedges, topiaries or formal geometric shapes. These tools are designed to cut several stems at once. Though they speed up the process, they eliminate the natural shape of the plant and create lots of stubs that make perfect entryways for insects and diseases.

Disinfecting tools can help reduce the spread of disease. Treat pruning blades in a 10% bleach or alcohol solution between cuts to avoid spreading a disease throughout the plant.

bowling ball bugs

Retiring an old bowling ball? Create a striking ladybug for the garden! These adorable critters are as easy as 1-2-3.

Our readers are constantly coming up with great ways to recycle old items to use for budget-friendly backyard projects. So, our staff joined the fun; we made our own ladybug family out of old, unused bowling balls. Now we're sharing this easy project (and tips we learned along the way) with you. And if we can do it. . .you can, too!

A few tips to get you started: (1) Have the "antennae" cut at the hardware store—you'll save time by not doing it yourself. (2) We used caulk to secure the beads onto the wire, but a polyurethane glue works, too. (3) A quart is the smallest can of mixed paint you can buy at the hardware store, but smaller quantities of acrylic hobby paint are available at craft stores. If you do have extra, use it to make a colony of bugs (or gifts for envious neighbors)!

1 Prime and paint the bowling ball (we used three coats of red paint). After the paint is completely dry, apply painter's tape in the desired pattern. Stipple on black paint with a stenciling brush or sponge for texture.

2 Make your own stencil by cutting differently sized circles from two pieces of painter's tape put top to bottom. We used 2-1/2-inch- and1-3/4-inch-diameter dots. Stipple the dots. After paint dries, remove the tape.

3 Fill the thumb hole with black caulk. Set in two antennae made from lengths of copper wire with painted wooden beads affixed to the top. You may need to prop them up so they don't droop while drying for 24 hours.

Photos: Jim Wieland/RP Photo

Supplies:

Bowling ball

Black silicone caulk

Two 8.5-inch lengths of #6 copper wire (have the hardware store cut it for you)

Two 1-inch round wooden beads

1 quart Kilz exterior primer

1 quart red exterior latex paint

1 quart black exterior latex paint

Painter's tape

Utility knife or scissors

Stenciling brush or sponge

Jim Wieland/RP Photo

15 Secrets to a care-free garden

By Mindy Brooks
Senior Editor

No matter how much you enjoy working in the yard or puttering around the garden, it always feels good to take a few time-consuming chores off of your to-do list. With a little planning and some good advice, you can save yourself hours of extra work for years to come. The difference between labor and leisure starts here!

1 Whether you're starting from scratch or making over an existing landscape, start with a plan. Think about how you want to use your space, how much money you want to spend and how much time you want to devote to creating and maintaining a landscape. Then stick with your plan to keep your workload to a minimum.

2 Despite the appeal of a large yard with expansive beds, your maintenance obligations increase with your landscape's size. Reducing the scale of your project translates into less work.

3 For years of reliable blooms and foliage, nothing beats the ease of hardy perennials, like rudbeckia (above). To keep the workload down, choose varieties that don't need frequent dividing or deadheading and that are drought-tolerant or disease- and pest-resistant.

4 Keep your landscape plans manageable. Don't let yourself be tempted into taking on a bigger project than you have time for. And, no matter how appealing, avoid plants that need lots of attention, outgrow their space or become invasive.

5 Identify the ongoing maintenance headaches that require your attention year after year and commit to finding long-term solutions. Crossing known problems off your maintenance list will lighten your workload all season long.

6 Container gardens are a favorite for outdoor decor, but they often require daily watering and frequent fertilizing to look their best. To reduce the workload, cluster your containers for convenient watering, use large pots to prevent the soil from drying out quickly, incorporate a slow-release fertilizer into the soil and try self-watering pots.

7 Don't waste time and money adding fertilizer and other products to your soil until you know what's necessary. Learn about your soil's pH levels, nutrient deficiencies and texture by getting a soil test through your county Extension service or a soil-testing lab.

8 When it comes to fertilizers, slow-release products require fewer applications than fast-release ones, and in general, less is better than

Keep container gardening low-maintenance.

6

Jim Wieland/RP Photo

Slow-release fertilizers are a good choice.

RDA/GID

Aphid infestation

RDA/GID

Fix problem spots with ground covers.

provenwinners.com

more. For overall soil improvement, consider using compost, which you can prepare right in your yard.

9 Controlling insect-related damage is easiest when you catch it early. Make it part of your routine to check for spots and holes on leaves and blooms, and examine any wilted, stunted or discolored plants for signs of infestation.

10 For precise and consistent watering without lifting a finger, install an automatic irrigation system. You can buy do-it-yourself systems at home and garden centers or hire a professional to do the job.

11 Trees and shrubs anchor a landscape for the long term. Avoid those that drop fruit or are susceptible to disease or pests. Keep their mature sizes in mind when planting, so they won't have to be moved or need frequent pruning.

12 Save time by organizing your landscape by care requirements. Some plants suffer in summer's heat and need frequent watering, while others thrive on neglect.

13 Make sure you have easy access to water all around your property, including outdoor spigots, sprinklers and hoses. This helps to keep your plants watered with minimal effort throughout the growing season.

14 Handling a lawn mower on a steep slope is hard work and potentially dangerous. Consider modifying the grade by terracing it. Or replace a hillside of grass with ground cover.

15 Ground covers are practical, low-maintenance choices for challenging landscape areas. Before you plant, kill the grass and weeds in the desired bed and double-check to make sure the plant you select is not invasive.

A Birdhouse with Country Charm

Made from scraps of vinyl siding and wood, this birdhouse is economical and as down-home as it gets.

This clever "bird barn" is sure to add a touch of the country to your backyard, whether it's in the city or along a rural back road.

Harlan Olson of Manitowoc, Wisconsin has given away dozens of these birdhouses. To his surprise, some of the recipients refuse to hang them outdoors.

"They say they're too nice to put outside," Harlan chuckles. "So they keep them inside for decoration."

Harlan designed the barn-style birdhouse in 1997, when a contractor was putting new vinyl siding on his house. "I asked him to leave the scraps behind, figuring I'd think of some use for them," he recalls. "Eventually, I came up with this birdhouse pattern that worked with the leftover siding.

"I made four or five barns from the stuff and gave them to relatives. Later, my nephew tore down a shed and had a bunch of extra siding. I really got busy building!"

Since then, Harlan has built nearly 50 of these barns and was getting ready to make "another 10 or 20" when we spoke to him.

He painted the first houses he made red, but now Harlan's tinkering with different shapes and designs. "The possibilities are endless," he says.

Your possibilities are endless, too. You can paint the birdhouse barn-red, develop your own color scheme or perhaps find some scraps of real weathered barn wood.

However, we recommend using light-colored siding or painting dark siding a light color before assembling. This will help keep the house cooler for the birds inside when the sun is shining.

When you're finished, go ahead and hang the birdhouse outside—no matter how pretty it is! The birds will love its country decor.

Here's What You'll Need...

- ❑ One 2-foot 1-inch x 10-inch No. 2 pine board
- ❑ 20 inches of double 4-inch vinyl siding
- ❑ 1-1/4-inch galvanized deck screws
- ❑ 1-1/4-inch wire brads
- ❑ 1/4-inch dowel (optional for perch)
- ❑ Glue stick
- ❑ Two screw eyes and chain for hanging the birdhouse

Recommended Tools...

- ❑ Table saw
- ❑ Saber saw
- ❑ Utility knife
- ❑ Hot-melt glue gun (optional)
- ❑ Hand saw
- ❑ Power drill
- ❑ Router (optional)

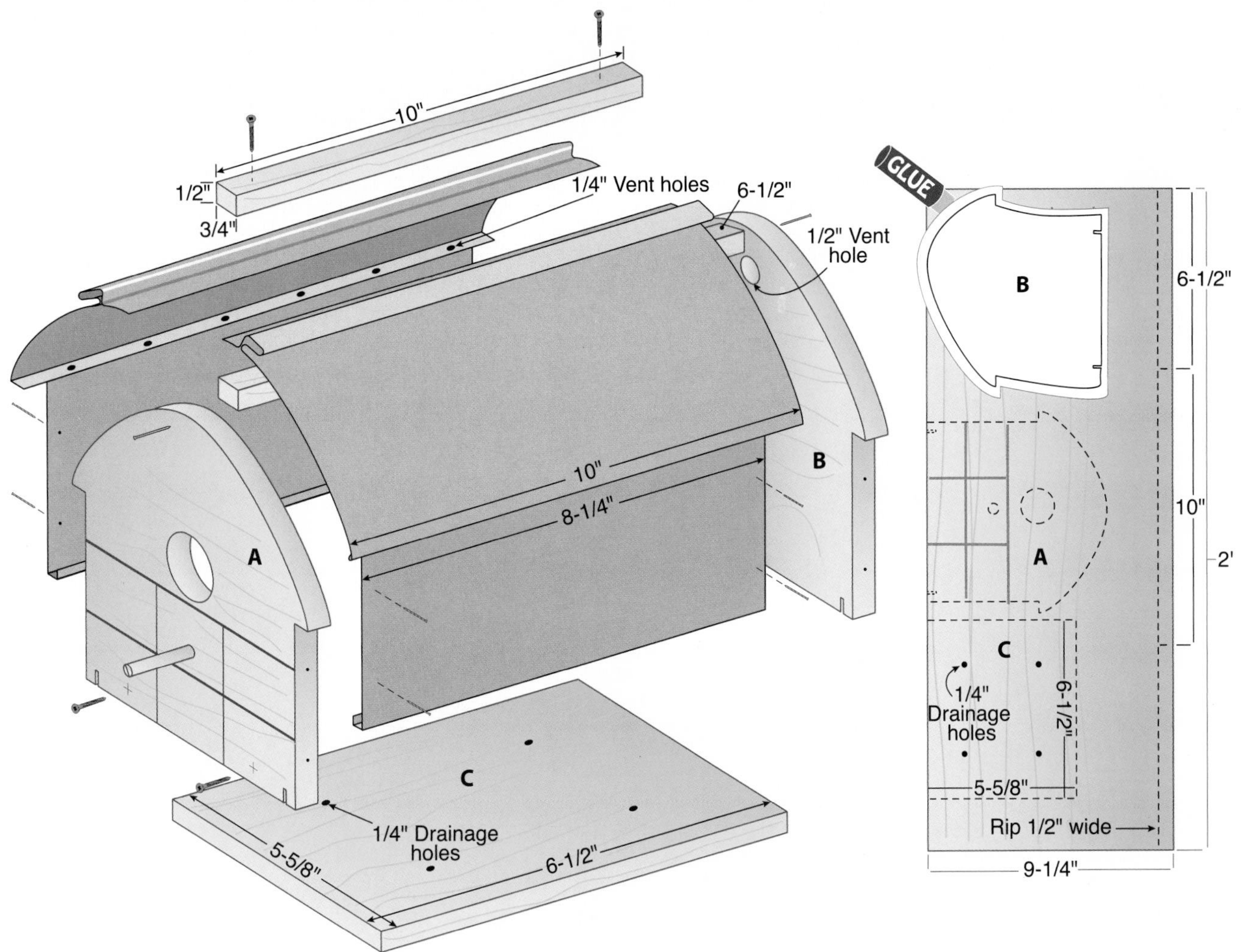

1. Begin by making two copies of the full-size pattern shown on the next page—one for the front of the birdhouse and one for the back. Cut the paper patterns out with a scissors about 1/2 inch outside the guidelines.

2. If you like the optional router cuts pictured on the front of the barn, it's important to make them before cutting the front and back pieces from the pine board.

To do this, lay the patterns on a 2-foot-long piece of 1-inch x 10-inch pine, making sure the grain runs horizontally. Lightly trace the pattern onto the wood, then mark where you'd like to route the grooves.

If you don't have a router or just want to keep things simple, move on to the next step.

3. Use a glue stick or spray adhesive to affix the patterns to the 1-inch x 8-inch board, but apply it sparingly so they'll peel off easily later. Again, make sure the grain runs horizontally.

4. Cut out the front and back pieces with a saber saw or band saw. It might be tempting to cut the board in half and stack the two pieces of wood to cut them both at once, but we don't recommend it—most saber saws are made to cut material 1 inch thick or less.

Your cuts must be precise for the vinyl siding to fit properly. Cut carefully along the guideline, then peel off the pattern. If any adhesive remains on the wood, remove it by lightly sanding.

5. On the bottom edge of the front and back pieces, make a 5/16-inch deep cut with a hand saw, 1/4 inch in from each corner. The bottom edge of the siding will fit into this slot.

6. Drill the entrance hole with a spade bit to a size appropriate for the type of bird you'd like to attract. (See page 250 for recommended hole sizes.) If you'd like an optional perch, drill a 1/4-inch hole 1 inch below the entrance hole. Cut a 3-inch piece of 1/4-inch dowel and glue it into the hole.

7. From the remaining pine board, cut a piece 5-5/8 inches x 6-1/2 inches for the floor. Predrill holes through the front and back pieces and into the floor board and secure it with 1-1/4-inch deck screws. (After nesting season, when it's time to clean out the birdhouse, remove the screws and the floor.) Add 1/4-inch drainage holes in the floor and vent holes under the barn eaves. Also add a 1/2-inch vent hole near the top of the back piece.

8. Rip a 2-foot 3/4-inch x 1/2-inch strip from the pine board. Cut two pieces from it—one 6-1/2 inches long (the inside roof beam) and another 10 inches long (the outside roof beam). Glue the inside roof beam to the front and back pieces and attach with 1-1/4-inch wire brads nailed through the front and back to hold it in place. Lay the outside roof beam aside.

9. Cut two pieces of double 4-inch vinyl siding into 10-inch lengths. (It's really 8 inches from top to bottom, but has two 4-inch sections molded into it.) Trim only the bottom 4-inch section with a utility knife to "indent" it 7/8 inch on each end. (The finished width of the bottom section should be 8-1/4 inches.) The wider top section provides an overhang.

10. Slip the bottom lip of the siding into the slots, then fasten

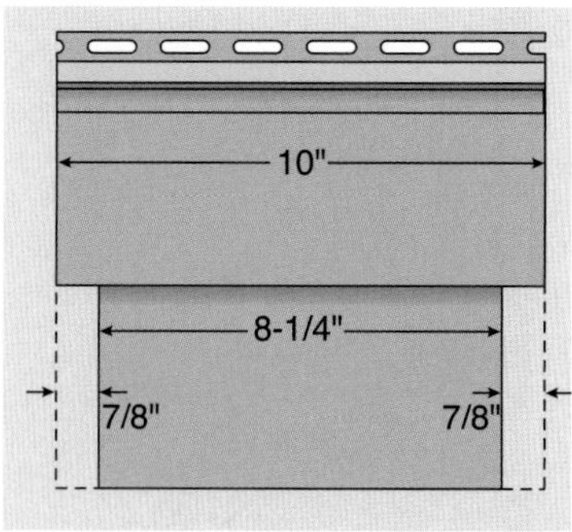

the bottom sections of the siding to the front and back pieces with wire brads.

11. Roll the siding so each piece meets and overlaps at the peak of the roof. To help hold them in place, tack with hot-melt glue. Then place the outside roof beam into the channel formed by the siding as it meets at the peak. Predrill two holes to fasten the beam to the front and back pieces. Attach with two 1-1/4-inch deck screws. Be careful not to tighten the screws too much, or the wood may split.

12. You can use just about any type of strong chain or wire to hang this birdhouse.

We don't recommend rope or twine because it can break or be chewed by predators. If you want to use two screw eyes and a chain (like we did in the photo on page 236), use two small pliers to twist open the screw eyes. Before adding the chain, screw the eyes into the outside roof beam between the galvanized screws. Then insert the ends of the chain into the screw eyes and close them with a pliers.

Your country-style barn is now ready for some feathered "livestock" to move in!

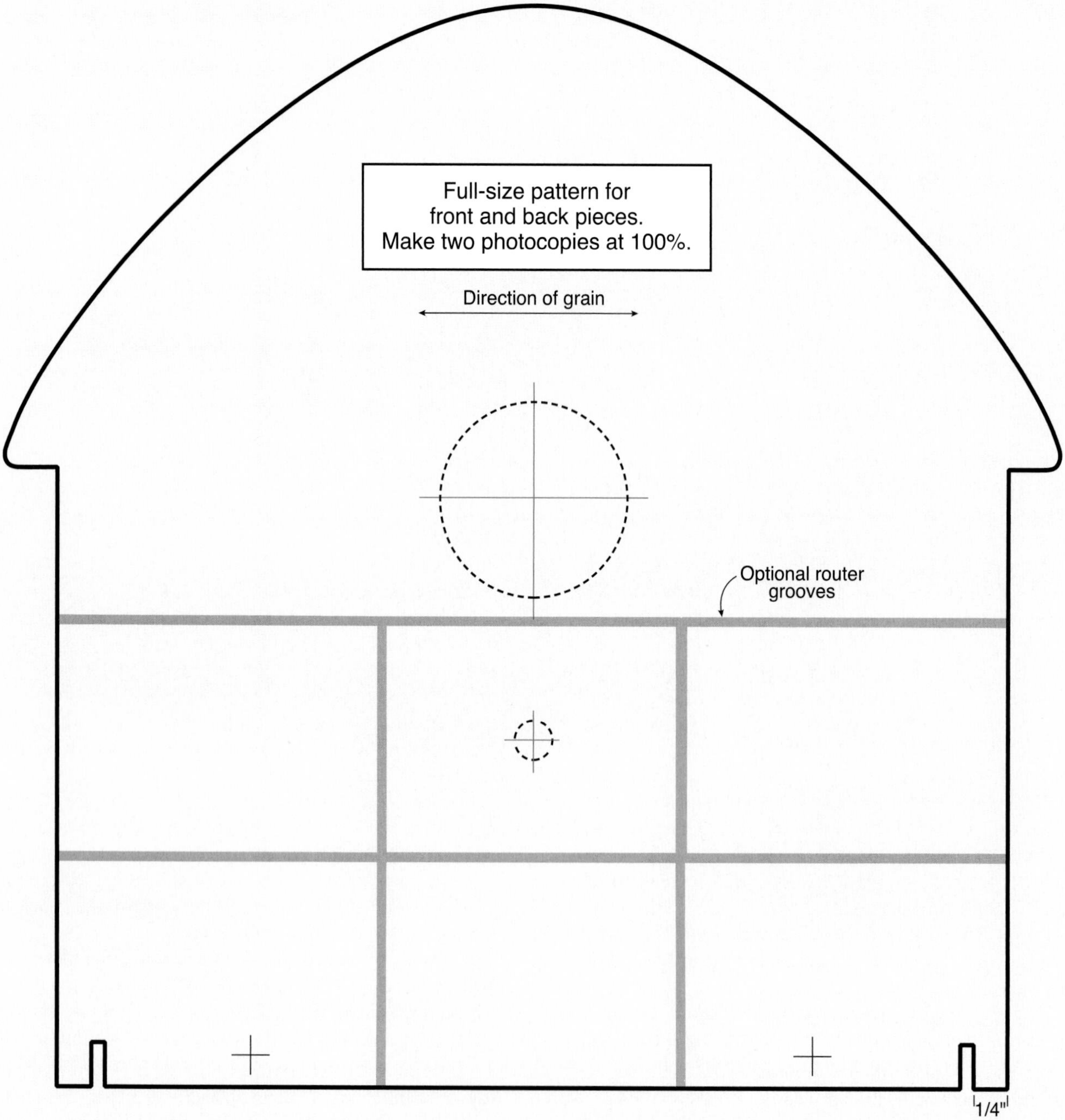

Full-size pattern for
front and back pieces.
Make two photocopies at 100%.

Direction of grain

Optional router grooves

1/4"

Hassle-free herb garden

1• 2• 3 project

Herb or strawberry pots—tall pots with holes around the sides—are ideal for growing a selection of herbs like this thyme. Herb pots are especially useful, since they have protruding cups to give support to the plants growing inside.

But there is a danger with these kinds of tall pots. . .plants at the top may well become waterlogged while the ones at the bottom dry out.

To make sure that water spreads evenly through the pot, include a central core of fine gravel when you plant. This simple solution will keep your herbs well hydrated.

your best bet

Trailing-herb varieties like thyme and oregano are good choices for multitiered containers.

Supplies:

Herb pot
1″ plastic plumbing pipe or cardboard tube
Soilless potting mix
Gravel or small stones
Assorted herbs

Photos: RDA/GID

1 Position a pipe in the center of the herb pot. An offcut of plastic plumbing pipe or the cardboard tube from a roll of paper towel will do.

Hold the pipe steady; then fill around it with potting mix as far as the first holes.

2 Start introducing the plants. Always plant trailing varieties in the side holes and bushier herbs in the top.

Push the herbs through the holes from the inside, and firm the compost around the plants as you go. Work your way up the pot until you reach the top.

3 Before you can plant in the space at the top of the pot, fill the pipe with gravel (inset photo) to the level of the compost in the pot.

Gently ease the pipe out, leaving the core of gravel behind; then put the plants in the top.

Catering to Caterpillars

To attract butterflies, you also need to invite these tiny crawlers over for dinner.

TIME TO DINE. Caterpillars (like the monarch, above) see your garden as a big buffet.

Nancy Rotenberg

One of the best ways to attract butterflies is to fill your garden with plants for caterpillars to eat. You can even combine the plants to create a garden that caters to butterflies and caterpillars.

Don't worry—the caterpillars won't destroy all your plants. That's a common misconception. Most garden butterfly species lay only one or two eggs on each host plant before moving on to another plant.

As a result, the caterpillars aren't plentiful enough to greatly harm any one plant. In addition, very few butterflies lay their eggs in clusters, as several moths are known to do.

Knowing the proper host plants is the secret to attracting butterflies. A good place to start is with black swallowtails, a species found throughout much of the United States. This butterfly is easy to please and will feed on plants in the carrot family. While they especially like fennel, they will also lay their eggs on dill, carrots and parsley.

Plants to Ponder

If you live in a warmer climate, passionflowers appeal to gulf fritillaries and zebra longwings. Use native plants if possible for these species, since the butterflies will not feed on some of the hybrid passionflowers. Two favored types are maypops and corky-stemmed passionflower, both native to the South.

Plant your passionflowers in sunlit areas to attract gulf fritillaries, or in the shade for zebra longwings. Variegated fritillaries also use passionflowers as a host, but they seek out flax, pansies and violets as well.

Violets are a popular host plant for many fritillary butterflies. In addition to the variegated species, violets will attract great spangled, Aphrodite and Atlantis fritillaries—all common in the eastern U.S.—as well as most of the western fritillaries (like the callippe, Mormon and zerene).

So no matter where you live, adding violets in shady garden spots should catch the attention of members of this family (just don't let them invade your lawn). Keep in mind that while you may see the fritillaries in summer, the caterpillars won't show up until the following spring.

And don't forget to plant some trees and shrubs, too. Sassafras and spicebush are the host plants for the spicebush swallowtail. These caterpillars always fold the leaf along the upper surface, lining it with silk. The shelters are easy to see, and the green caterpillars inside will amaze you with their large false eyespots.

There are many other options for common host plants you can add to your garden to attract caterpillars. The list at right is a good place to get started. After all, it's only polite to invite these crawling visitors to join your outdoor buffet. Then sit back and enjoy the beautiful butterflies as they flit in your garden!

A Garden for Butterflies

Illustration: Elizabeth Roska

Do you dream of a yard filled with the fluttering wings of monarchs, tiger swallowtails and painted ladies? If so, the plants in this garden are a great start. There are a few popular butterfly favorites like butterfly bush and lantana, as well as caterpillar host plants, including everlasting and dill.

When planning a garden for butterflies, it helps to include a few stones for butterfly sunbathers, as well as a spot of wet sand, where some butterflies will perch to sip nutrients from the moisture.

Backyard WINGS TIP

In a butterfly garden, put the tallest flowers in back so you can see the blooms and the butterflies that visit.

10 plants that create a butterfly buffet

To attract butterflies, variety is key. Select a mix of colorful, nectar-rich plants, as well as caterpillar host plants, that will please both you and the butterflies.

1 **Salvia**
Salvia splendens
Annual

2 **Butterfly weed**
Asclepias tuberosa
Perennial, Zones 3 to 9

3 **Butterfly bush**
Buddleja davidii
Shrub, Zones 4 to 9

4 **Daylily**
Hemerocallis
Perennial, Zones 3 to 10

5 **Dill**
Anethum graveolens
Annual

6 **Clematis**
Clematis
Perennial, Zones 3 to 9

7 **Lantana**
Lantana camara
Annual (Perennial in Zones 9 to 11)

8 **Impatiens**
Impatiens
Annual

9 **Pansy**
Viola x wittrockiana
Most are annuals

10 **Everlasting**
Anaphalis margaritacea
Perennial, Zones 3 to 8

Best Annuals for Birds

Plant these seven pretty annuals, and you'll create a bird buffet, with no waiting.

RDA/GID

Cleome

Also Known As: Spider flower.
Botanical Name: *Cleome hassleriana.*
Bloom Time: Midsummer to first frost.
Size: 4 to 6 feet high, 2 feet wide.
Flower: Pink, purple and white airy, spiderlike flowers.
Light Needs: Full sun to partial shade.
Growing Advice: Plant seeds or container-grown plants after danger of frost has passed. In northern areas, give seeds a head start indoors.
Prize Picks: Queen Mix, Sparkler Blush.

RDA/GID

Cosmos

Botanical Name: *Cosmos bipinnatus.*
Bloom Time: Summer to late fall.
Size: 1 to 6 feet high, 1 to 2 feet wide.
Flower: Single or double daisy-shaped blooms in pink, white, red and purple.
Light Needs: Full sun.
Growing Advice: Place tall varieties near a fence or provide stakes to help the plants stand up to winds and rain.
Prize Picks: Diablo, Sea Shells, Sonata Series.

RDA/GID

Nasturtium

Botanical Name: *Tropaeolum majus.*
Bloom Time: Early summer until frost.
Size: Climbing varieties reach 10 feet, dwarf varieties form mounds that are up to 15 inches tall, 12 to 24 inches wide.
Flower: Bright yellow, red, cream, apricot and salmon.
Light Needs: Full sun.
Growing Advice: Sow directly in most gardens after last frost. Plant 3/4-inch deep and 8 to 12 inches apart. Thin plants as they become crowded.
Prize Picks: Alaska Series, Whirlybird.

RDA/GID

Bachelor's buttons

Also Known As: Cornflower.
Botanical Name: *Centaurea cyanus.*
Bloom Time: Late spring through summer.
Size: 2 to 3 feet tall.
Flower: About 1-1/2-inch-wide purple and bluish flowers shaped like buttons.
Light Needs: Full sun.
Growing Advice: Plant 9 to 12 inches apart in well–draining soil; will tolerate poor soil and drought. For spring blooms, sow seeds in early fall.
Prize Picks: Black Magic, Blue Boy, Jubilee Gem, Polka Dot.

RDA/GID

Four-o'clocks

Botanical Name: *Mirabilis jalapa.*
Bloom Time: Midsummer through fall. Blossoms open in midafternoon and fade before sunrise.
Size: 1-1/2 to 3 feet high, 1 to 3 feet wide.
Flower: Purplish-red, yellow, pink, white and lavender blooms, sometimes on the same plant. Some varieties have striped flowers.
Light Needs: Full sun.
Growing Advice: Four-o'clocks will reseed, so avoid disturbing soil in spring. Grows as perennial in Zones 7 to 11. All plant parts are poisonous.
Prize Picks: Jingles.

RDA/GID

Marigold

Botanical Name: *Tagetes.*
Bloom Time: Summer through autumn.
Size: 6 inches to 3 feet high, 6 to 15 inches wide.
Flower: Yellow, orange, gold, bronze and creamy white.
Light Needs: Full sun.
Growing Advice: Directly sow into the garden after the threat of frost has passed. Lightly cover seeds with soil and keep moist until they germinate.
Prize Picks: French marigold (*Tagetes patula*) is compact and grows from 6 to 15 inches tall. African marigold (*Tagetes erecta*), with its enormous blooms, can reach 3 feet tall.

Sunflower

Botanical Name: *Helianthus annuus.*
Bloom Time: Summer to early autumn.
Size: 2 to 15 feet high, 18 to 24 inches wide.
Flower: Mainly yellow. Some varieties may be red or brown; large, daisy-like ray of bright florets with a dark center.
Light Needs: Full sun.
Growing Advice: Sow seeds 6 inches apart in spring. Thin to the strongest growers so the plants are 18 to 24 inches apart
Prize Picks: Russian Giant, Autumn Beauty.

www.ParkSeed.com

Best Perennials for Birds

These 21 "flowering feeders" will return to bloom in your garden year after year.

Rugosa rose

Also Known As: Beach rose, Japanese rose, and salt-spray rose.
Botanical Name: *Rosa rugosa.*
Hardiness: Zones 2 to 8.
Bloom Time: Spring to autumn.
Size: 3 to 8 feet high, 8 feet wide.
Flower: Cupped and fragrant white, red or pink flowers that appear as singles, doubles or in small clusters.
Light Needs: Full sun.
Growing Advice: Plant small bare-root roses while dormant in spring. Container plants may be added to your landscape any time during the growing season.
Prize Picks: Seek out alba for white flowers blooming from pale-pink buds.

Coreopsis

Also Known As: Tickseed.
Botanical Name: *Coreopsis.*
Hardiness: Both annual and perennial varieties are available; zones vary by variety.
Bloom Time: Late spring through late summer.
Size: 8 to 48 inches high, 8 to 36 inches wide.
Flower: Yellow, orange, maroon, red and pink; daisy-like single, semi-double or double blooms 1/2 to 3 inches wide. Petals are often notched.
Light Needs: Full sun.
Growing Advice: Keep the soil around newly planted coreopsis moist, but resist the urge to overwater once established. Check the soil first. If the top 3 inches or so are on the dry side, then you can pull out your watering can. This plant is drought-tolerant.
Prize Picks: Perennial threadleaf varieties like Moonbeam offer distinctive foliage and pastel yellow flowers, and require little maintenance. Closely related *Coreopsis rosea* bears pink blooms and tolerates dry conditions; it's a good ground cover for arid slopes. Other excellent choices include Sunray and Early Sunrise.

Photos this page: RDA/GID

Blanket flower

Also Known As: Gaillardia.
Botanical Name: *Gaillardia* x *grandiflora.*
Hardiness: Zones 3 to 9.
Bloom Time: All summer.
Size: 2 to 3 feet high, 1 to 2 feet wide.
Flower: Red or yellow with yellow or purple centers.
Light Needs: Full sun.
Growing Advice: Sow perennial types in spring or early summer. Start annual types indoors 4 to 6 weeks before planting outdoors. Wait for frost danger to pass before planting outside.
Prize Picks: New hybrid Fanfare sports a distinctive ruby center and golden, trumpet-shaped outer florets.

Blazing star

Also Known As: Blazing star, gayfeather.
Botanical Name: *Liatris* species and cultivars.
Hardiness: Zones 3 to 9.
Bloom Time: Summer.
Size: 2 to 5 feet high, 1 to 2 feet wide.
Flower: Pink-purple or white flower heads, produced in dense spikes.
Light Needs: Full to partial sun.
Growing Advice: Once established, its tuberous rootstock will anchor it and enable it to survive drought amazingly well.
Prize Picks: Kobold (or Goblin), though no higher than 2 feet tall, has large, deep-purple blooms.

RDA/GID

Stokesia

Also Known As: Stoke's aster.
Botanical Name: *Stokesia laevis.*
Hardiness: Zones 5 to 9.
Bloom Time: Early summer through fall.
Size: 1 to 2 feet.
Flower: 3- to 5-inch-wide blue, lavender or pink blooms with ragged-toothed petals around a creamy white center.
Light Needs: Full sun to partial shade.
Growing Advice: Plant 15 inches apart; divide every 3 to 4 years. Regular deadheading will extend bloom time.
Prize Picks: Blue Danube, Silver Moon.

RDA/GID

Amaranth

Also Known As: Love-lies-bleeding, tassel flower.
Botanical Name: *Amaranthus caudatus.*
Hardiness: Zones 10 and 11; grow as an annual elsewhere. Reseeds.
Bloom Time: Summer to early autumn.
Size: 3 to 5 feet high, 1 to 2-1/2 feet wide.
Flower: Shades of red, purple, and green form 18-to 24-inch cascading "ropes" of tiny flower clusters.
Light Needs: Full sun.
Growing Advice: Sow seeds in spring after the last frost. It will reseed year after year.
Prize Picks: It's fairly easy to find the "red" or "green" flowered ones in major seed catalogs. A named variety called Emerald Tassels is especially desirable for its lime-green blooms.

Globe thistle

RDA/GID

Botanical Name: *Echinops ritro.*
Hardiness: Zones 3 to 10.
Bloom Time: Midsummer.
Size: Up to 4 feet-tall.
Flower: Dense, silvery or bright-blue, spherical flower heads up to 1 to 2 inches in diameter, with small spiny petals.
Light Needs: Full sun in poor, sandy soil.
Growing Advice: Space 15 to 18 inches apart in well-draining soil.
Prize Picks: Taplow Blue, Veitch's Blue.

Goldenrod

Botanical Name: *Solidago* species.
Hardiness: Zones 3 to 9.
Bloom Time: Summer to fall.
Size: 8 to 48 inches high, 24 to 30 inches wide.
Flower: Yellow.
Light Needs: Full sun.
Growing Advice: Deadhead flowers to promote continued blooming. Give them plenty of room to spread.
Prize Picks: Golden Fleece is a dwarf variety with arching clusters; Fireworks is known for its unique flowering stems; Golden Baby is compact and blooms early; sweet goldenrod has showy flowers and anise-like scented leaves.

Donna and Tom Krischan

RDA/GID

Baptisia

Also Known As: False indigo, wild indigo.
Botanical Name: *Baptisia.*
Hardiness: Zones 3 to 9.
Bloom Time: Late spring to early summer.
Size: 3 to 5 feet high, about 2 feet wide.
Flower: Pea-like blooms, usually blue. Interesting seedpods.
Light Needs: Full sun.
Growing Advice: Plant with ample elbow room in a spot where you won't have to move it, because it develops a deep taproot.
Prize Picks: While the blue of Baptisia australis is vivid and beautiful, also consider Baptisia alba, which blooms with white flowers and sometimes purple petals.

RDA/GID

Joe Pye weed

Botanical Name: *Eupatorium purpureum.*
Hardiness: Zones 4 through 9.
Bloom Time: Late summer and fall.
Size: 4 to 7 feet.
Flower: Large, rounded heads of medium-pink, vanilla-scented flowers with foot-long, whorled leaves.
Light Needs: Full sun or light shade.
Growing Advice: Grow in average to moist soil. Pinch back early in the growing season to grow shorter plants and boost flower production.
Prize Picks: Atropurpureum, Gateway.

RDA/GID

Coral bells

Also Known As: Heuchera.
Botanical Name: *Heuchera.*
Hardiness: Zones 3 to 9.
Bloom Time: Varies by cultivar, but most coral bells typically bloom from late spring into early summer.
Size: 8 inches to 3 feet high, 12 to 24 inches wide.
Flower: Bell-like blooms in purple, red, black, silver, amber, orange and bronze.
Light Needs: Partial to full shade.
Growing Advice: Plant in early spring, choosing soil that's moist, rich and well draining.
Prize Picks: Plum Pudding sports both attractive foliage and flowers. Purple Petticoats has ruffled foliage.

RDA/GID

Lupine

Botanical Name: *Lupinus perennis.*
Hardiness: Zones 3 to 7.
Bloom Time: Late spring and early summer.
Size: 3 to 4 feet.
Flower: Spires of pea-like blooms.
Light Needs: Full sun to mild shade.
Growing Advice: Plant 2-1/2 feet apart; deadhead flowers to promote continued blooming.
Prize Picks: Longtime garden favorite Russell hybrids, Gallery dwarf hybrids.

RDA/GID

Purple coneflower

Also Known As: Echinacea.
Botanical Name: *Echinacea purpurea.*
Hardiness: Zones 3 to 9.
Bloom Time: Midsummer to early fall.
Size: 2 to 5 feet high, 2 feet wide.
Flower: Purple, pink, crimson, white and new varieties like yellow and orange; daisy-like drooping petals surround a bristly cone-shaped center.
Light Needs: Full sun; will tolerate light shade.
Growing Advice: Plant bare-root perennials in spring or container-grown specimens anytime during the growing season. To propagate, sow seeds in fall or early spring (it may take 2 to 3 years to flower).
Prize Picks: Magnus, the 1998 Perennial Plant of the Year, has showy flat flower heads up to 7 inches across. The smaller White Swan has white petals and produces fewer seedlings. Orange Meadowbrite and Mango Pixie are lively orange versions that sport light fragrances.

Autumn Joy sedum

RDA/GID

Botanical Name: *Sedum* Autumn Joy or *Sedum* Herbstfreude.
Hardiness: Zones 3 to 8.
Bloom Time: Late summer until first frost.
Size: 2 feet high.
Flower: Star-shaped blooms form clusters that start out pale green then become burgundy.
Light Needs: Full sun to partial shade.
Growing Advice: Plant 15 inches apart from spring through early fall. Divide in spring.
Prize Picks: Closely related Vera Jameson features pink flowers against dusky, purple-tinged foliage—lovely!

Phlox

Also Known As: Garden phlox.
Botanical Name: *Phlox.*
Hardiness: Zones 4 to 8.
Bloom Time: Summer.
Size: 24 to 36 inches high, 30 to 36 inches wide.
Flower: Pink, white and purple.
Light Needs: Full sun.
Growing Advice: Deadhead flowers to promote continued blooming.
Prize Picks: David and the Flame Series resist powdery mildew.

Penstemon

Also Known As: Beardtongue.
Botanical Name: *Penstemon.*
Hardiness: Zones 3 to 9.
Bloom Time: Summer.
Size: 18 to 36 inches high, 12 to 24 inches wide.
Flower: White, yellow, orange, red, pink and purple.
Light Needs: Full sun to light shade.
Growing Advice: Sow seed outdoors from late winter through early summer. Plant nursery-raised seedlings in late spring and water well until established.
Prize Picks: Gorgeous Husker Red owes its name to its reddish foliage and stems; the flowers are white with a pink cast. *Penstemon barbatus* has striking scarlet flowers; *Penstemon gloxinoides* comes in various attractive hues.

Lavender

Botanical Name: *Lavendula.*
Hardiness: Zones 5 to 9.
Bloom Time: Summer.
Size: 24 to 36 inches high, 30 to 36 inches wide.
Flower: Purple, blue.
Light Needs: Full sun.
Growing Advice: Plant in well-drained soil, in spring in northern areas. Place in groups to showcase scent.
Prize Picks: Hidcote Blue.

Yarrow

Botanical Name: *Achillea.*
Hardiness: Zones 3 to 9.
Bloom Time: Summer.
Size: 6 to 52 inches high, 12 to 24 inches wide.
Flower: Yellow, white, red, and pink.
Light Needs: Full sun.
Growing Advice: Sow seeds outdoors in spring or early summer. Divide in spring. Long-lasting when cut or dried.
Prize Picks: Moonshine is indispensable for abundant bright, light-yellow flowers. *Achillea millefolium* Paprika, Christel and Red Beauty contribute pink and red but can be weedy; *Achillea filipendulina* is not weedy.

RDA/GID

Hollyhock

Botanical Name: *Alcea rosea.*
Hardiness: Biennial and short-lived perennial in Zones 3 to 9.
Bloom Time: Early to midsummer.
Size: 3 to 8 feet high, 1 to 3 feet wide.
Flower: Funnel-shaped or double blooms in numerous bright and pastel hues including red, pink, yellow, white and purple.
Light Needs: Full sun.
Growing Advice: Plant seeds in midsummer for blooms the following year. Or force blooms during the first summer by sowing indoors in late winter and transplanting in early spring.
Prize Picks: Try Chater's Double for double blooms or Nigra for striking, dark-maroon flowers that appear almost black.

Jim Wieland/RP Photo

Black-eyed Susan

Botanical Name: *Rudbeckia.*
Hardiness: Varies; most are Zones 3 to 9.
Bloom Time: Summer through autumn.
Size: 1 to 6 feet high.
Flower: Yellow, orange, and russet petals with black-brown or green centers.
Light Needs: Full sun; will tolerate light shade.
Growing Advice: Sow seeds directly in the soil in early spring or fall by scattering them on loosened soil. Potted plants transplant easily and need ample water until established.
Prize Picks: Popular perennials include Rudbeckia hirta and *Rudbeckia fulgida*; Goldstrum is a classic flower, prized for its beauty and durability. *Rudbeckia maxima* makes a statement, with plants soaring as high as 6 feet when in full bloom.

www.ParkSeed.com

Gazania

Botanical Name: *Gazania.*
Hardiness: Zones 9 to 11; annual elsewhere.
Bloom Time: Late spring to fall.
Size: 3 to 8 inches high, 8 to 10 inches wide.
Flower: Brightly colored, daisy-like blooms; bronze, shades of orange, pink, yellow, white red, brown and green.
Light Needs: Full sun.
Growing Advice: Plant in sandy, well-drained soil.
Prize Picks: Chansonette Series, Daybreak Red Stripe.

Birdhouse Guidelines

Customize your designs for your favorite feathered friends.

Species	Dimensions	Hole	Placement	Color	Notes
Eastern bluebird	5" x 5" x 8"h.	1-1/2" centered 6" above floor	5-10' high in the open; sunny area	light earth tones	likes open areas, especially facing a field
Tree swallow	5" x 5" x 6"h.	1-1/2" centered 4" above floor	5-8' high in the open; 50-100% sun	light earth tones or gray	within 2 miles of pond or lake
Purple martin	multiple apts. 6" x 6" x 6" ea. (minimum)	2-1/8" hole 2-1/4" above floor	15-20' high in the open	white	open yard without tall trees; near water
Tufted titmouse	4" x 4" x 8"h.	1-1/4"	4-10' high	light earth tones	prefers to live in or near woods
Chickadee	4" x 4" x 8"h. or 5" x 5" base	1-1/8" centered 6" above floor	4-8' high	light earth tones	small tree thicket
Nuthatch	4" x 4" x 10"h.	1-1/4" centered 7-1/2" above floor	12-25' high on tree trunk	bark-covered or natural	prefers to live in or near woods
House wren	4" x 4" x 8"h. or 4" x 6" base	1" centered 6" above floor	5-10' high on post or hung in tree	light earth tones or white	prefers lower branches of backyard trees
Northern flicker	7" x 7" x 18"h.	2-1/2" centered 14" above floor	8-20' high	light earth tones	put 4" sawdust inside for nesting
Downy woodpecker	4" x 4" x 10"h.	1-1/4" centered 7-1/2" above floor	12-25' high on tree trunk	simulate natural cavity	prefers own excavation; provide sawdust
Red-headed woodpecker	6" x 6" x 15"h.	2" centered 6-8" above floor	8-20' high on post or tree trunk	simulate natural cavity	needs sawdust for nesting
Wood duck	10" x 10" x 24"h.	4" x 3" elliptical 20" above floor	2-5' high on post over water, or 12-40' high on tree facing water	light earth tones or natural	needs 3-4" of sawdust or shavings for nesting
American kestrel	10" x 10" x 24"h.	4" x 3" elliptical 20" above floor	12-40' high on post or tree trunk	light earth tones or natural	needs open approach on edge of woodlot or in isolated tree
Screech owl	10" x 10" x 24"h.	4" x 3" elliptical 20" above floor	12-40' high on tree	light earth tones or natural	prefers open woods or edge of woodlot
			Nesting Shelves		
American robin	6" x 6" x 8"h.	none—needs roof for rain protection	on side of building or arbor or in tree	light earth tones or wood	use is irregular
Barn swallow	6" x 6" x 8"h.	none—does not need roof	under eaves of building	light earth tones or wood	prefers barns or outbuildings
Phoebe	6" x 6" x 8"h.	none—does not need roof	under eaves of building	light earth tones or wood	prefers water nearby

Note: With the exception of wrens and purple martins, birds do not tolerate swaying birdhouses. Birdhouses should be firmly anchored to a post, a tree or the side of a building.

Source: *Garden Birds of America* by George H. Harrison. Willow Creek Press, 1996.

What's Your Zone?

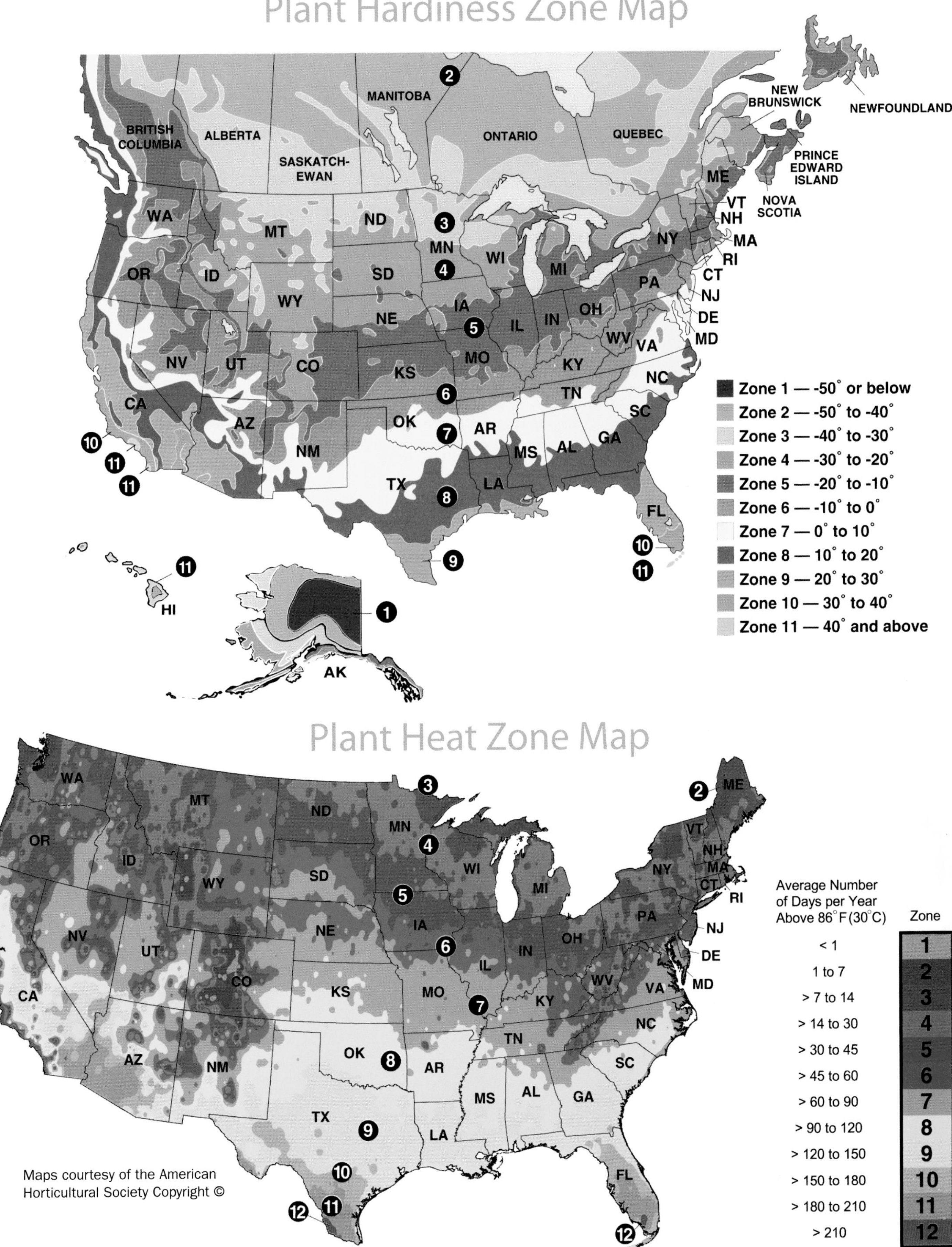

Index